William Hargreaves

Alcohol and Science

William Hargreaves

Alcohol and Science

ISBN/EAN: 9783743315006

Manufactured in Europe, USA, Canada, Australia, Japa

Cover: Foto ©ninafisch / pixelio.de

Manufactured and distributed by brebook publishing software (www.brebook.com)

William Hargreaves

Alcohol and Science

OR,

ALCOHOL: WHAT IT IS, AND WHAT IT DOES.

BY

WM. HARGREAVES, M.D.

AUTHOR OF "OUR WASTED RESOURCES," "MALT LIQUORS, THEIR NATURE AND EFFECTS," "ALCOHOL AND MAN," ETC.

LONDON:
WILLIAM NICHOLSON AND SONS,
20, WARWICK SQUARE, PATERNOSTER ROW, E.C.,
AND ALBION WORKS, WAKEFIELD.

500 DOLLAR PRIZE ESSAY.

THE following is the report of the committee, appointed by the Seventh National Temperance Convention at Saratoga, N. Y., to co-operate with Job H. Jackson, of Pennsylvania, in an effort to secure an American standard work on Temperance:

"To HON. WM. E. DODGE, President of the National Temperance Society and Publication House:

"SIR: The undersigned appointed by the Seventh National Temperance Convention, held at Saratoga, N. Y., August 26 and 27, 1873, to secure an '*American Standard Work on Temperance*,' 'presenting the status of the temperance question and argument in the present light of science,' etc., availing themselves of the fund then secured by the worthy efforts of Job H. Jackson, of West Grove, Pa., decided to divide the work into three parts, and to offer two prizes for essays upon each part, to be open to all writers who choose to compete therefor in this and other countries.

"In February, 1874, they publicly, and as widely as possible, announced two prizes for Part First.

"1. The Scientific, embracing the Chemical, Physiological, and Medical aspects.

"2. The Historical, Statistical, Economical, and Political.

"3. The Social, Educational, and Religious.

"For the best essay adjudged satisfactory, the sum of $500; for the second-best essay, the sum of $300. Manuscripts with the names and addresses of the writers by whom forwarded for competition, enclosed in separate sealed envelopes, not to be opened until after the award was made, to be forwarded to the Chairman of the Committee, 58, Reade Street, New York, by January 1, 1875. Accepted MSS. to become the property of the National Temperance Society.

"Early in January, 1875, the Committee met and had laid before them a number of competing MSS. Each member of the Committee has in turn read these papers; and we report great gratification that the plan adopted had presented for adjudication so many very interesting, able, and thoughtfully prepared papers.

"Assembled for final adjudication, the Committee unanimously adjudged the manuscript entitled 'Alcohol: What it Is, and what it Does' the best essay, satisfactory, and award to its author the first prize of $500. Upon opening the accompanying sealed envelope, we find its author to be William Hargreaves, M.D., of Philadelphia, Pa.

"Very respectfully,
"A. M. POWELL,
"JAMES BLACK,
"ROBT. C. PITMAN,
"A. A. MINER,
"NEAL DOW.

PREFACE.

IN preparing this Essay, it has been our aim, not merely to present our own views, but to furnish a treatise on the Alcoholic Controversy, embodying some of the early, as well as the latest experiments and demonstrations of science, on the controvertible points of the inquiry.

To present the subject fairly, nearly all the chief experiments and observations made by scientific men, within the last fifty years, have been noted. Though we do not agree with all the conclusions, yet we have presented them, in order that all the points in the controversy might be clearly understood; and also, that those who hold differing views, should not have ground to complain, that we had only presented one side of the question.

These demonstrations and testimonies of chemists and physicians, are presented to the consideration of the reader, in the hope that the nature and effects of the Alcohols, with their merits and demerits, will be clearly understood, not only by those learned in science, but by the general community.

If, from further investigations, the Alcohols shall be found useful, the prayer of the author is, that the medical profession shall be fully agreed for what to use them, how to use them, and when to use them.

THE AUTHOR.

CONTENTS.

PART I.

WHAT IS ALCOHOL?

	PAGE.
Chemical History of Alcohols	11
Alcoholic or Vinous Fermentation	18
Composition of Beer, Wines, &c.	22

PART II.

WHAT BECOMES OF ALCOHOL WHEN INGESTED. 24

Is Alcohol Eliminated from the Human Body?	26
Alcoholic Alphabet	29
Elimination of Alcohol only Partial	31
Experiments of Dr. Subbotin	32
Dr. Anstie's "Final Experiments"	33
Remarks on the Elimination of Alcohol	34
Dr. Richardson's Cantor Lectures, extracts from	36

PART III.

PHYSIOLOGICAL ACTION OF ALCOHOL .. 37

Dr. Richardson's Experiments	37
Action of Butylic Alcohol	39
Action of Amylic Alcohol	40
Action of Ethylic Alcohol	41
Experiments of Dr. Parkes and Count Wollowicz	44
Effects of Alcohol on the Human Body	48
Experiments of Dr. Hammond	50
Action of Alcohol on Colloidal Matter	52

	PAGE
Action of Alcohol. Dogiel's results	54
Dr. Carpenter's Observations	55
Summary of the Action of Alcohol	56

PART IV.

IS ALCOHOL A POISON?	57
Alcohol a Poison	59
Alcohol a Poison. Dr. Percy's Experiments	60
Alcohol is Poisonous to all Animals	62
Effects of continued use of Alcoholics	63
Effects of Alcoholics on Man	64
Poisoned by Whiskey.—Children	65
Alcoholic Poisoning	67

PART V.

IS ALCOHOL FOOD?	67
Nutrition and Alcohol	70
Is Alcohol Respiratory Food?	79
Nitrogenous Substances are not the only Sources of Force	80
Does Alcohol Produce Heat	87
Effects of Alcohol on the Temperature of the Body	93
Does Alcohol Retard the Waste of Tissue	98
Dr. Parkes' Experiments on the effects of Alcohol and Exercise on the Body	102
Dr. Parkes' Conclusions	104
Is Alcohol a Solvent of Food?	108
Does Alcohol Aid Digestion?	110

PART VI.

DOES ALCOHOL SUSTAIN VITALITY?	112
Does Alcohol Promote Health, &c., when used as a Beverage?	116
Longevity and Total Abstinence	119
Mortality of Liquor Sellers, and Abstainers	124
Effects of Alcohol on the Medical Profession	126

CONTENTS.

	PAGE.
State Board of Health, of Massachusetts	128
The Death Rate of Liverpool	130
Morbid Effects of Alcohol, &c.	134
Will Alcoholics Prevent Disease?	136
Total Abstinence Prevents Cholera, &c.	140

PART VII.

DISEASES CAUSED BY ALCOHOL	143
The Effects of Alcohol on the Stomach	143
The Effects of Alcohol on the Liver	154
The Effects of Alcohol on the Kidneys, &c.	158
Effects of Alcohol on Stomach, Liver, Heart and Kidneys	160

PART VIII.

NERVOUS DISEASES FROM ALCOHOL	162
Alcoholic Drinks cause Paralysis	162
Alcoholic Paresis and Paraplegia	162
Alcohol causes Thrombosis of the Cerebral Arteries	164
Alcohol the Cause of Insanity	165
Different Alcoholic Liquors and Insanity	170
The Increase and Number of the Insane	174
Dipsomania	176
Intemperance a Disease	178

PART IX.

ALCOHOL; ITS EFFECTS ON PROGENY	181
Hereditary Effects of Intoxicating Drinks	182
Physical Degeneracy in Children by Intemperance of Parents	187

PART X.

IS ALCOHOL A MEDICINE?	192
Medical Science, What is it?	192

CONTENTS.

	PAGE
The Use of Alcohol as a Remedy for Debility, &c.	199
Alcohol Impairs the Vitality of the Blood Discs	201
Is Alcohol a Stimulant or a Narcotic?	202
Experiments on the use of Wine	207
Recovery Retarded by the use of Wine	209
Violent Inflammation Excited by Alcohol	210
Influence of Alcoholism on Traumatic Lesions	211
Stimulants During Hemorrhage	212
Alcoholic Stimulants in Typhus Fever	214
Alcohol as a Cure for Dyspepsia	216
Alcohol in Consumption	217
The influence of Alcoholic Drinks on the Development and Progress of Pulmonary Tuberculosis	218
Alcohol as a Cure for Bronchitis and Heart-disease	221
Alcoholic Stimulants in Child-Birth	222
The Use of Alcohol by Nursing Mothers	224
Stimulants and Death-Rate	230
The Use of Alcoholic Liquors in Workhouses	231
Medical Experience	232
Council of the British Medical Temperance Association	237
Concluding Remarks	240

PART I.

WHAT IS ALCOHOL?

THE CHEMICAL HISTORY OF ALCOHOLS.

THE term alcohol, is not restricted to an isolated compound, as there are several kinds of alcohols, of which that met in wines, beer, brandy, &c., is only a representative of an active series of compounds known under the same name. Alcohols are substances more or less resembling common alchol, which has the formula of $C_2 H_6 O$, and corresponds among organic substances, to the hydro-oxides in inorganic chemistry, and we may suppose them to be derived from water, by substituing an organic radical for hydrogen.

Thus:—Both common alcohol and caustic potash we may suppose to be obtained from water, by substituting for hydrogen, in the one case, potassium, in the other the organic radical ethyl.

Water.	Caustic Potash.	Alcohol.
$\left.\begin{array}{c}H\\H\end{array}\right\} O.$	$\left.\begin{array}{c}K\\K\end{array}\right\} O.$	$\left.\begin{array}{c}C_2\ H_5\\H\end{array}\right\} O.$

Or, alcohol may be defined a compound of a hydro-carbon radical, with hydroxyl,—Thus, ethyl alcohol is, $C_2 H_5 H O$.

2. The alcohols, in their reactions with acids, resemble the metallic hydro-oxides. Methylic Alcohol or Carbinol

$\left.\begin{array}{c}C H_3\\H\end{array}\right\} O.$ or $C. \left\{\begin{array}{c}H\\H\\H\\HO\end{array}\right.$ may be regarded as *marsh gas*, in which one atom

of hydrogen has been replaced by hydroxyl. It is possible to obtain methyl alcohol from its elements, for marsh gas can be prepared from carbon and hydrogen; and if acted upon by chlorine in the sun-light, it forms methyl chloride. If methyl chloride be heated in close tubes, with caustic potash, methyl alcohol is obtained:—

$$C H_3 cl + K H O = K cl + C H_3 H O.$$

3. Methyl alcohol is commonly termed, *Wood Spirits*, and is the product of the distillation of wood. The products of this distillation are, acetic acid, methyl alcohol, and some other substances. Methyl alcohol is a colourless liquid, having a burning

$C_? \ H_{12} \ O_?$ $C_4 \ H_{12} \ O_2$

ALCOHOL AND SCIENCE.

taste, and smelling sometimes like ordinary alcohol. It mixes in all proportions, with water; boils at 66° C, and has a specific gravity of 0.8142, and burns like common alcohol, for which it is often substituted; being cheaper. It is allowed in England, to be mixed with *ethylic* or common alcohol, and sold for manufacturing purposes free of duty.

4. The following are the principal alcohols:

Name.	Chemical composition.	Vapour density.	Specific gravity water 100.	Boiling Point.	
				Centigrade.	Fahr.
Methylic Alcohol	$C \ H_4 \ O$	16	.814	60	140
Ethylic ,,	$C_2 \ H_6 \ O$	23	.792	78	172
Propylic ,,	$C_3 \ H_8 \ O$	30	....	96	205
Butylic ,,	$C_4 \ H_{10} \ O$	37	.803	101	230
Amylic ,,	$C_5 \ H_{12} \ O$	44	.811	132	270
Caproylic ,,	$C_6 \ H_{14} \ O$	51	.821	150	302

5. Ethylic, or common alcohol, is a compound composed of carbon 2, hydrogen 6, and oxygen 1:—$C_2 \ H_6 \ O$. Though it can be prepared snythetically, yet it is always produced by the fermentation of sugar. Under the influence of yeast, the sugar splits up into carbon dioxide—carbonic acid—and alcohol; thus:—

Sugar.   Alcohol.   Carbon Dioxide.

$$C_6 \ H_{12} \ O_6 = 2 \ C_2 \ H_6 \ O + 2 \ C \ O_2.$$

6. Fermented liquors contain diluted alcohol and other substances. The crude spirit is obtained by distillation, which still contains a considerable proportion of water, and other impurities, one of which is fusel oil, especially found in spirits, from Indian corn and potatoes. Distillation alone will not free it from water. To accomplish this, some substance having a strong affinity for water must be employed; quick lime being commonly used, to produce anhydrous alcohol, or absolute alcohol, As alcohol possesses a strong affinity for water, really pure absolute alcohol is very difficult to obtain; for when it is mixed with water, it evolves heat, and undergoes contraction; so that 53.7 vols. of alcohol and 48.9 vols. of water, produce only 100 vols. of dilute alcohol.

7. The construction of *ethylic*, common alchol, in a chemical sense, is water ($H_2 \ O$) in which the organ radical *ethyl*, also composed of carbon and hydrogen, ($C_2 \ H_5$), replaces one atom of hydrogen of the water, thus:

$\left.\begin{array}{c} H \\ H \end{array}\right\} O$ Water, $C_2 \ H_5$ Ethyl, $- H = C_2 \ H_6 \ O$ Alcohol.

8. Ethylic alcohol when oxidized yields a variety of compounds according to the character of the oxidation. The result may be the oxidation of two atoms of hydrogen by which water is only produced, which will leave a fluid with the water having the composition of $C_2 \ H_4 \ O$, called *aldehyde;* or, the oxidation carried further, and an equivalent of oxygen added, the resulting com-

pound will be $C_2 H_4 O_2$ *acetic acid*. If the oxidation be intense, as the burning of alcohol in a lamp, the carbon, which in preceding examples was not touched, is now directly oxidized with the hydrogen, and the result will be the formation of dioxide of carbon, carbonic acid, CO_2, and water, $H_2 O$.

9. Taking ethylic alcohol as a type of the other five alcohols of the table, we will study their properties. Methylic alcohol, the first on the list, as already seen, page 11,) is produced in the destructive distillation of wood, and is commonly termed woodspirits, or naphtha. It differs from common—*ethylic*—alcohol, being a compound in which the organic radical methyl $C H_3$ replaces an atom of hydrogen of the water. Thus:

$$\left.\begin{matrix} H \\ H \end{matrix}\right\} O \text{ Water, } C H_3 \text{ Methyl, } - H = C \left.\begin{matrix} H_3 \\ H \end{matrix}\right\} O \text{ Methylic alcohol.}$$

This methylic alcohol, whose composition is $C H_4 O$, when slowly oxidized yields an aldehyde called formaldehyde, to produce which, two atoms of hydrogen of the methyl alcohol are oxidized, forming one equivalent of water $H_2 O$ and formaldehyde $C H_2 O$, a gas. If the oxidation is carried still further, an equivalent of oxygen is added, and formic acid is the result, analogous to acetic acid. By burning it in a lamp, the carbon and oxygen are both oxidized, and carbonic acid $C O_2$ and water $H_2 O$ are formed.

10. The other alcohols, propylic, butylic, amylic, and caproylic, have all the same plan of construction as common, or ethylic, that is, one atom of the hydrogen of water ($H_2 O$) is replaced by an organic radical. In propylic alcohol, the radical is *propyle* ($C_3 H_7$;) in butylic alcohol, *butyle* ($C_4 H_9$;) in amylic alcohol, *amyle* ($C_5 H_{11}$;) in caproylic alcohol, *coproyle* ($C_6 H_{13}$). In each the change is the same as in the ethylic alcohol, and by their oxidation the corresponding aldehydes and acids are formed.

11. If heavier alcohols are burned in a lamp, the oxygen in the air is not sufficient to consume all the carbon, and hence a large amount of free carbon will be deposited as soot. The methylic and ethylic alcohols burn without depositing soot; the propylic alcohol will give a faint deposit; butylic more; amylic, still more; while the caproylic yields a still larger amount of carbon.

12. It will be seen by referring to the table, that in the proportion carbon and hydrogen are increased, so is the fluid's vapour density, fluid density, and higher boiling point. All these differences modify the physiological action of the alcohol. Another peculiarity is that while methylic and ethylic alcohol mix, in all proportions, with water, butylic is soluble in water in the proportion of one part to one and a half, only, but amylic and caproylic are insoluble.

13. The atmosphere is composed of oxygen, hydrogen, nitrogen and carbon, from which all vegetable forms upon the surface of the earth derive their nourishment. The chemical elements of

the air are the same in all parts of the earth; so are those of the plants, for the elements of the atmosphere, oxygen, hydrogen, nitrogen and carbon, compose almost the entire vegetable kingdom.

14. CARBON is commonly known as charcoal, but is mixed with several earthy substances, and is solid. In diamonds carbon is in absolute purity. Carbon is endowed with a considerable range of affinity, forming, as already seen, two gases by its union with oxygen.

15. HYDROGEN has special affinity for oxygen, uniting with it to form water. Upon the exercise of this affinity the decay of all substances depends, and many of the most nutritive processes of plants originate in the attempt to gratify this affinity. In a gaseous state of hydrogen is the lightest body known and very combustible. It is never found in nature in an isolated state; water is its most common combination.

16. OXYGEN is a gaseous element, and composes about one-fifth of the atmosphere and one-third of the crust of the earth. It has a powerful attraction for other elements, combining with them with such force as to produce combustion. It is superor in the extensive range of its affinities to all other elements, affecting the union and disunion of a great number of compounds.

17. NITROGEN, in its chemical character, is opposed to carbon and hydrogen, and its chief characteristics, are indifference to all other substances and a reluctance to unite with them; and when forced by peculiar circumstances, it seems to be inert, so that a very slight change causes a disunion or decomposition. Yet nitrogen is an invariable constituent of all plants, and is subject to the control of the vital power during their life; but when it ceases to exercise its power, nitrogen resumes its chemical character, and causes the decay of vegetable substances by escaping from the compounds of which it formed a constituent.

18. These elements form organic bodies. Plants do not use them in their simple state to build up their structures; but in the form of carbonic acid, ammonia and water.

19. ALIMENTARY SUBSTANCES.—Although the elements employed by nature are so simple, and limited in number; yet the vegetable products constructed from them are almost boundless in variety and number. Alimentary substances are divided into non-nitrogenized and nitrogenized.

20. The non-nitrogenized are divided into three groups, differing in the relative proportions of the elementary atoms composing them. The following are the NON-NITROGENIZED.

21. First Group: Sugar and allied substances. These all appear to contain six atoms of carbon, or a multiple of that number united with hydrogen and oxygen, in the proportion in which they combine to form water. They may be divided as follows:

THE CHEMICAL HISTORY OF ALCOHOLS.

GROUP FIRST—FORMULA $C_{12}H_{22}O_{11}$.

Cane sugar, or sucrose—from sugar cane,
Milk sugar, or lactose—in milk of mammalia.
Mycose, or trehaloze.
Melezitose.
Mycose.

GROUP SECOND—FORMULA $C_6H_{12}O_6$.

Grape sugar, or dextrose—in grapes.
Fruit sugar, or levulose—in honey and fruits.
Galactose.
Sorbin.
Eucolin.

GROUP THIRD—FORMULA $C_6H_{10}O_5$.

Starch—in roots, stems and seeds of plants, as wheat, corn, potatoes, &c.
Glycogene.
Dextrine—obtained by heating starch from 150° F. to 200° F.
Inuline.
Gums.
Cellulose—from the woody fibre of plants.

22. The *grape sugar* and *starch* may be expressed thus:

Grape Sugar.		Starch.	
Carbon,	6 atoms.	Carbon,	6 atoms.
Hydrogen,	12 atoms.	Hydrogen,	10 atoms.
Oxygen,	6 atoms.	Oxygen,	5 atoms.
Total,	24 atoms.	Total,	21 atoms.

Or, they may be expressed in the usual form, $C_6H_{12}O_6$ grape sugar; and $C_6H_{01}O_5$ starch. In the grape sugar and starch, the atoms of carbon are the same, and the hydrogen and oxygen atoms are in exact proportion to form water, (H_2O). The same is true of lignin and gums; hence the three groups are simply charcoal and water.

23. The second group of non-nitrogen substances, the vegetable acids, malic and citric acids, that give the sour flavour to fruits, are very differently composed, as will be seen by examining the formula:

Malic acid $= C_4H_9O_5$.
Citric acid $= C_6H_8O_7$.

There is a variable amount of carbon and oxygen in excess.

24. THE THIRD GROUP of NON-NITROGENIZED SUBSTANCES, are the FATS and OILS, which differ from both *starch* and *fruit acids*, in having hydrogen and carbon largely in excess, and in having little oxygen, thus:

Stearic acid $= C_{18}H_{36}O_2$.
Margiric acid $= C_{17}H_{34}O_2$.

25. It was supposed by Liebig that the above groups of non-nitrogenized aliments are designed principally to be burned up in the animal system, to produce heat, and that they are decomposed during the process of respiration, into carbonic acid (CO_2) and water (H_2O); and are called elements of respiration. It is clear that the amount of heat produced by their decomposition will vary as the amount of hydrogen and carbon varies in their composition. As the fats and oils contain the most carbon and hydrogen, they give the most heat; next the sugars and starch; while lastly the vegetable acids give the least amount of heat.

26. We find in the arrangement and economy of nature, that these substances are distributed to meet the wants of the animal kingdom, according to the conditions of climate and season. Thus, animal oil and blubber are furnished for the inhabitants of the higher latitudes of the POLAR REGIONS; the fruits, acids and starch for those within the Tropics; while they are varied and blended between the two extremes of heat and cold. Thus the different necessities of the whole animal kingdom are provided for.

27. THE NITROGENIZED OR TRUE NUTRITIVE, COMPOUNDS, are the second class of alimentary principles; and are formed by the addition of nitrogen to the elements composing the first class; hence they are called nitrogenized aliments; they are vegetable albumen, vegetable fibrin, and vegetable casein. Albumen, fibrin, and casein are regarded by some chemists as compounds of the same primary substance (proteine), combined with different proportions of sulphur and phosphorus. The composition usually assigned to these substances is $C_{18} H_{27} N_4 O_6$. They are the true builders of the animal, being transformed into the various tissues. The flesh or animal albumen, animal fibrin, animal casein and animal gluten, being identical with vegetable albumen, fibrin, casein and gluten; containing the same proportion of nitrogen.

28. PROTEIN COMPOUNDS.—The nitrogenous compounds, or albuminoid elements, are the true formers of the muscles and tissues of the animal system. These compounds have a strong tendency to decomposition, to putrify under favourable circumstances, and destroy sugar when brought into contact with it.

29. The gases are simple compounds, containing a pair of elements, with only 2, 3 or 4 atoms; but substances that vegetables form out of them, consist of three or four distinct kinds of matter, having a large number of atoms. The greater the number of elements a substance contains, the more numerous the attractions, and the easier the composition is broken up by the disturbing forces brought to bear upon them. The forces which produce growth, readily derange the equilibrium in which they are held, when they are decomposed and changed into simpler and more permanent conditions.

30. THE DECOMPOSITION OF MATTER.—The decomposition of compounds of organized substances, and the relapse of atoms to the inorganic condition, takes place under many circumstances,

and gives rise to almost as many products, as the conditions under which the decomposition occurs. For example: from wood, allowed to decay, in contact with air and moisture, humus, humeric acid, &c., &c., are formed: substances of an entirely different nature. If allowed to decay under water, as in marshes and ponds, with mud and peat, an inflammable gas is generated; but if heated with partial admission of air, as in coal pits, carbonic acid, water, and charcoal are produced; and if heat be applied to the wood with entire exclusion of air, destructive distillation takes place, when charcoal, tar, pyroligneous acid, creosote, and illuminating gas are formed; but when wood is burned in the open air, the oxygen seizes upon the carbon and hydrogen, and returns it to carbonic acid and water; the original elements of the wood. In all the above processes of the destruction of wood, the attraction which held together its atoms is broken up, and the atoms again combine in other proportions, thus giving rise to new and entirely different substances, which are all intermediate states in the processes of decomposition or disorganization; and the return of the atoms to their original condition of carbonic acid and water.

31. PUTREFACTION OF NITROGENIZED SUBSTANCES.—Nitrogenous aliments are the most transient and changeable of all organized matter. At the common temperature, under the influence of moisture and oxygen, their decomposition, or putrefaction, rapidly takes place. Milk, meat, dough, &c., containing large quantities of nitrogenous matter, when placed in a moist condition, rapidly become putrid. The nitrogenized substances not only become rapidly putrid themselves, but communicate putrefaction to the non-nitrogenized. Pure starch, sugar, &c., are very enduring, and are able to resist putrefaction for a long time; but when brought into contact with nitrogenized substances in the process of decay they are at once affected, and go on to the same condition. "The substances," says Liebig, "which constitute the principal mass of every vegetable, are compounds of carbon with oxygen and hydrogen, in the *proper relative proportion for forming water*. For example; a rotten peach or apple, placed in contact with one that is sound, soon causes it to rot; and its atoms return to their original condition, or elements; carbonic acid and water.

32. FERMENTATION is the term applied to the change which occurs in one organic substance when brought into contact with, and influenced by another in a state of decay or putrefaction. The process was originally understood to include all the changes which the substances of plants and animals undergo, when disunited from *living force;* but is now restricted to certain changes which all organic matter undergo.

33. Starch, sugar, &c., have no power of themselves to pass into decay; while albumen, fibrin, casein, gelatinous tissues, mucus, &c., when exposed to moderately heated air in a moist condition, begin to putrify more or less rapidly. The sub-

stances that spontaneously pass into a state of change or putrefaction are called *ferments*, and when they are brought into contact with sugar, &c., which would not otherwise be altered, cause the latter to be broken up into simpler compounds; it is this process that constitutes fermentation. The ferment is always a substance that has the power of rotting or becoming putrid.

34. Every substance that is liable to putrefy becomes, while putrefying, a *ferment;* and in this condition acquires the property of inducing or starting the process of *fermentation* in other bodies capable of it, and retains that power till it is so far decomposed, that putrescence is over. *Ferments* are very widely distributed in inorganic bodies, and therefore when an animal or a plant dies, the process of *fermentation* proceeds more or less rapidly.

35. ALCOHOLIC OR VINOUS FERMENTATION is the *fermentation* which will claim our particular attention, as being the principal process in the production of alcoholic liquors; beer, wine &c.

36. Vinous fermentation is the decomposition that the different kinds of sugars undergo, by which the elements combine to form new compounds, and under like conditions, are always the same. These conditions consist mainly in the action of a peculiar ferment, called yeast, upon a saccharine liquid; when sugar $C_6 H_{12} O_6$, is decomposed into two atoms of alcohol each $C_2 H_6 O$, and two atoms of carbonic acid, each $C O_2$. It was formerly supposed that *all* the sugar was transformed into alcohol and carbonic acid; but that is not the case, as about 6 per cent of it is changed, thus:—

    3.5 per cent. are converted into Glycerine.
    0.5 per cent. are converted into Succinic acid.
    1.5 per cent. are converted into Cellulose.
    0.5 per cent. are converted into Carbonic acid.

37. Without going into the different theories of the causes of the changes occurring in the process of vinous fermentation; there is very strong evidence that in all cases living organisms are present. Yeast, when examined under the microscope, is seen to be made up of organized cells, or globules, which are either vegetable or animal. When these living organisms are added to grape juice, or an infusion of malt, fermentation begins. The yeast cells increase in number, and go through various changes, and the result of their life-action is the conversion of sugar into alcohol and carbonic acid. These cells consists of two parts, the cell wall composed of matter, termed *cellulose*, and the contents of the cell resembling fat or oil. The idea that yeast was an organized living plant, was strongly opposed by both Berzelius and Liebig, but by the microscope they were convinced both of the organization and vitality. The scientific name is *Fermentum cervesia*, or *torula* cervisia.*

---

* Schnetzler says: "That alcoholic fermentation, with evolution of gas, is caused by living cells of the *fungus* known as *saccharomyces*, present in the ferment; and that there are cases in which other species of *fungus*, as *mucus*, *aspergillus* and *penicillium*, present in the same liquid, produce fermentation with evolution of gas."—*Annual Record of Science and Industry*, 1873.

38. Vinous fermentanion proceeds best at a temperature ranging from 60° to 80° F., the mean and more desirable temperature being about 70° F. The process itself causes the development of heat, and confirms the organic theory, which is, that the yeast cells or ferment, feed upon the vegetable substances, multiply, evolve heat, and give off as excretions alcohol and carbonic acid. According to every theory, fermentation is the process by which the food of man is destroyed and alcohol produced. The results invariably are that by the fermentation of sugar, new substances are produced, by a new grouping or arrangement of its elements; the elements of the body which excites the fermention, taking no share in the transformation.

39. It has been shown by very exact experiments, that 100 parts of cane sugar, give from 50.3, to 50.27 parts of carbonic acid, and 52.62 parts of alcohol; the sum of 103.89. The excess is found in the alcohol formed as oxygen and hydrogen, in the proportion to form water. It is therefore certain, that in the fermentation of *cane* sugar, the elements of one atom of water, have a share in the transformation. M. M. Duplaise says: "Among the proximate principles of organic substances, sugar alone gives occasion to vinous fermentation, from which alcohol is derived."

40. This fermentation requires the concurrence of five agents, each acting in a different direction, the union of which is indispensable, viz.: 1st, sugar or saccharine principle; 2d, water; 3d, heat; 4th, a ferment; 5th, atmospheric air. If one of these agents is suppressed, vinous fermentation will not take place, and consequently alcohol will not be produced. The action of each is of more or less importance, and fermentation absolutely depends on their employment and combination.

41. Sugar, as we have said, is the only constituent element that can produce alcohol; the other agents are merely auxiliaries to the decomposition. According to the principles of chemistry, sugar, when dissolved and brought in contact with a ferment, is transformed into alcohol and carbonic acid; composed, by weight, 42.47 parts of carbon, 50.73 of oxygen, and 6.90 of hydrogen.

42. The great French chemist, A. F. Fourcroy, says:* "The fermentation of alcohol takes place at the expense of the *destruction* of a *vegetable principle;* thus: spirituous fermentation is a commencement of the destruction of principle *formed* by vegetation. The acid or acetous fermentation, is the *second natural movement* which contributes to reduce vegetable compounds to more simple states of composition. Wine, in turning sour, absorbs air; so that certain portions of the oxygen of the atmosphere appear to be necessary to the formation of the acetous acid. Finally, after vegetable liquors, or their solid parts moistened, have passed to the acid state, their decomposition continuing, under unfavourable circumstances, (namely, a warm temperature, exposure to air, and the contact of water,) leads them into putrefaction, which terminates in volatilizing most of the principles, under the form of

---

* Philosophy of Chemistry, Ch. XII., 1785.

gas. Water, carbonic acid, carbonated and even sulphurated hydrogen gas, volatile oil in vapour, and sometimes even azotic gas and ammonia, are evolved; and after this, there remains nothing but a brown or black residuum, known by the name of mould. Though all the circumstances of putrefaction are not described, or ever known, we have discovered that they are confined to the conversion of *complex substances* into simple substances, *less compounded;* that nature restores to new combinations, the materials which it had but lent, as it were to vegetables and animals; and that she thus accomplishes the perpetual circle of compositions and decompositions, which attests her power, and demonstrates her fecundity, while it announces equal grandeur and simplicity in the course of her operations."

43. The juices of all vegetables and other liquids containing sugar, are capable of alcoholic or vinous fermentation, when sufficient albuminous matter is present to produce and sustain the process, which is usually the case when the juice of apples, pears, peaches, currants, grapes, &c., are employed as sources of alcohol.

44. As already seen, there are several kinds of sugar. *Grape sugar* is alone capable of being directly converted into alcohol; the others must be transformed into grape sugar before they are susceptible of vinous fermentation.

45. Though the cereals, as rye, wheat, barley and Indian corn, contain but little sugar, they consist of a large proportion of starch, which is capable of being converted into sugar. This change is caused by *diastase*, a peculiar ferment, that is developed during the germination of all seeds. An impure solution of *diastase* is produced, by adding one part of hot water to two parts of ground malt, or freshly germinated barley, after standing for a short time. The proportion of *diastase* in malt is not more than one part in 500; yet, this small quantity, at a temperature of 150° Fahr., is powerful enough to change 2000 parts of starch into *dextrine*, and then into *grape sugar*. In the operation of malting this principle is made available. *Malt* is barley or other grain, caused to germinate and the germination arrested by heat. If bruised malt is mingled with the ground meal of any other grain, and water at the requisite temperature, the *diastase* of the malt converts the additional STARCH into SUGAR. This sweet liquid contains the newly formed grape sugar, and can be changed into alcohol by fermentation.

46. Fermented liquors are alcoholic beverages; the principal, being the different kinds of *ale* and *beer*, made by fermentation of an infusion of malt, chiefly of barley, but sometimes of other grains. Wine is the fermented juice of the grape; cider the fermented juice of apples; perry that of pears, palm wine of the sap of the different kinds of palms. Fermented liquors called wines, are also made from the juices of various kinds of fruit. Mead is a fermented liquor, made from honey. From every kind of fermented liquor alcohol can be obtained by distillation.

47. Pure Ethylic Alcohol, is a colourless transparent liquid, of an agreeable fruity odour, and a penetrating burning taste; its specific gravity or weight is .792°, or, about one fifth lighter than water, for which it has such a strong affinity or attraction, that when bottles containing it are left uncorked, it withdraws water from the atmosphere and becomes heavier. Therefore the weight of the mixture is used to determine the alcoholic per centage contained. As already shown, alcohol contains two atoms of carbon, six atoms of hydrogen and one atom of oxygen; it is therefore highly inflammable, and burns with a lambent blue flame, producing no soot, a small amount of light, but intense heat; hen e it is admirably adapted to the wants of the chemist, to be burned in lamps, as a source of heat. It is also used as a solvent of many substances, that water will not dissolve. It is a powerful antiseptic, and prevents the putrefaction of animal and vegetable substances, immersed in it; hence physicians and naturalists use it to keep dead bodies from decomposition.

48. The difference between fermented and distilled liquors, is only one of degree, the essential ingredient alcohol, being the same in quality in each. As alcohol is always generated in a liquid solution of sugar, a portion of water must be mingled with it. Distillation is the process used to separate the water from the alcohol or spirit. Though the term is usually employed to designate malting, mashing fermentation, and the final separation of the spirituous product from the water, yet, it but strictly applies to the last process. Alcohol, being a light fluid, boils, or is converted into vapour at a heat forty degrees lower than is required to boil, or vapourize water; hence a heat that would not convert water into steam, raises alcohol to the state of vapour, which is passed through the WORM of the *still* surrounded with cold water, and is here condensed into a liquid. The first product is by no means pure; for the powerful chemical attraction of alcohol for water, retains a portion of it in combination as it passes through the vapourous state. A second distillation reduces the proportion of water, which is termed *spirits* of *wine*. Another distillation renders it still stronger, forming *rectified spirits* of wine, which still contains from 10 to 20 per cent of water. The remaining water can only be separated entirely by powerful chemical means.* The common commercial alcohols contain very variable proportions of water.

49. Fermented and spirituous liquors, not only mainly differ from each other in their proportions of alcohol and water; but also in colouring matter and flavour, sugar and gummy extractives, and in various foreign and adulterating ingredients, added either during their manufacture, or afterwards by their vendor. According to Brande, and Dr. Bence Jones, rum, whiskey, brandy and gin, contain from fifty-three to fifty-seven per cent. of alcohol; port wine, twenty-two; Champagne, twelve; cider, five to nine; and beer, four to six per cent. The distinguished chemist, Prof,

---

* See Section 6.

John C. Draper, of the University Medical College, New York, made a chemical examination of the liquors sold at the first-class drinking-places of that city. The alcoholic percentage is given below, also the number of ounces of alcohol in an imperial pint, in samples of beer, wine, spirits, &c., in the food collection of South Kensington Museum, London. Some of which will be found in the following table:

	Alcoholic Percentage.			Number of ounces in imperial pt. of 20 ozs.
	By Brande	By Bence Jones	By Prof. Draper.	
Bourbon,	....	....	28. to 55	
Whiskey,	54.11	....	29. to 49	
Rum,	53.68	72.0 to 77.1		
Brandy,	53.39	50.4 to 53.8	22. to 56	10½ ounces.
Holland Gin	51.60	49.4 to	31.	
Raisin Wine	25.12			
Madeira,	24.17	19.0 to 19.7	....	4 ounces.
Port,	22.96	20.7 to 23.2	....	4 ounces.
Sherry,	19.17	15.4 to 24.7	....	4½ ounces.
Claret,	15.10	9.1 to 11.1	....	2 ounces.
Burgundy,	14.57	10.1 to 13.2	....	2½ ounces.
Champagne,	12.80	14.1 to 14.8	....	3 ounces.
Elderberry,	8.79			
Cider,	7.54	5.4 to 7.5		
Perry,	7.26			
Strong ale,	6.20			
Brown stout	6.80	....	....	1½ ounces.
Porter,	4.20	....	....	1½ ounces.
Small beer,	1.28	....	....	¾ ounce.

COMPOSITION OF BEER, WINES, &c.

In the food collection, at the South Kensington Museum, London, there are samples of various kinds of beer, wines, and spirits, with tables attached, showing the ingredients of which they are composed. Thus: according to this scale,

An imperial pint of malt liquors, contains:—

	Water.	Alcohol.	Sugar.	Acetic acid.
London stout,	18½ ounces.	1½ ounces.	281 grains.	54 grains.
London porter,	19¼ ounces.	¾ ounce.	267 grains.	45 grains.
Strong ale,	18 ounces.	2 ounces.	136 grains.	54 grains.
Mild ale,	18¾ ounces.	1¼ ounces.	280 grains.	38 grains.
Pale ale,	17½ ounces.	2½ ounces.	240 grains.	40 grains.

An imperial pint of wine, contains:

	Water.	Alcohol.	Sugar.	Tartaric acid.
Port,	16 ounces.	4 ounces.	1 oz. 2 grs.	80 grains.
Brown sherry,	15½ ounces.	4½ ounces.	360 grains.	90 grains.
Claret,	18 ounces.	2 ounces.	....	161 grains.
Burgundy,	17½ ounces.	2½ ounces.	....	160 grains.
Hock,	17¾ ounces.	2¼ ounces.	....	127 grains.
Mozelle,	18¼ ounces.	1¾ ounces.	0.9 grains.	140 grains.
Champagne,	17 ounces.	3 ounces.	1.133 grains.	90 grains.
Madeira,	16 ounces.	4 ounces.	0.400 grains.	100 grains.

An imperial pint of spirits, contains:—

	Water.	Alcohol.	Sugar.
Brandy,	9½ ounces.	10½ ounces.	80 grains.
Rum,	5 ounces.	15 ounces.	
Gin, (best,)	12 ounces.	8 ounces.	
Gin, (retail,)	16 ounces.	4 ounces.	½ ounce.

Even the home-made wines are often stronger of alcohol than the imported, depending upon the amount of sugar added to the fruit. That made from raisins is even stronger than port, and elder wine is as strong of alcohol as cider, or the strongest malt liquors; hence home-made wines are far from being the innocent, harmless beverages, some of our mothers were apt to think, when they told us there was nothing in them to hurt any one, as they knew they had put nothing in the wine, but the juice of the fruit, and the sugar to sweeten the juice.

50. The alcohol in the above-named liquors, is not in a state of chemical combination, but exists in a free state, in the mixture.

51. Thus we understand the true derivation of alcohol. No matter what form it may assume, it has one origin, the *destruction of sugar*. It is not a product of vegetable growth, like the substances created to nourish man. "Nature," says Count Chaptal, "*never forms spirituous liquors;* she rots the grape upon the branch, but it is *art* which converts the juice into wine." No chemist has ever yet found it among the substances formed by plants. Nature in the laboratory of vegetation, takes the poisonous gases and splits them up, and then puts the atoms into new groups, capable of nourishing the animal system. But alcohol is the product of dissolution, the wreck, the disorganization of human food; it is in reality a product of decomposition. The juices of the fruits, by the influence of that *fungus yeast*, are turned to rottenness, and then, and then *only*, is alcohol generated, out of the destruction of the organic sugar. It has the same orign as the malignant and fatal exhalation of the pestilence—the death and putrefaction of organic substances. Hence it is no more the gift of the Creator, than the malarial poison that breathes its contagion, and strikes down the young and the old, with disease and death.

PART II.

WHAT BECOMES OF ALCOHOL, WHEN INGESTED?

52. THE precise action of alcohol within the human system, has long been, and still is, an unsettled question. The points that seem determined, are, that alcohol absorbed into the blood current, is carried to all parts of the system, and some according to Dr. Anstie, and all according to Lallemand, Perrin and Duroy, passes out in all the excretions. Not many years ago, the celebrated Liebig, had, on incidental investigation, announced the theory that no alcohol left the body in an unchanged condition, but that it furnished heat, and combining with oxygen, passed out as carbonic acid and water.

53. This theory, incidentally promulgated by such an authority, for a time satisfied many, but has since been shown to lack adequate proof. Nothing, however, in it is really opposed to the practice of total abstinence, for, by his own showing, alcohol was of less value as a heat producer, than fat.

54. It was taken for granted that from its highly combustible nature, it would change into carbonic acid and water, when brought into relation with oxygen in the capillaries of the lungs. The fact that alcohol is rapidly eliminated unchanged with the urinary excretion, and escapes from the system with the pulmonary and cutaneous exhalations, as indicated by the alcoholic odour in the breath, and perspiration, is a very strong argument against the doctrine that alcohol undergoes changes, and is used up by a combustive process.

55. Then again, we know of no alimentary substance that passes from the system unchanged, by the excretory processes, except when the organic functions are deranged, as in *diabetes* and *albuminaria*.

56. That alcohol enters the circulation and remains unchanged in the system, was stated by Dr. James Kirk, of Scotland, in an address in 1830, to the VALE OF LEVEN TEMPERANCE SOCIETY, who said: "I dissected a man who died in a state of intoxication after a debauch. The operation was performed a few hours after death. In two of the cavities of the brain—the lateral ventricles—was found the usual quantity of limpid fluid. When we smelled it, the odour of whiskey was distinctly perceptible; and when we applied a candle to a portion in a spoon, it actually burned blue, the lambent blue flame, characteristic of the poison, playing on the spoon for some seconds." Doubts being expressed as to the truth of Dr. Kirk's statements, Dr. Ogston, of Aberdeen, said: "I am happy to be able to add one case to the number. The body of a woman, aged forty, of the name of Cattie, who was believed to have drowned herself, in a state of intoxication, was found, on the 23rd of August, 1831, in the Aberdeen canal. In company with another medical man, I was requested to examine the body. * * We discovered nearly four ounces of fluid in the ventricles, having all the physical qualities of alcohol, as proved by the united testimony of two other medical men, who saw the body opened and examined the fluid."

57. To test these statements, Dr. Percy* instituted a series of experiments, partly on human subjects, but chiefly on dogs. He did not rely upon the odour or inflammability of the fluid, as evidence that it was alcohol, but by distillation he procured a sufficient quantity, which, when treated with subcarbonate of potash, proved its alcoholic character, not only by its inflammability, but by its power to dissolve camphor.

58. These facts were ascertained by introducing alcohol into stomachs of several dogs, sometime in quantities sufficient to produce the common manifestations of alcoholic intoxication. He had no difficulty in extracting alcohol from the blood, and from the substance of the brain, but was unable to detect it in the fluids in the ventricles of the brain. The amount that he obained from the brain was larger than from an equivalent amount of blood.

59. Hence there seemed to exist a kind of affinity between alcohol and the substance of the brain. He also separated alcohol from the substance of the liver, and the bile; and detected it in the urine of men and dogs. He also showed that when alcohol was introduced into the circulation, it caused death, by it specific effect upon the nerve centres, and not by coagulating the blood as stated by Orfila. By his experiments he also furnished strong proof that the effects of alcohol are due to its absorption and conveyance in substance to organs on which its peculiar influence is exerted, except in cases where the introduction of large doses of alcohol act so powerfully, as to produce a shock to the nerve-centres, similar to a blow in the region of the stomach. Dr. Percy's experiments were either not well known, or not appreciated, else the Liebigian theory of the food value of alcohol could not have been so generally admitted. But modern science takes nothing for granted. It demands that everything shall be demonstrated; and proof that alcohol undergoes a combustive process is still wanting. It has been observed by some experimenters, that there is less carbonic acid exhaled after taking alcohol; and to account for this, it is taken for granted that the

---

* An experimental inquiry concerning the presence of alcohol in the ventricles of the brain, after poisoning by that liquid. By Dr. Percy, of Nottingham, 1839.

alcohol is decomposed; and, as hydrogen in alcohol bears a larger proportion to the carbon than it does to other hydro-carbons in the blood, a greater portion of the inspired oxygen, it is supposed, is converted into water, and a smaller into carbonic acid.

60. To solve the question of the combustion, or non-combustion of alcohol in the animal body, the derivatives of alcohol have been sought for in the blood.

61. The first derivative formed by oxydizing alcohol is aldehyde; that is, alcohol minus two atoms of hydrogen, which unites with oxygen to form water.

62. The second is acetic acid, which results from further oxydation, in which the two equivalents of hydrogen removed to form water are replaced by an additional equivalent of oxygen.

63. If these two derivatives were found in the blood, it would indicate that some oxydation had taken place. Alcohol, it was asserted by Bouchardat and Sandras, is burned off by the respiration to form at once carbonic acid and water; and that they had sometimes discovered in the vapour from the lungs small quantities of alcohol and acetic acid. They thought that death from alcohol was due to its greed for oxygen, which it attracts from the other constituents of the blood; producing the same effects as if the animal had been asphyxiated in an atmosphere containing no oxygen.

64. Then again, M. Duchek tried to prove that when alcohol entered the circulation it was changed, first into aldehyde, then to acetic acid, which gave rise to oxalic acid, before being finally disposed of, as carbonic acid and water. It would certainly be a strong argument in favour of combustion, if it could be proved that these changes had taken place.

65. But Buckheim, a much higher authority on these matters, questioned Duchek's conclusions, and proved that there was not enough evidence to confirm the assumption that aldehyde was present in the blood of animals poisoned by alcohol, but that the facts were strongly against the assumption. He also proved the presence of alcohol in the condensed products of perspiration, and also in the urine, but failed to detect either acetic acid or oxalic acid or anything else in the blood or excretions, that indicated the metamorphosis of alcohol within the body. This was the aspect of the question, of the action of alcohol in the body, prior to 1860, there being no proof that it is decomposed in the system, but facts pointed strongly against that presumption.

IS ALCOHOL ELIMINATED FROM THE HUMAN BODY?

66. MM. Lallemand, Perrin, and Duroy* who had been engaded for several years examining anæsthetics, discovered a mode of detecting the presence of chloroform in the blood and tissues of

* Du Role l'Alcool, et des Anesthesiques dans l'Organisme, Racherches Experementales. Paris, 1860.

the body; and established also, that when this agent is inhaled, it is received in substance in the blood, and carried to the brain, and may be extracted after death; that when inhalation is suspended the chloroform is rapidly eliminated in substance with the breath from the lungs.

67. Encouraged by their success, they extended their method of inquiry to other anæsthetics, and substances having affinity with them. Their attention was naturally turned to alcohol being related to the anæsthetics in chemical composition and physiological action. They employed, as Dr. Percy had done, the methods of distillation and condensation to detect the presence of alcohol, in their earlier experiments, and proved, as he had done, that alcohol received into the stomach is rapidly absorbed into the blood, and then into the substance of the nerve centres. They used the same means in searching for alcohol in the exhalations of the lungs. Two men, who had taken brandy, were caused to expire through an apparatus fitted to condense the vapour of the breath; but on distilling the liquid, they failed to obtain a trace of alcohol.

68. It fortunately happened that they had placed at the extremity of the apparatus a tube containing a solution of bichrommate of potash in sulphuric acid, a red liquid, which changes to emerald green, when certain organic compounds are mixed with it. They observed that the expired air, separated from its watery parts, rapidly produced this change, in passing through the tube, and that persons who had not taken alcohol might breathe through the tube for any length of time without producing any change; and therefore justly concluded that the change in the colour of the solution indicated the presence of alcohol, or some of its derivatives. Experiments were carefully made to discover if *aldehyde* was present in the blood of animals, having received alcohol in their stomachs, without the least trace being found; but aldehyde was readily detected, when administered, clearly proving that alcohol is not converted into *aldehyde*.

69. They found that if alcohol remained in the stomach a certain length of time, a trifling amount was changed into acetic acid, by the influence of the ferment in the gastric juice; but traces of acetic acid being also found when alcohol has not been taken, it is no evidence that alcohol is converted into acetic acid in the blood.

70. The chromic test being conclusively established, a series of fresh experiments were made, to ascertain how alcohol was disposed of in the living animal.

71. A solution of bichromate of potash in sulphuric acid, of known strength, being prepared, a definite measure of it was put into a glass tube of fixed diameter, and air containing alcoholic vapour passed through it, the red colour of the solution was changed to emerald green, which afforded a definite standard of comparison; so that by substituting one tube for another, as the

conversion was complete in each, until no further change was perceived, the proportional amounts of alcoholic vapour given off in different experiments were readily ascertained by the total quantity of solution changed; and, as the time required for the conversion of the quantity of air passing through the tube was the same, it gave the measures; which was a very ready and useful application in the process of detecting alcohol in products of respiration.

72. To make the matter still clearer, we will give one or two of the investigations. In one experiment a man took a litre of red wine, containing 16 per cent. of alcohol, his meal terminating at 10½ A. M. His breath at 1 P. M. was found to convert a centimetre of the test liquid in two minutes; at 2 P. M. in four minutes; at 4 P. M. in ten minutes; and at 5 P. M, in fifteen minutes; whilst at 6 P. M., after fifteen minutes, the colour of the liquid was but slightly changed; at 7 P.M. no change was perceived. By this gradual diminution, the period of entire cessation of the elimination of alcohol, by the pulmonary exhalations, was definitely indicated.

73. The urine of the same person, was also subjected to the chromic test at similar intervals, when it was found that 60 grammes of that excretion, passed at mid-day, gave alcoholic vapour enough to change the colour of 16 cubic centimetres of the test liquid; the same quantity, passed at 2 P. M. produced the like effect on 15 cubic centimetres: at 4 P. M. on 12; at 6 P. M. on ten; at 8 P. M. on four; at 10 P. M. on one; whilst that passed at midnight gave but a faint trace of the re-action. By this method they were not only able to test the excretions of the lungs and kidneys, but to detect the presence of alcohol in the vapour exhaled from the skin of a dog, in a state of alcoholic intoxication. They also traced the passage of alcohol in the blood-currents and all the tissues of the body; the liver and the brain being the parts in which it tended most to accumulate; but the proportion notably differed in these two organs, according as the alcohol had been taken into the stomach, and passed through the portal circulation, in direct relation to the liver substance; or was brought into the general circulation at once by injection.

74. In the former case if the proportion of alcohol obtained from a given weight of the blood, be represented by 100, the proportion by the same weight of brain tissue and liver, were 1.34 and 1.48 respectively. But in the latter, from the same weight of brain and liver, the proportions were 3,000 and 1.75 respectively.

75. In both cases the proportion obtained from muscular flesh was much less than was yielded from the blood. By these and other experiments, varied and repeated, these gentlemen were fully satisfied that alcohol was separated from the blood, by the tissues, and particularly by the substance of the brain and the liver, and that the organs are continually engaged in eliminating it, even when the quantity introduced into the system was small;

while the larger the quantity of alcohol taken into the body, the longer the period required for its entire elimination from the system.

76. MM. Lallamand, Perrin, and Duroy, by their experiments, felt justified in drawing the conclusion that alcohol is not decomposed, but when taken into the body, is excreted as alcohol. So that it has no claims to be ranked as a food; but must be classed among those poisonous and medical agents, whose presence in the animal system exert a powerful influence for good or evil, without entering into composition with any of the components of the body.

77. While they did not claim, in every instance, that they had succeeded in reproducing the whole amount of alcohol taken or introduced into the system, yet they very justly claimed that such demonstration cannot fairly be expected, or reasonably exacted. For, while on one hand there is entire absence of any proof whatever, that alcohol is eliminated by the process of combustion; the assumption that it is eliminated by combustion, is met by the fact that none of the derivatives of alcohol are detectable in the blood; for if they were really there, their presence could easily be detected; and that alcohol is decomposed, is rendered still more improbable by the length of time which it can be shown that it remains in the body, even when taken in small quantities.

78. While, on the other hand, we have positive evidence that it is eliminated unchanged in any of its characteristics as alcohol, by the excretions of the lungs, kidneys, and the skin; and that it is found in the substance of the brain, liver, and blood, after persons have died from alcoholic poisoning. In one case, after drinking a litre of brandy, although emetics and other remedial agents were early used, the man died; when alcohol was found in the brain, liver, and blood, thirty-two hours after the brandy was taken.

79. The results of these experiments we learn from the following translation, by Dr. Lees, who styles it the:

ALCOHOLIC ALPHABET.

A. Alcohol ingested into the stomach, applied to the skin, or introduced as a vapour into the lungs, is absorbed into the veins, and carried by the blood into all the tissues.

B. The injection of alcohol produces upon animals an intoxication, that is marked by a progressive series of functional disturbances, and alterations, the intensity of which corresponds with the quantity of alcohol absorbed.

C. It manifests itself at first by a general excitement, but very soon the respiration and circulation are relaxed, and the temperature lowered.

D. Muscular power is weakened and extinguished; always beginning at the extremities.

E. The insensibility gradually extends to the centres (as in dead drunkenness).

F. The heart is the last to die (ultimum moriens).

G. The time that elapses between the beginning of intoxication and death varies from forty-five minutes to three hours.

H. When the dose is not sufficient to induce death; the excitability of the nervous system returns after a time, varying, with circumstances.

I. The arterial blood remains bright, and preserves all its apparent qualities, nearly up to the moment of death.

J. *Alcoholized blood contains, during life and after death, a great number of free, fatty globules, visible to the naked eye.*

K. The pathological alterations are; *vivid inflammation* of the *mucous membrane* of the *stomach;* the accumulation of the blood in the right chamber of the heart and the large veins; congestion of the meninges, and especially of the lungs.

L. All solids or liquids in union with alcohol, are easily separated by distillation, proportionately by the method of volumes.

M. Alcohol taken by the stomach enters into the liver, and the substance of the brain; if in the blood it is represented as 1.0; in the brain it is 1.34, in the liver 1.48.

N. Diluted alcohol produces the same effect when introduced by injection into the veins, as when introduced into the stomach, but operates more rapidly. The animal succumbs in less than twenty minutes.

O. Alcohol injected into the veins, spreads to all the tissues, but accumulates most largely in the brain; being in the liver 1.75, in the cerebral matter, 3.

P. Death by alcoholic poisoning, is due primarily to its special action upon the nervous centres.

Q. After the injection of a small dose of brandy (25 grammes =360 grains), the blood continues to manifest the presence of alcohol by chemical re-action for many hours.

R. *We never found in either the blood or tissues, any of the derivatives of alcohol.*

S. Only in the stomach was found a trace of acetic acid, generated from alcohol by the ferment of the gastric juice.

T. Alcohol is rejected from the vital economy by divers systems of elimination; by the lungs, the skin and the kidneys.

U. These organs are found to eliminate alcohol after the ingestion of very small doses.

V. The elimination lasts many hours; even after an ingestion very moderate, the kidneys continue longest to reject it.

X. Aldehyde, introduced into the stomach, is readily found in the blood.

Y. The aldehyde is, in great part, eliminated, partly transformed into acetic acid.

Z. Alcohol has the same action, and produces the same effects upon men and upon the lower animals.

80. By these different experiments we find that when alcoholic drinks are used, the alcohol enters into the blood current and permeates every part of the body; that it undergoes no chemical change in the system, but is eliminated through the excretory organs, particularly the lungs and the kidneys, within a few hours; that while the blood is circulating through the body, the sensibility of the brain and the nervous system is diminished by the alcohol, as by other anæsthetics; which retard the active and normal changes of the tissues, and consequently diminishes eliminations.

81. If these are facts and scientific truths, we must conclude that the food hypothesis is a myth; and that the old doctrine must make way for the new.

82. If alcohol is food, so is ether, chloroform, &c., the difference in their action being only secondary; for alcohol taken into the stomach (or the vapour of ether or chloroform inhaled by the lungs,) as soon as received into the blood current is treated as an intruder, a foreign invader, and removed as quickly as possible by the excretory organs. But as might be expected, the conclusions of these French experiments excited an animated and interesting discussion, in which Baudot, Trousseau, Schulinus, Edward Smith, Anstie, Thudicum, Duprè, Parkes, Subbotin, Richardson and others took a part. While all agreed that a part of the alcohol passed out of the body unchanged, they were not, as will be seen, agreed as to what became of the remainder.

ELIMINATION OF ALCOHOL ONLY PARTIAL.

83. A. Duprè, Ph. D., read a paper on the subject before the Royal Society of London, the substance of which may be summed up as follows: The amount of alcohol eliminated per day does not increase with the continuance of the use of alcohol; therefore all the alcohol consumed daily, must of necessity be disposed of daily; and, as it certainly is not eliminated within that time, it must be destroyed in the system.

84. The elimination of alcohol following the ingestion of a dose or doses, ceases in from nine to twenty-four hours after the last dose. The amounts of alcohol eliminated both in the breath and urine are a minute fraction only of the amount taken.

85. Dr. Duprè, states that after six weeks' abstinence, and even in the case of a teetotaller, he discovered a substance eliminated in the urine, and perhaps also in the breath, which, though apparently not alcohol, gives all the reactions ordinarily used for the detection of traces of alcohol, viz.: it passes over with the first portions of the distillate; it yields acetic acid on oxydation; gives the usual green reaction with bichromate of potash and strong sulphuric acid; yields iodoform, and its aqueous solution,

has a lower specific gravity, and a higher vapour tension than that of water.

86. It was found that after the elimination of injected alcohol had ceased, the amount of this substance eliminated in a given time was below the quantity normally excreted, and only gradually rose again to the normal standard.

87. The main point raised by Dr. Duprè's experiments is, that, "The amount of acohol per day does not increase with the continuance of the use of alcohol; therefore it must be somehow destroyed in the system."

EXPERIMENTS OF DR. SUBBOTIN.

88. The method employed by Dr. Subbotin, to establish the presence of alcohol, consisted in its conversion into acetic acid by chromic acid. Sometimes he used the pure chromic acid, sometimes a proportional mixture of bichromate of potash and sulphuric acid. He mixed first the chrome salt, or chromic acid, with the liquid to be tested, and then added the sulphuric acid, much diluted, closed the vessel, and kept the whole warm for 24 hours.

89. The acetic acid was then obtained by distillation, and its amount estimated by soda solution. These experiments were made, on the principle of Pettenkoffer's breathing apparatus.

90. The diluted alcohol (29 per ct. of absolute), was thrown into the stomach of an animal through the opened œsophagus in quantities of 5 to 10 to 15 cubic centemeters.

91. The expired air was first passed through a vessel of distilled water, and then through a series of pipes containing chromic acid solution, and the last two, a strong solution of caustic soda. The first pipe was, during the experiments, warmed by means of a water bath.

92. Experiments on rabbits gave the following results

1st. In the first five hours after the injection of the alcohol, a not inconsiderable quantity of it was excreted by the lungs, skin and kidneys. 2nd. Through the skin and lungs at least twice as much alcohol was separated, as through the kidneys, in opposition to the assertions of Lallemand, Perrin and Duroy. 3rd. The amount of alcohol obtained is only a fraction of what is really excreted, because so much is lost in various ways, and because the experiments only lasted some five or six hours; whereas excretion is lively even after 24 hours, if the dose has been large. He came to the conclusion that in 24 hours after the ingestion of the alcohol at least 16 per cent of it is excreted unchanged (or as aldehyde '

DR. ANSTIE'S "FINAL EXPERIMENTS."

93. In "The Practitioner," for July, 1874, the late Dr. Anstie, published a series of experiments, under the title of "FINAL EXPERIMENTS ON THE ELIMINATION OF ALCOHOL FROM THE BODY," which were prophetically "his final experiments," as he died suddenly from a dissection wound, September 12, 1874, three months after their publication.

94. These experiments were made to decide, if possible, whether alcohol in any appreciable extent escaped unchanged from the body. With this view, the excretions, which might be the channels of the elimination, were examined.

95. Dr. Anstie considers that the subject of elimination of unchanged alcohol, may now be considered as closed, and that we can see our way to the discussion of other very important questions, respecting the physiological role of alcohol. He says:

96. "It is impossible to fully appreciate the importance of the further inquiries which must be made, respecting the action of alcohol, unless we remember the actual state of physiological knowledge respecting the process of alimentation. No physiologist, of any standing at the present, doubts that the hydrocarbons (fats,) and hydrates of carbon (starch, sugar,) by their consumption produce available force within the body, and in fact, that the bulk of the work done in the organism, is obtained from these substances."

97. "Alcohol," as Dr. Pavy remarks, "stands in a peculiar position, being intermediate, as to composition, between these two classes of foods (Hydro-carbons and Carbohydrates.) Being, as it is, a most highly oxydizable substance, it would be strange indeed, if its oxydation did not prove to be the mode by which alcohol disappears within the organism."* * *

98. I think I may take it as conceded that quite 600 grains of absolute alcohol, can be disposed of daily, within the organism of an adult male, without any perceptible injurious effect upon the bodily functions.

99. "Now this quantity of alcohol is (theoretically) capable of generating an enormous amount of force," (and how much force practically,) "but it is equally certain, that that force does not show itself under the form of heat. It is scarcely possible, therefore, but that the solution of the question as to the action of alcohol in the body, will also bring about the discovery of new physiological facts of great interest and importance: 1st. If alcohol be a force-producing food, as seems by far the most likely, it is probably of great value in that capacity, on account of the rapidity with which its transformations take place. It is, however, abundantly certain, that beyond a certain dosage (which is pretty clearly made out for the average, though, of course, there are individual exceptions in both directions), it becomes a narcotic poison of a dangerous character in every

respect, not the least disadvantage being that it cannot be eliminated to any considerable extent. 2nd. If alcohol does not disappear by oxydation, it must undergo some, as yet quite unknown transformations, after which it must escape unrecognized in the excretions. I have heard various attempts to suggest such modes of disappearance, but nothing, so far, which wears any air of probability. 3rd. If alcohol, however, be indeed oxydized, and yet does not beget force which can be used in the organism, this would be the strangest possible discovery, considering the very high theoretical force value of the 600 to 800 grains of absolute alcohol, which millions of sober persons are taking every day, we may well be hopeless of any reasonable answer to the question. Why does not this large development, of wholly useless force within the body, produce some violent symptoms of disturbance?"

REMARKS ON THE ELIMINATION OF ALCOHOL.

100. The foregoing are some of the chief experiments and views, regarding the elimination of alcohol from the body. Is the evidence for or against the total elimination of alcohol, strong enough for us to decide that all is eliminated? or shall we conclude that only a small portion is cast out unaltered, as alcohol? Though it must be owned that there is still room for further investigation, yet it is very probable that the greater portion passes out of the body unchanged. The important points in the question are:—Does alcohol arrest oxydation, or does it undergo oxydation? Are the alcohols burned in the body, and do they yield the same products of combustion:—carbonic acid and water, as when burned in a lamp, or are they burned at all? The evidence, as we have seen, is conflicting. On one side there is that of Percy, Lallemand, Perrin and Duroy, which goes to prove that alcohol is laid up in the tissues, until it is eliminated by the excretory organs. Then there are the experiments of Thudicum, Duprè and Anstie, showing that although when the body was super-saturated with it, free alcohol passed off by the urinary organs, yet this bears but a small proportion to what ought to be found, if the whole was eliminated in the form of alcohol.

101. Each and all agree, that it passes off by the urine, in certain stages of intoxication, as alcohol, but as the whole is not accounted for by their experiments, they therefore beg the question by assuming that the remainder is consumed by the system.

102. It must be admitted that great difficulties are in the way of the performance of all the necessary experiments, yet, it is clearly not sufficient to collect the alcohol only for a short time, and then infer that it always passes off at the same rate; nor to collect it merely at one or two outlets, when the presumption is that it must pass out at all of them. Before concluding that because only a small part of what is injected, is collected as alcohol, the remainder is consumed in the system, we must know how

much the body will hold, and how much can be held in combination with the water of the tissues, as the blood alone contains about 790 parts of water in 1000; and also how long a time must pass, before a given quantity of alcohol is actually removed from the tissues with the excretions.

103. From the well-known greed of alcohol for water, there can be but little, or no doubt, that a large quantity taken will become absorbed with the water in the tissues; and hence remain within the system long after the period when it ceases to be detected in the excretions of the lungs, skin, kidneys, &c.

104. It is scarcely presumable that all the alcohol taken into the body could be detected in the excretions, yet failing to detect it, is made the test of the value of alcohol as a food. As Dr. Parkes well said in reply to Dr. Anstie:* "Even if complete destruction within certain limits were quite clear, this fact alone would not guide us to the dietetic use of alcohol. We have first to trace the effect of the destruction, and learn whether it is for good or evil."

105. To claim because alcohol is not detected that it must be oxydized in the body, is claiming more for the action of alcohol in the system than for the action of other drugs. It is not reasonable or fair to assume because it is not collected from the tissues and excretions that it must be food. Its mode of destruction, if it be destroyed, is not known, and there is no chemical law that will warrant the claim that it must be food, if it is not found in the excretions. We are unable to conceive of the very high theoretical force value of the 600 or 800 grains of absolute alcohol, that Dr. Anstie says, "millions of sober persons are taking daily." * * He asks: "Why does not this large development of wholly useless force within the body produce some violent symptoms of disturbance?"

106. While we do not believe in the "force value of the 600 or 800 grains of alcohol daily taken," we have no difficulty in perceiving "some violent symptoms of disturbance."

107. These disturbances are seen everywhere among the users of alcohol, and the doctor need not search far to find them, as will be shown hereafter when we notice the diseases produced by alcoholics. Alcohol can give no force, as it cannot give nutrition in any form or quantity. True there appears to be an increase of temperature, in the first stage of alcoholic excitement; but it is brief, and we may justly apprehend it to be the effect of local irritation and paralysis of the nerves, and not an augmentation of force: for no sooner does alcohol find its way into the organism, and diffuse itself through the fluids, than depression takes place, respiration is impeded, carbonic acid is decreased, muscular power diminished, and the sensibility and consciousness blunted.

108. If active combustion or oxydation of alcohol took place within the body, we should reasonably expect that the tempera-

---

* Practitioner, 1872, p. 85.

ture would be permanently increased; but all will agree that the temperature generally declines after the ingestion of alcohol. It is impossible when the animal system is burning faster than is normal, that it should be colder than it is naturally.

109. A slight oxydation may occur when the blood, diluted with alcohol, is carried by the circulating current to the lungs, and exposed to the air, for this will occur if diluted alcohol is left exposed to the air, out of the body. It is also possible that acid oxydation may take place, as is demonstrated, by free acid sweating, and the acid secretions from the intestines after alcoholic intoxication, especially by wine and malt liquors. This acid oxydation may perhaps mainly proceed from the fermentation that sometimes occurs within the stomach, caused by the drinking of wines and malt liquors that have been imperfectly fermented.

110. Another fact opposed to the combustive theory of alcohol in the body is this, that none of its derivatives are found in the system, unless they have been taken independently of or in addition to the alcohol. Lallamand, Perrin and Duroy failed to discover any aldehyde, except that which had been administered, when it was readily detected. When we see ashes, there is the evidence that something has been burned; as aldehyde, a derivative of alcohol, has not been detected in the animal system, as an evidence that alcohol has been decomposed, it is very clear that it does not undergo in the animal the combustive process claimed for it.

111. The weight of evidence shows that it enters the animal system, alcohol, and leaves it, the same compound. It must also be borne in mind, that alcohol will accumulate in the brain, spinal cord and nerves, as was shown by Dr. Hammond, in his New York lecture; and it is also well known that it accumulates in the blood, liver, and other organs, and tissues; hence it is reasonable to expect that but a small portion would escape with the excretions. And further, as alcohol is found and extracted from the organs and tissues long after its ingestion, it must be very evident, that it had not undergone the process of oxydation; hence we must still doubt that it is decomposed in the animal body, or in any way serves to build up the tissues, or produce force.

EXTRACT FROM DR. RICHARDSON'S CANTOR LECTURES.

112. Dr. Richardson, in his late lectures,* after speaking of the various experiments to discover the mode by which alcohol is removed from the organism, says: "It is a subject on which I

---

* Six Cantor Lectures, delivered at the request of the Council of the Society of Arts, before the Society, November, December, January and February, 1874-5. P. 72-3.

hope, with some degree of experimental certainty. * * * I may venture to add in advance two or three suggestions to which my researches, as far as they go, point.

113. "Firstly, I believe there is a certain determinable degree of saturation of the blood with alcohol, within which degree all the alcohol is disposed of by its decomposition. Beyond that degree the oxydation is arrested, and then there is an accumulation of alcohol, with voidance of it, in the unchanged state, in the secretions.

114. "Secondly, the change or decomposition of the alcohol in its course through the minute circulation, in which it is transformed, is not into carbonic acid and water, as though it were burned, but into a new soluble, chemical substance, probably aldehyde, which returns by the veins, into the great channels of the circulation."

"Thirdly, I think I have made out that there is an outlet for the alcohol, or for the fluid product of its decomposition, into the alimentary canal, through the secretion of the liver. Thrown into the canal, it is, I believe, subjected there to further oxydation, is in fact oxydized by a process of fermentation attended with the active development of gaseous substances. From this surface the oxydized product is in turn re-absorbed in great part and carried into the circulation, and is disposed of by combination with bases or by further oxydation. Here, however, I leave the theoretical point to revert to the practical, and the practical is this: that alcohol cannot by any ingenuity of excuse for it, be classified amongst the foods of man. It neither supplies matter for construction nor heat. On the contrary, it injures construction, and it reduces temperature."

PART III.

PHYSIOLOGICAL ACTION OF ALCOHOL.

115. WHAT alcohol does, or its physiological action while in the body, has claimed considerable attention from scientific investigators. The most important and conclusive of these experiments and observations are those of Dr. B. W. Richardson, F. R. S., of England. From these experiments the progress to complete intoxication is shown to be through four distinct stages. These stages vary with the different alcohols used, and whose narcotic action increases in proportion to the weight of the carbon and hydrogen which they contain.

116. Of methylic alcohol, the lightest of the series, Dr. Richardson says:*—"The first stage is that of excitement of the nervous organization; the pulse is quickened, the breathing is quickened, the surface of the body is flushed, and the pupil dilated. After a little time there is a sense of languor, the muscles falling into a state of prostration, and the muscular movements become irregular.

117. Thereupon the second stage follows, if the administration be continued. In this second stage, the muscular prostration is increased, the breathing is laboured, and is attended by deep sighing movements, at intervals of about four or five seconds, followed by further prostration, rolling over of the body upon the side, and distinct signs of intoxication.

118. From this condition the subject passes to the third stage, which is that of entire intoxication, complete insensibility to pain, with unconsciousness of all external objects, and with inability to exert any voluntary muscular power. The breathing now becomes embarrassed and blowing, with what is technically called "bronchial rale," or rattle, due to the passage of air through fluid which has accumulated in the finer bronchial passages. The heart and lungs, however, even in this stage, retain their functions, and therefore recovery will take place, if the conditions for it be favourable. Also, if the body be touched or irritated in parts, there will be response of motion, not from any knowledge or consciousness, but from what physiologists call "reflex action;" that is to say, the impression we have made by irritation upon the surface of the body, has travelled by its usual route through the nerves to its centre, in the brain; and uncontrolled there by consciousness has rolled back again, stimulating in its course some muscular fibre to motion. Probably the reason why the heart, which is a muscle, and the breathing muscles continue to beat while all the other portions are at rest, is due to this fact, that the blood which the heart drives to the brain and other nervous centres, conveys to the centres which supply the heart a wave of motion, that rolls back upon these vital muscles, and sustains them still in rhythmical motion." We also learn that:

119. "During these stages there is no violent convulsive action from this alcoholic, no distinct tremor," but the marked phenomena through all of them is a reduction of animal temperature. The body exposed even 80° (summer heat), will begin to cool (Cantor Lect., p. 32), from the first, and will continue through all the stages, so that at last, the loss of heat will become dangerous, for the cold body cannot throw off water freely, and there is risk of suffocation, like that of drowning. The "decline of temperature from methylic alcohol in animals narcotized by it, proceeded to the loss of eight degrees of heat on Fahrenheit's scale, when insensibility was at its extreme point."

* Cantor Lectures, English Edition, page 31.

120. "Presuming that the administration of the methylic alcohol be continued, when the third stage has been reached. there is a last stage, which is that of death. The two remaining centres which feed the heart and respiration cease simultaneously to act, and all motion is over. After death the blood throughout the body is found charged with the alcohol. The circulation of the blood over the lungs has continued to the last, and so the lungs are found containing blood in both sides of the heart; the vessels of the brain are engorged with blood, as are the other vascular organs. The blood itself is not materially changed in physical quality, but coagulates, or forms into clots rather more slowly than usual."

121. "If, at the third stage of insensibility, the administration of methylic alcohol is stopped, recovery takes place if the body is kept dry and warm, from four to five hours, but the restoration of the animal temperature is not perfected under seven hours." These facts are drawn from careful observation, and though methylic alcohol is the lightest and less potent than the others; its use, if long continued, would lead to structural changes, and pervert the natural functions of the organism. "An agent (Cantor Lec., p. 33,) that causes congestion of the brain, cannot be employed many times without destroying the delicate organization of the vascular structure of the brain, neither can it influence the other vascular organs in the same way without prejudice to their structure; neither can it destroy the functions of the nerves of the muscles, and of the organs of the senses without prejudice to their functions."

THE ACTION OF BUTYLIC ALCOHOL,

122. Butylic alcohol is the third in the series, (see p. 20), and one of the heavier bodies of the group, containing a larger proportion of carbon and hydrogen than the methyl and ethyl alcohols. It is not obtained by special distillation, but is produced with other alcohols in the process of fermentation, and is obtained by distillation, at a certain fixed temperature, from fusel oil, or from the oil of beet-root, or from molasses after distillation of common alcohol.

123. "The action of butylic alcohol (Cantor Lec., p. 34,) on the animal body is divisable into four stages," the same as "methylic spirits, but the periods required for producing the different stages are greatly prolonged; and when the third stage, that of insensibility is reached, there is added a new phenomena. which does not belong to any of the lighter alcohols.

124. "In this third degree, after the temperature of the body is depressed to the minimum by the butylic spirit, distinct tremors occur throughout the whole body. * * * The tremors themselves are not positively muscular contractions, but are rather vibrations, or wave-like motions through the muscles,

and are attended with an extreme deficiency of true contractile power in the muscular fibres. * * * So long as these tremors are present, the temperature of the body is depressed, falling even half a degree; but when they cease, the temperature rises again, not to the natural standard, but to, or near that which existed before the tremors were excited. * * * They are the tremors which occur in man during the stage of alcoholic disease, when there is set up that malady," called '*delirium tremens*.' In this condition "the voluntary system of nerve and muscle is well-nigh dead, and recovery will rest entirely on the maintenance of the organic nervous power. Still, recovery will take place if the body be sustained by external heat, and by internal nourishment.

125 In the extreme stage of intoxication from butylic alcohol, the red blood in the arteries loses its rich colour, and the blood from the veins which flows with difficulty, is of a dirty hue.

126. The blood coagulates readily, but the clot is loose, and the fibrin of which it is composed, separates in a coarse net-work or mesh. The little corpuscles of the blood run into each other, forming rolls or columns. Indeed, it is wonderful how the blood circulates through the structures it should nourish. The vascular membranes of the brain are found charged with this tary blood; the brain structure is softened, and gives the odour of the poison, and the muscles, when divided by the knife, cut without firmness, yielding from numerous points the same tar-like blood.

127. The vascular organs—spleen, liver, lungs, kidneys,—are equally changed in a similar manner, Their fine structures are infiltrated with the deteriorated vascular fluid which was intended for their maintenance, and even the secretions and the cavities of the body are perverted by being charged with fluid derived from unnatural blood. This is the state of the body of one who dies insensible after the delirium and tremors, which characterize the human malady, self-inflicted and terrible, known as *delirium tremens*."—(See plate VI.)

THE ACTION OF AMYLIC ALCOHOL.

128. Amylic alcohol is the fourth of the series, and is obtained by the fermentation of potato-starch, or starch of grain, as corn, rye, &c., and is commonly known as *fusel oil*. It has a burning, acrid taste, and is itself practically insoluble in water, but when diluted with ethylic, or common alcohol, it dissolves freely in water, and hence is often used to adulterate or give a strong, burning taste to liquors, after their strength has been reduced, to increase the profits of the dealers. When used, as it often is, to adulterate *common alcohol*, it is very dangerous. A man whose business, he informed me, was to mix liquors for the retail dealers, called upon me for one dram of burnt sugar, one dram of tincture of capsicum, and one dram of fusel oil. He said by adding the above to five gallons of common whiskey, it could be

diluted with five gallons of water, and thus make ten gallons of whiskey, as good as is generally sold in the retail drink shops.

129. Dr. Richardson says (Can. Lect. p. 37): "Its action on the body is about the same as *butylic* alcohol. It produces three stages of insensibility, ending in the profoundest narcotism or coma, followed by reduction of temperature and by muscular tremours." * * * "In all respects the phenomena induced are the same as are observed from butylic alcohol, except that they are much more prolonged, from two to three days being sometimes required for the complete restoration of the animal temperature. The reason of this prolongation of action lies in the greater weight and the greater insolubility of this spirit; that is to say, the force required to decompose it, or mechanically to lift it out of the body when it has once entered it, is so much greater than is required for the lighter spirits, which diffuse more readily through the secretions, volatilize by the breath, or possibly undergo rapid decomposition."

130. The action of these heavier alcohols has been noticed, from the consideration that they are often mixed with common alcohol and may aid us to account for many effects that follow the use of common alcohol.

THE ACTION OF ETHYLIC ALCOHOL.

131. Ethylic alcohol, as already seen, is the spirit which enters into, and is the essential intoxicating principle of wines, malt, and spirituous liquors. On the action of this alcohol, within the body, Dr. Richardson says (Can. Lec. p. 41): "Suppose then a certain measure of alcohol be taken into the stomach, it will be absorbed there; but previous to absorption it will have to undergo a proper degree of dilution with water, for there is this peculiarity respecting alcohol when it is separated by an animal membrane from a watery fluid like the blood, that it will not pass through the membrane until it has become charged to a given point of dilution with water. It is itself so greedy for water it will pick it up from watery tissues, and deprive them of it until, by its saturation, its power of reception is exhausted, after which it will diffuse into the current of circulating fluid. * * Alcohol, therefore, entering the veins, makes its way * * * through the right heart, through the lungs, through the left heart, through the body at large by the arteries. * * What does it do in making this round?"

132. "As it passes through the circulation of the lungs it is exposed to the air, and some little of it raised into vapour by the natural heat, is thrown off in expiration. If the quantity be large this loss is considerable, and the odour of the spirit may be detected in the expired breath. If the quantity be small the loss will be comparatively small, as the spirit will be held in solution by water in the blood. * * * In its passage through the minute

circulation the alcohol finds its way to every organ. To the brain, the muscles, the secreting and excreting organs, nay even into the bony structure, it moves with the blood. In the parts not excreting it remains for a time diffused; and in the parts where there is a large percentage of water it remains longer than in other parts. From organs which have an open tube for conveying fluids away, as the liver and kidneys, it is thrown out or eliminated, and in this way a portion of it is ultimately removed from the body.

133. "The rest passing round and round with the circulation, is probably decomposed and carried off in new forms of matter." Dr. Richardson says of its action on the blood, "If however, the dose taken be poisonous or semi-poisonous, then the blood, rich as it is in water (790 parts in 1000) is affected." "The alcohol diffusing through the water, comes in contact with the other constituents, with the fibrine, that plastic substance, which, when blood is drawn, clots and coagulates, and which is present in the proportion of two to three parts in a thousand; with albumen which exists in the proportion of seventy parts in a thousand; with the salts, ten parts in a thousand; with the fatty matters: and lastly with the minute round bodies, the blood globules or corpuscles, which are in fact cells, red in colour, and give the colour to the blood. Besides these red corpuscles there are others called the white corpuscles. These different cells float in the blood stream within the vessels. The red corpuscles perform the most important functions in the economy, as they absorb in great part the oxygen which we inhale in breathing, and carry it to the extreme tissues of the body; they absorb in great part the carbonic gas which is produced in the combustion of the body in the extreme tissues, and bring that gas back to the lungs, to be exchanged for oxygen there; in short they are the vital instruments of the circulation."

134. "With all these parts of the blood, with the water, fibrine, albumen, salts, fatty matter and corpuscles, the alcohol comes in contact when it enters the blood, and if it be in sufficient quantity, it produces disturbing action. * * * It may cause the corpuscles to run too closely together, and to adhere in rolls; * * it may change the round corpuscles into the oval form; or in very extreme cases it may produce * * * a truncated form of corpuscles in which the change is so great that if we did not trace it through all its changes, we should be puzzled to know whether the object looked at was indeed a blood-cell. "All these changes are due to the action of the spirit upon the water contained in the corpuscles; upon the capacity of the spirit to extract water from them. During every stage of the modification of the corpuscles thus described, their function to absorb and fix gases is impaired; and when the aggregation of the cells in masses is great, other difficulties arise, for the cells united together pass less easily than they should through the minute

vessels of the lungs and of the general circulation, and impede the current, by which local injury is produced.

135. "A further action upon the blood instituted by alcohol in excess, is upon the fibrine, or the *plastic* colloidal matter. On this the spirit may act in two different ways, according to the degree in which it affects the water that holds the fibrine in solution. It may fix the water with the fibrine, and thus destroy the power of coagulation; or it may extract the water so determinately as to produce coagulation. These facts bear on a new and refined subject of research, with which I must not trouble you except to add that inquiry explains why in acute cases of poisoning by alcohol the blood is sometimes found quite fluid, at other times firmly coagulated in the vessels."

136. Dr. Richardson by various experiments has established the fact that alcohol paralyzes the minute blood vessels and allows them to become dilated with the flowing blood; and says, (Can. Lec. p. 49:) "If you attend a large dinner party you will observe, after the first courses, when the wine is beginning to circulate, a progressive change in some of those about you who have taken wine. The face begins to get flushed, the eye brightens, and the murmur of conversation becomes loud. What is the reason of that flushing of the conntenance? It is the same as the flush from blushing, or from the reaction of cold, or from the nitrite of amyl. It is the dilatation of the vessels following the reduction of nervous control, which reduction has been induced by the alcohol. In a word, the first stage of vascular excitement from alcohol, has been established. The action of alcohol extending so far, does not stop there. With the disturbance of the power in the extreme vessels, more disturbance is set up in other organs, and the first organ that shares in it is the heart. With each beat of the heart a certain degree of resistance is offered by the vessels when their nervous supply is perfect, and the stroke of the heart is moderated in respect to both tension and to time. But when the vessels are rendered relaxed, the resistance is removed, the heart begins to run quicker, like a watch from which the pallets have been removed, and the heart-stroke, losing nothing in force, is greatly increased in frequency, with a weakened recoil stroke. It is easy to account in this manner for the quickened heart and pulse which accompany the first stage of deranged action from alcohol, and you will be interested to know to what extent this increase of vascular action proceeds. * * * I traced in these observations an increase of beats of the heart amounting, in the course of two hours, to one-fourth beyond what was natural." Dr. Richardson, referring to the experiments of Dr. Parkes and Count Wollowicz, said, "Their results are stated by themselves, as follows:

ACTION OF ALCOHOL ON THE HEART—EXPERIMENTS OF DR. PARKES AND COUNT WOLLOWICZ.

137. "The average number of beats of the heart in 24 hours, (as calculated from eight observations made in 14 hours,) during the first or water period, was 106,000; in the earlier alcoholic period it was 127,000, or about 21,000 more; and in the later period it was 131,000, or 25,000 more. The highest of the daily means of the pulse observed during the first or water period was 77.5; but on this day two observations are deficient. The next highest daily mean was 77 beats. If instead of the eight days, or 73.57, we compare the mean of this one day, viz., 77 beats per minute, with the alcoholic days, so as to be sure not to overestimate the actions of alcohol, we find:—

On the 9th day, with one fluid ounce of alcohol, the heart beat 4.300 times more.
On the 10th day, with two fluid ounces of alcohol, 8,172 times more.
On the 11th day, with four fluid ounces of alcohol, 12.960 times more.
On the 12th day, with six fluid ounces of alcohol, 30.672 times more.
On the 13th day, with eight fluid ounces of alcohol, 23.904 times more.
On the 14th day, with eight fluid ounces of alcohol, 25.488 times more.

138. "But as there was ephemeral fever on the 12th day, it is right to make a deduction, and to estimate the number of beats in that day as midway between the 11th and 13th days, or 18,432. Adopting this, the mean daily excess of beats during the alcoholic days was 14.492, or an increase of rather more than 13 per cent. The first day of alcohol gave an excess of 4 per cent., and the last 23 per cent.; and the mean of these two gives almost the same percentage of excess as the mean of the six days.

139. "Admitting that each beat of the heart was as strong during the alcohol period as in the water period (and it was really more powerful,) the heart on the last two days alcohol, was doing one-fifth more work.

140. "Adopting the lowest estimate which has been given of the daily work of the heart, viz.: as equal to 122 tons lifted one foot, the heart, during the alcoholic period, did daily work in excess equal to lifting 15·8 tons one foot, and in the last two days did extra work, to the amount of 24 tons lifted as far.

141. "The period of rest for the heart was shortened, though perhaps not to such an extent as would be inferred from the number of beats, for each contraction was sooner over. The heart, on the fifth and sixth days after alcohol was left off, and apparently at the time when the last traces of alcohol were eliminated, showed in the sphygmographic tracings signs of unusual feebleness, and, perhaps, in consequence of this, when the brandy quickened the heart again, the tracings showed more rapid contractions of the ventricles, but less power in the alcoholic

period. The brandy acted in fact on a heart whose nutrition had not been perfectly restored."

142. Dr. Richardson, upon the above experiments (Cantor Lect. p. 52,) said : "It will seem, at first sight, almost incredible that such an excess of work could be put upon the heart, but it is perfectly credible when all the facts are known. The heart of an adult man makes, as we see above, 73.57 strokes per minute. This number, multiplied by sixty per hour, and again by 24 hours for the entire day, would give nearly 106,000 as the number of strokes per day. * * * * * With each of these strokes, the two ventricles of the heart, as they contract, lift up into their respective vessels three ounces of blood each, that is to say, six ounces with the combined stroke, or 600,000 in 24 hours.

143. "The equivalent of work rendered by this simpler calculation would be 116 foot tons ; and if we estimate the increase of work induced by alcohol, we shall find that four ounces of spirit increase it one-eighth part, six ounces one-sixth part, and eight ounces one-fourth part.

144. "The stage of primary excitement of the circulation thus induced, lasts for a considerable time, but at length the heart flags from over-action, and requires the stimulus of more spirit to carry on its work. Let us take what we may call a moderate amount of alcohol, say two ounces by volume, in the form of beer, or wine, or spirits, * * it matters not which, if the quantity of alcohol be regulated by the amount present in the liquor imbibed. When we reach the two ounces a distinct physiological effect follows, leading on to the first stage of excitement. * * The reception of spirit arrested at this point, there need be no important injury done, (?) but if the quantity imbibed be increased, further changes quickly occur. * * * All the organs of the body are built upon the vascular structures, and therefore it follows that a prolonged paralysis of the minute circulation must, of necessity, lead to disturbance in other organs than the heart.

145. "By common observation, the flush seen on the cheek during the first stage of alcoholic excitement, is presumed to extend merely to the parts actually exposed to view. It cannot, however, be too forcibly impressed, that the condition is universal in the body. If the lungs could be seen, they too would be found with their vessels injected ; if the brain and spinal cord could be laid open to view, they would be discovered in the same condition ; if the stomach, the liver, the spleen, the kidneys, or other vascular organs or parts, could be exposed, the vascular engorgement would be equally manifest.

146. * * * "I once had the unusual though unhappy opportunity of observing the * * phenomena in the brain structure of a man, who, in a paroxysm of alcoholic excitement, decapitated himself under the wheel of a railway carriage, and whose brain was instantaneously evolved from the skull by the crash. The

brain itself, entire, was before me three minutes after death. It exhaled the odour of spirits most distinctly, and its membranes and minute structures were vascular in the extreme. It looked as if it had been recently injected with vermilion. The white matter of the cerebrum, studded with red points, could scarcely be distinguished when it was incised, by its natural whiteness; and the pia-mater, or internal vascular membrane covering the brain, resembled a delicate web of coagulated red blood, so tensely were its fine vessels engorged. * * This condition extended through both the larger and smaller brain, the cerebrum and cerebellum, but was not so marked in the medulla or commencing portion of the spinal cord."

147. "The action of alcohol continued beyond the first stage, the function of the spinal cord is influenced. * * There follows quickly upon this a deficient power of co-ordination of muscular movement. The nervous control of certain muscles is lost, and the nervous stimulus is more or less enfeebled. The muscles of the lower lip in the human subject usually fail first of all, then the muscles of the lower limbs, * * the tensor muscles give way earlier than the flexors. The muscles themselves by this time, are also failing in power; they respond more feebly than is natural to the nervous stimulus; their structure is becoming temporarily deranged, under the depressing influence of the paralyzing agent, and their contractile power is reduced. This modification of the animal functions under alcohol, marks the second degree of its action.

148. If alcohol is carried still further, "the brain centres become influenced; they are reduced in power, and the controlling influence of *will* and *judgment* are lost. * * The rational part of the nature of man, gives way before the emotional, passional, or organic part. The reason is now off duty, or is fooling with duty, and all the mere animal instincts and sentiments are laid atrociously bare. The coward shows up more craven, the braggart more boastful, the cruel more merciless, the untruthful more false. 'In vino veritas,' expresses even indeed to physiological accuracy, the true condition. The reason, the emotions, the instincts, are all in a state of carnival, and in chaotic feebleness.

149. "Finally, the action of the alcohol still extending, the superior brain centres are overpowered; the senses are beclouded, the voluntary muscular prostration is perfected, sensibility is lost, and the body lies a mere log, dead by all but one-fourth, on which alone its life hangs. The heart still remains true to its duty, and while it just lives, it feeds the breathing power. And so the circulation and the respiration in the otherwise inert mass, keeps the mass within the bare domain of life, until the poison begins to pass away, and the nerves revive again. It is happy for the inebriate that, as a rule, the brain fails so long before the heart, that he has neither the power or the sense to continue his process of destruction, up to the act of death of his circulation, therefore he lives to die another day.

150. "Thus there are four stages of alcoholic action in the primary form, (*a*) a stage of vascular excitement and exhaustion; (*b*) a stage of excitement and exhaustion of the spinal cord with muscular perturbation; (*c*) a stage of unbalanced reasoning power, and of volition; (*d*) a stage of complete collapse of nervous function."

151. These are the stages of the action of alcohol upon those unaccustomed to it, and who have not become habituated to its use; "but if the experiment be repeated too often and too long, if it be continued after the term of life when the body is fully developed, when the elasticity of the membranes, and of the blood-vessels is lessened, and when the tone of the muscular fibre is reduced, then an organic series of structural changes, so characteristic of the persistent effects of spirits, become prominent and permanent. The external surface becomes darkened and congested, its vessels in part visibly large; the skin becomes blotched, the proverbial red nose is defined, and those other striking vascular changes which disfigure many who may probably be called moderate alcoholics, are developed." Dr. Richardson, speaking of these experiments and observations,[*] said: "For my own part I was ignorant, and that is why I sought for certain knowledge. To the research I devoted three years, viz.: from 1863 to 1866, modifying experiments in every conceivable way, taking advantage of seasons, and varying temperature of seasons, extending observations from one class of animals to another, and making comparative researches with other bodies of the alcohol series, than the *ethylic*, or common alcohol."

152. "The results, I confess were as surprising to me, as to any one else. They were surprising from their definiteness and their uniformity. They were most surprising from the complete contradiction they gave to the popular idea of alcohol as a supporter and sustainer of the animal temperature. * * I placed alcohol and cold side by side in experiment and found that they ran together equally to fatal effect, and I determined that in death, the great reduction of animal temperature was one of the most pressing causes of death." Again he said, in summing up his researches:[*]

153. "What I call the preliminary and physiological part of my research was now concluded. I had learned purely by experimental observation that in its action on the living body, this chemical substance, alcohol, deranges the constitution of the blood; unduly excites the heart, and respiration; paralyzes the minute blood vessels; increases and decreases according to the degree of its application, the functions of the digestive organs, of the liver, and of the kidneys; disturbs the regularity of nervous action; lowers the animal temperature; and lessens the muscular power. Such, independently of any prejudice of party or influence of sentiment, are the unanswerable teachings of the

---

[*] At the Medical Conference in the Sheldonian Theatre, Oxford, October 30, 1876.

sternest of all evidences, the evidences of experiment, of natural fact revealed to man by experimental testing of natural phenomena. If alcohol had never been heard of, as nitrite of amyl and many other chemical substances I have tested, had never been heard of by the masses of mankind, this is the evidence respecting alcohol which I should have collected, and these are the facts I should have recorded from the evidence. * * * This record of simple experimental investigation and results respecting the action of alcohol on the body were incomplete without two other observations which come in as a natural supplement. It will be asked, *was there no evidence of any good service rendered by the agent in the midst of so much obvious bad service?* I answer to that question THAT THERE WAS NO SUCH EVIDENCE WHATEVER, AND IS NONE."

THE EFFECTS OF ALCOHOL ON THE HUMAN BODY.

154. Dr. Parkes and Count Wollowicz undertook a series of experiments to demonstrate the physiological and dietetic effect of alcohol and to clear up several doubtful points.*

155. The subject of the experiments was an intelligent healthy soldier, 28 years old, five feet six inches in height, weighing from 134 to 136 lbs., clear, smooth skin, a clear bright eye, good teeth, largely developed, powerful muscles, and but little fat. Having been accustomed to smoke, he was allowed half an ounce of tobacco daily, lest being deprived of it, might disturb his health.

156. Though the amount of alcohol administered varied, it never was carried so far as to produce narcotic symptoms. For 26 days he remained on a diet precisely similar as to food and times of meals in every respect, except that for the first eight days he took only water (in the shape of coffee, tea, and simple water); for the next six days, he added to this diet rectified spirits, in such proportions, that he took, in divided quantities, on the first day, one fluid ounce (=28 C. C.) of absolute; on the second day two fluid ounces; on the third day four ounces; and on the fifth and sixth day eight ounces each day. He then returned to water for six days, and then for three days took each day, half a bottle— (=12 ounces, or 341 C. C.) of fine brandy, containing 48 per cent of alcohol. Then for three days he returned to water.

157. Thus, there were five periods of drinking, viz.: of water, alcohol, water, brandy, and water. The man who before commencing the experiments had been accustomed to take one or two pints of beer daily, abstained altogether from alcoholic liquors for ten days.

158. During the first few days, there was a gradual increase in weight, owing probably to the food being rather more and the exercise less than before; the equilibrium was reached on the

---

* See paper read at the Royal Society, May 18, 1870. In the Proceedings of the Royal Soc., XVIII. 1870.

eighth day, and the weight remained almost unchanged during the alcoholic period. There was a slight decrease after using alcohol, and on the last brandy day a slight increase, which was maintained in the after period.

159. The general result (other conditions remaining constant), appears to be, that the effect of alcohol in modifying weight is quite unimportant. The temperature of the axilla and rectum was but little changed when the alcohol and brandy were taken as described; what effect there was being rather in the direction of an increase than a diminution. It was found that the pulse was increased both in volume and frequency, rising in number from 77.5 before alcohol, to a maximum of 94.7 with the largest doses. The capillary circulation was increased, shown by flushing of neck, face, etc.

160. From the sphygmographic observations that were made, there was increased frequency of the ventricular contractions of the heart, and increased rapidity of each contraction; the ventricles therefore were doing more work in a given time. The period of the beat being much shortened, and the blood moving more freely through the capillaries; the increased quantity of blood, which is to be presumed was thrown into the arteries, was very quickly got rid of. In the renal secretions, there was a decided increase in the amount of water eliminated, but in opposition to previous experiments, they demonstrated that as long as the ingress of nitrogen is the same, 8 oz. of absolute alcohol, and 12 oz. of brandy, have no effect, or only a trifling effect on the processes which end in the elimination of nitrogen by the urine, and most decidedly do not lessen the elimination.

161. The influence of alcohol on the eliminations of chlorine and phosphoric acid, and upon the free acidity of the urine is inconsiderable. The action of alcohol on the elimination of nitrogen by the alvine discharges was inconsiderable; no experiments were made as to its effects on the pulminary excretions.

162. From these experiments, the evidence derived from the pulse as felt by the finger; from the state of the cutaneous vessels; and from the sphygmographic tracings, it seems fair to conclude that the chief effects of alcohol are on the ventricles; the rapidity with which contractions are accomplished being greatly increased, and on the capillaries, which are dilated, and allow blood to pass more freely through them.

163. From the colour test, they are of the opinion that a large portion of the alcohol is eliminated by the lungs, and still more by the skin; and only a small portion is given off by the renal and alvine discharges.

164. It was found that one or two ounces of absolute alcohol, in divided doses, increased the appetite; 4 oz. lessened it, and larger quantities almost entirely destroyed it. Estimating the daily work of the heart at 122 tons lifted one foot, during the alcoholic period, the heart's daily work in excess was equal to

lifting 158 tons one foot, and in the last two days did extra work equal to lifting 34 tons. After omitting the alcohol, the heart showed signs of weakness. The experimenters say:

165. "It is quite evident that alcohol is not necessary for him; that is, that every function of life was perfectly performed without alcohol, and that even one ounce in twenty-four hours, produced decided effects upon his heart, which was not necessary for his health, and perhaps, if the effect, continued, would eventually lead to alterations in circulation, and to degeneration of tissue.

166. These careful observations furnish satisfactory proof of the perfect safety of abstinence from alcoholics. They also say: "In spite of our previous experience in the use of alcohol and brandy, we were hardly prepared for the ease with which the appetite may be destroyed, the heart unduly excited, and the capillary circulation improperly increased. Considering its daily, and almost universal use, there is no agent which seems to us to require more caution, and more skill to obtain the good and to avoid the evil which its use entails."

THE EXPERIMENTS OF DR. HAMMOND.

167. Dr. W. A. Hammond caused a dog to take into its stomach three ounces of strong alcohol, diluted with a corresponding quantity of water. The animal, immediately on receiving it, retired to a corner of the room and laid down. At the end of five minutes he endeavoured to make him walk about the room, which he did with evident reluctance, but without staggering, at this time.

168. Alcohol was detected in the expired air in forty-eight seconds after its administration. After eight minutes the animal walked with difficulty, the posterior extremities were beginning to be paralyzed, which gradually increased, and the gait became more and more staggering, when, at the end of fourteen minutes, the animal could no longer move; the paralysis having now reached the anterior extremities.

169. "Now," in the language of Dr. Hammond, "sensitiveness was still present, though evidently lessened in acuteness, loud noises were perceived, and the eyes involuntarily closed, when the motion of striking was made before them. The respiration was hurried, and the action of the heart was greatly accelerated. The pupils were at first contracted, but became dilated in about fifteen minutes, and remained in that condition throughout the experiment. In thirty minutes the animal was in a state of profound coma.

170. "Sensibility, even of the cornea, was destroyed, the limbs were in a state of complete resolution, the respiration was hurried, the heart beat rapidly, but feebly, and the temperature had fallen from 101° F., which it was before the ingestion of the alcohol, to 98.5°.

171. "The animal remained in a comatose state, and died in one hour and twenty-two minutes after the ingestion of the alcohol."

172. In another experiment, he introduced into the stomach of a large dog, one ounce of strong alcohol, diluted with the same amount of water.

173. During the first few minutes, no change worthy of note occurred. Then the motion of the heart was accelerated, and also the respiration. Sensibility and power of motion were not affected. In twelve minutes the gait of the animal was uncertain, the limbs were lifted higher than natural, the body swaying from side to side, with an occasional strong effort being made to maintain the erect position.

174. The pupils were still contracted, and sensibility appeared to be intact. This condition lasted twenty-two minutes, and then the pupils began to dilate. The posterior extremities were so far weakened, as to render locomotion impossible, while the sensibility of the posterior portions of the body was materially impaired. The respiration was irregular; the pulse still rapid, but weaker than at first. Slight coma followed in less than an hour, which lasted about twenty minutes. The animal recovered; the phenomena of intoxication passed off in an inverse order to their supervention.

175. Dr. Hammond desiring to ascertain whether alcohol increased or diminished the amount of blood circulation in the cranium, performed the following experiment: Trephining a dog, he screwed a cephalohalmometer into the opening made in the skull by the trephine. An ounce of alcohol, diluted with one ounce of water, was then administered. Alcohol was detected in the expired air in fifty seconds. In four and one-half minutes, respiration was accelerated, the action of the heart more rapid and strong; the pupils began to contract, but as yet there was no increase in the intercranial pressure; hence the amount of blood on the brain was not increased. Though in six minutes and a half, the dog's gait was staggering, and his movements uncertain, there was no paralysis; and the inter-cranial pressure remained unaltered. But after the fluid had remained stationary for seventeen minutes, it began to rise slowly; and with the increase of inter-cranial pressure, paralysis of the posterior extremities supervened. As the amount of blood increased in the cranium, the paralysis extended, the pupils dilated, and coma ensued.

176. The return to sensibility and power of motion, was attended with a diminution of the inter-cranial pressure. The deductions of Dr. Hammond from these experiments are: "That the first symptoms which result from the ingestion of alcohol, are due to the presence of this substance in the brain, while the

later phenomena are in part, at least, the results of cerebral congestion."*

THE ACTION OF ALCOHOL ON COLLOIDAL MATTER.

At the opening meeting of the Hunterian Society, Dr. Richardson, F. R. S., delivered a most interesting lecture on the above subject.

177. "The characteristic of colloid is its aqueous or watery condition, that of pectous is its thickened state. The aqueous is the active and living, the pectous is the passive or dead condition of organized matter.

178. "In the form of colloid, exists all the matter in nature which is capable of assuming the organized motion, which elements can be substituted by others.

179. "In colloid water combines more or less loosely with albumen, or some other substance. Particles of water seem to substitute particles of albumen. Where the adhesion is slight, on the faintest disturbance the water may be displaced, and the particles, under the attraction of cohesion, may rush together. The resistance is so feeble in fibrine, that the merest accident may suffice to break the aqueous connection, and permit the molecular cohesive attraction to operate. The aqueous colloid of nervous matter is equally or even more sensitive. In the brain it is the colloid matter that is impressed by external vibrations, and on which external impressions are made."

180. "In considering the effects of alcohol on colloid, it must be remembered that this substance has a remarkable tendency to diffuse itself through water. The mobility of the particles of alcohol is so great, that one drop can be perfectly mixed with a pint, a quart, or a gallon of water."

181. "Let us see what are the effects produced by alcohol on the system. *First.* When alcohol is imbibed, it permeates the moist mucous membrane in its way to the stomach; coming in contact with peripheral extremities of the colloid of the nerves supplying the gastric tract, the effect is reflected on the vessels of the skin. Hence there is a temporary flushing and the escape of heat, and an agreeable but temporary sensation of warmth is caused.

182. "*Second.* Whilst it is producing this effect on the peripheral nerves, it finds its way, through the lymphatics and veins into the blood. Here it comes in contact with free colloid, and with that of the corpuscles—of which there are millions and billions, which are carriers of oxygen from the lungs to the tissues. In proportion as they abound and are in good working order, so there is purity of blood, a vigorous vitality, and a strong tendency to mental and muscular activity. Under the influence of alcohol the colloid of the affected corpuscles loses a portion of its water;

---

* The "EFFECTS OF ALCOHOL" an address before the New York Neurological Society, May 4th, 1874.

it contracts, it is paralyzed, and neither brings oxygen to nor from the tissues. The chemical changes in the tissues are diminished, there is lessened combustion, a lessened production of ash, and lessened heat. The slackening of chemical activity has a soothing effect on the nerves, which, whilst not nourished, are free from wear and tear. This is a second source of the agreeable feeling which the drinker experiences.

183. "*Third.* By far the greater change caused by the contact of alcohol, takes place in the brain. Here we have the colloidal matter in the most favourable condition for permeation by alcohol, and therefore the most marked effects here become apparent. The brain contains a larger amount of blood than any other organ of its size, and its tissues are more aqueous than are any other. Hence, when alcohol enters the system, a larger quantity can be found here than in any other part of the body; and so far as observation has gone, it appears to be found in this organ for a longer period than in any other. As we have seen the contact of alcohol with tissues—water disturbs the relation between it and the tissues. But any change in the condition of nerve tissue produces a proportionate evolution of nerve force. Hence the conversability, the animation, exhilaration and tendency to indulge in muscular activity which is so frequently manifested when alcohol is partaken of. The face is flushed, the eyes sparkle, the nerves of the face are fuller; there is the evident increased flow of blood to the brain and the surface of the body, as there had just previously been to the stomach and skin. There is no doubt in each case an illustration of the principle "*Ubi stimulus ibi fluxus.*"

184. "*Fourth.* The contact of alcohol with the nerve tissue has been productive of two effects. First, the conversion of the active colloid into the inactive pectous. The matter which just previously blazed up, is now a burnt out cinder Instead of the nerve cells going gradually through the cycle of growth and decay, disintegration, solution, and removal, they have suddenly become hardened and effete, and are sources of obstruction until they are displaced.

185. "But second, the stimulus produced by the atom of alcohol has been reflected to vaso-motor centre, and there has been a consequent increase of blood to the part. But owing to the presence of dead matter, there is no activity, the vessels cannot be relieved of their contents, there is no interchange, and hence for a time there is congestion. Thus after the excitement, comes a state of oppression, of sluggishness, and disposition to sleep. This is the second or narcotic stage. The slumber is troubled and unrefreshing; the drinker wakes up in a state of discomfort, he is depressed and indisposed for action. Knowing this, how speedily he goes for renewed stimulation, and this is perhaps, irresistible, if liquor is obtainable. The alcohol again rouses and then depresses, and so the craving is apt to be kept

up. But this tampering with the most delicate texture and processes cannot be repeated time after time with impunity. An atheromatous condition of the vessels, or fatty degeneration of the heart or other tissues occur. The pectous membrane admits salines through it imperfectly. Dr. Richardson tells us, that if these or a fatty substance be presented to it in excess, it entraps them, so that fat or salts, which are not very soluble, become incorporated with its own structure. In this way is initiated heart disease, aneurism, apoplexy, dropsy, and a host of other maladies.

186. "In the change produced by alcohol on colloid, we perceive how it is that animals to which alcohol is frequently administered become stunted; there is a spoiling and waste of material, and development is restrained. We further see how it comes that an article which is highly combustible really stops combustion, and thus causes a diminution of heat, of carbonic acid gas (CO_2,) and of urea. We furthermore clearly understand how the craving for drink is engendered, and why it is that, even when used in moderation, alcohol is the genius of degeneration."[*]

THE ACTION OF ALCOHOL: DOGIEL'S RESULTS.

J. Dogiel arrives at the following results from his experiments.[†]

187. 1st. Ethyl-alcohol introduced into the stomach is absorbed by the veins and lacteal; and detected in the *chyle* of the *thoracic duct*, in the serous and arterial blood in about a minute and a half after its introduction.

188. 2nd. The excretion of alcohol beside the ways heretofore known is through the skin in frogs.

189. 3rd. It acts chiefly not by reduction in the blood, nor oxydation-products in the blood, nor through aldehyde or acetic acid, but as alcohol.

190. 4th. The action of alcohol differs according to its concentration and quantities on the blood from an artery, both in relation to its coagulation, the escape of the hæmoglobin from the blood corpuscles and its crystallization, &c.

191. 6th. Blood from an animal under its influence coagulates slower, and yields less fibrine than normal blood.

192. 7th. It rapidly causes the amœboid movements of the white corpuscles to cease, and to dissolve both the red and white corpuscles, at a certain concentration.

193. 8th. If added to blood drawn from an artery, it retards putrefaction, and prevents the development of low organisms. Arterial blood from an intoxicated animal is more quickly decomposed than normal blood.

---

[*] "Medical Temperance Journal," January, 1875.
[†] In a paper read before the Meeting of the Russian Savants at Kasan, in 1873. On Monatomic Alcohols (Pflüger's Archiv. Vol. viii. parts 11, 12.

194. 9*th.* Its action on the heart-beats consist in acceleration followed by retardation. When strong, its action is very pronounced in retarding the pulse, passing on to acceleration. These are due first, to the stimulation of the accelerating nerves of the heart, and second, on the increased and afterward diminished excitability of the inhibitory fibres of the pneumogastric nerves. It has also an effect on the cardiac muscles, which is indicated by the beats of the heart becoming slower and stronger.

195. 10*th.* It first increases and then diminishes the arterial blood pressure. The excitability of the vaso-motor centres runs parallel to the blood pressure.

196. 11*th.* It first increases and then diminishes the rapidity of the blood current in the carotid artery; but the greatest retardation of the blood current coincides with the stage of alcoholic narcotism (sleep).

197. 12*th.* By small doses respiration is accelerated, and large doses render it slow. The slow respiration is superficial; and inspiration becomes longer. The reflex action from the vagus on the inspiratory centre is generally evinced by the acceleration of respiration and becomes weaker as intoxication increases.

198. 13*th.* The temperature sinks under its influence.

14*th.* The reflex movements produced by irritating the skin in beheaded frogs, are first increased and then diminished by it.

199. 15*th.* By it the excitability of motor and sensory nerves is at first increased and then lowered.

200. 16*th.* The muscular contractions are affected in the same way.

201. 17*th.* Chyle from the thoracic duct is first increased and then diminished.

203. 18*th.* The same is true with regard to the secretions of gastric juice.

204. 19*th.* The urine is increased, though the peristaltic movements follow each other at increased intervals.

205. 20*th.* The secretions of saliva from the submaxillary gland is increased by alcohol.

206. 21*st.* Its actions on the nervous system is direct, but is not caused by changes of the blood or the circulation.

207. 22*nd.* Methyl, propyle, butyle, and amyle alcohols, act similarly to ethyl, but differ from each other in the intensity of their action. Methyl alcohol acts less intensely than ethyl, whilst propyl, butyl, and amyl act in the ascending scale much more intensely.

208. Dr. Carpenter says: "It would seem, that in whatever way the exertion of volitional power is related to the condition of the brain, this exertion is interfered with by the use of intoxicating agents, before there is any serious perversion of the automatic

activity. And this may be especially noticed in alcoholic intoxication; the usual tendency of which is to produce a greater change in the *actions* of the unhappy subject of it, than is ordinarily induced either by opiums, or by *Hasheesh*. For whilst the tendency of these is to act upon the moral feelings and sentiments, the action of alcohol more commonly manifests itself in the excitement of the lower propensities.

209. "As soon as the liquor begins to exert *any* effect upon the brain, its operations are quickened, either the ideational or the emotional activity, or both combined; and at the same time in weakening the volitional control. * * * Many men under this influence, are more generous and conceding, than in their perfectly sober condition; so that they are ready to grant favours and make agreements, which their better judgment disapproves; a circumstance of which those who have a point to gain from them, are not slow to take advantage. Those, on the other hand, in whose constitutions the lower animal propensities habitually predominate, are subjects of an exaltation of these from a very slight alcoholic stimulus; and their power of self-control being at the same time weakened, they become slaves of any brutal passion that the slightest provocation may arouse. It is in this primary stage of alcoholic excitement that a large number of crimes of violence as well as of minor offences are committed."

SUMMARY OF THE ACTION OF ALCOHOL.

210. These experiments of Drs. Richardson, Parkes, Count Wollowicz, Hammond, and others, demonstrate that alcohol, when administered in quantities to produce distinct effects, makes the blood unduly thin, or coagulates it according to the quantity carried into the circulation. It acts on the blood corpuscles, alters them in shape and size; and reduces their power of absorbing oxygen.

211. It so changes the action of the heart that it beats with undue rapidity; and in extreme cases, the heart of an adult man is driven to perform an excess of 25,000 strokes in 24 hours; being an increase of daily labour equal to lifting 24 tons one foot high, or nearly one-fourth more work. It also affects the respiration correspondently for evil. (See pp. 44, 45.)

212. It paralyzes the minute blood vessels that form the terminal arteries, in which are carried on the vital acts of nutrition, the production of heat and force. This effect is seen in the flushed face, &c., of persons under the influence of wine: which flush is extended to the brain, lungs, digestive organs, and all parts of the system. If the alcoholic influence is carried to its full extent, it becomes congestion; and in persons habituated to long excess the congestion becomes permanent, as seen in the blotched face; and often disorganization is produced in the lungs, liver, kidneys, and the brain. On the stomach it acts

according to the quantity taken. Small doses excite the mucous membrane to over exertion, leading some to think it aids digestion; while in larger doses it not only impairs secretion and weakens digestion, bnt produces organic disease of the stomach.

213. It paralyzes the nervous fibres of the organic and vegetative, nervous systems, controlling the minute vessels, by which a large supply of blood is driven by the heart to the nerve centres, first exciting and then blunting the nervous actions.

214. Not only are the brain and nerve centres paralyzed, but the vital organs; as the lungs, liver, kidneys, &c., &c., having their fine minute vascular structures governed by the nervous current; their weakened vessels are overcharged with blood, as is the skin and body of the drinker, when flushed with wine.

215. This flushing, supposed to be due to an increase of temperature, is nothing more than radiation from an enlarged surface of blood, and hence a more rapid cooling.

216. Hence, as already said, alcohol unnaturally excites the heart and respiration; disturbs the regularity of nervous action; increases and decreases the functions of digestion according to the degree of its application; lowers the temperature, and injures the body in many ways, without presenting evidence of a single beneficial service; but is evil always, and that continually.

PART IV.

IS ALCOHOL A POISON?

217. WHAT is a poison? "A poison," says Webster. "is any agent capable of producing a morbid, noxious, or dangerous effect upon anything endowed with life." Taylor says: "A poison is commonly defined to be a substance, which, when administered, or taken in small quantities, is capable of acting deleteriously on the body; in popular language this term is applied only to those substances which destroy life, in small doses. Perhaps the most comprehensive which can be suggested, is this: A poison is a substance which, absorbed into the blood, is capable of seriously affecting health, or destroying life.* Again he says: "It is not easy to define the boundary between a large dose of medicine and a poison. It is usually considered that a medicine in a large dose is a poison, and a small dose is a medicine; but a

---

* Taylor's Medical Jurisprudence, Vol. I. p. 175.

medicine, such as tartarized antimony, may be easily converted into a poison, by giving it in small doses at short intervals, either under states of the body not adapted to receive it, or in cases in which it exerts an injuriously depressing effect."

218. "Poisons," says COPLAND, in his Dictionary, "are substances which exert a deleterious influence on the human frame, when taken internally, or applied externally, as regards either nature or quantity of them employed; or which tend in either respect to destroy life when thus used."

219. In his "Treatise on Poisons," Prof. Christison divides them into three classes, viz.: 1*st*, IRRITANT POISONS, whose characteristic operation is to excite inflammation, among which are the three mineral acids; oxalic acid, iodine, etc., jalap, etc., cantharides, etc. 2*nd*, NARCOTIC POISONS, which act in a peculiar manner upon the brain and nerves, and include: opium, hydrocyanic acid, nitric oxide gas, etc.: chloroform, etc. 3*rd*, NARCOTIC ACRID POISONS: possessing a double action, being local irritants, like those of the first class; and subsequently producing effects on the nervous system like those of the second class, which includes nightshade, hemlock, foxglove, nux-vomica, camphor, tobacco, etc.; alcohol, ether, etc.

220. Alcohol is also described by Prof. Christison in his "Dispensatory," in its relation to the living animal system, as, 1*st*, a local irritant. 2*nd*, an astringent. 3*rd*, a sedative.

221. That alcohol is a poison, common and universal speech bears evidence. The literal meaning of the term commonly used to describe a person under the influence of alcoholic liquors, intoxicated, is—poisoned. The word intoxicated, is derived from the Greek *toxicum*, which signifies a *bow* or an *arrow;* the barbarians poisoned their arrows, hence, *toxicum* in Latin was used to signify poison; from this we have the term *toxicology*, signifying the science which treats of *poisons* and *poisoning*.

222. Intoxication, in plain English, though it signifies the state or condition of being poisoned, is limited to the poisonous effects produced by certain substances upon the nervous system, associated with mental disturbance, delirium or frenzy.

223. That *alcohol is a poison*, in large doses, is rendered obvious by its action upon the living body; for if introduced into the stomach in sufficient quantities, either in its pure state or when diluted, as rum, gin, brandy, etc., its results are fatal. Though men do not generally use absolute or pure alcohol, yet we have ample evidence of its effects upon animals, by Dr. Percy and others, that it is a poison.

224. Prof. Regnault says:—"Concentrated alcohol acts as a poison on the animal economy, and will produce death, when taken in large quantities. Injected into the veins it produces almost sudden death by coagulating the albumen of the blood.*"

---

* Regnault's Chemistry, vol. 2, page 515, 1852.

225. Flourens, a distinguished physiologist who made numerous experiments with alcohol upon animals, observed that it produced the same effects on the movements of birds as occasioned by the removal of the cerebellum, but with this difference, when alcohol was administered, the animal lost the use of its intellectual faculties; whereas when the cerebellum only was removed it preserved them.

226. From these and other observations it was concluded that alcohol, in a certain dose, acts on the cerebellum, and in larger doses it affects other parts; its action on the cerebellum being absolutely the same as a mechanical lesion.*

ALCOHOL: A POISON.

227. Dr. Mussey asks, "What is a poison?" "It is that substance, in whatever form it may be, which, when applied to a living surface, disconcerts and disturbs life's healthy movements. It is altogether distinct from substances, which are in their nature nutritious. It is not capable of being converted into food, and becoming a part of the living organs. We all know that proper food is wrought into our bodies; the action of animal life occasions a constant waste, and new matter has to be taken in, which, after digestion, is carried into the blood, and then changed; but poison is incapable of this. It may indeed be *mixed* with nutritious substances, but if it goes into the blood, it is thrown off as soon as the system can accomplish its deliverance, if it has not been too far enfeebled by the influence of the poison. Such a poison is alcohol—such in all its forms, mix it with what you may."

228. Dr. Chadwick, in his "Essay on Alcohol," says:—"When taken pure, or almost pure, and in sufficient quantity, it acts as a poison, and may produce death in a few minutes, or in the course of some hours from the time of taking it, and when taken in small quantities for a length of time, it tends to shorten the duration of life, and may produce many different diseases which terminate in death." Again he says, "But alcohol may be taken in quantities sufficient to cause death, without producing its effects immediately. In fact, when it does not kill a person by its direct effect on the stomach, and the consequent shock to the whole body, it may, nevertheless be absorbed into the blood, and be conveyed in the course of the circulation to the brain, and then cause death by depriving that organ of its sensibility."

229. Prof. Pereira, in his "Materia Medica," says:—"The local effects of alcohol, or rectified spirits, are those of a powerful irritant and caustic poison. To whatever part of the body this agent is applied, it causes contraction and condensation of the tissue, and gives rise to pain, heat, redness, and other symptoms of inflammation."

---

* Recherches un les functions et les proprietes, etc.

230. Says Dr. Gordon :—"It would be difficult to find a more destructive poison than ardent spirits."

231. Dr. C. A. Lee, says:—"All writers on materia medica, now rank alcohol among the most powerful and fatal of vegetable narcotic poisons."

232. Sir ASTLEY COOPER says:—"I never suffer ardent spirits in my house, thinking them evil spirits. If the poor could witness the white livers, the dropsies, the shattered nervous systems, which I have seen as the consequences of drinking, they would be aware that spirits and poisons are synonymous terms."

233. Dr. URE says:*—Of aqua vitæ, the name very absurdly given to (alcohol) intoxicating beverages.—"It has been *aqua mortis* (the water of death), to myriads of the human race; and will probably, ere long, destroy the native tribes of North America and Australia."

ALCOHOL: A POISON.

DR. PERCY'S EXPERIMENTS.

234. Dr. Percy injected 2½ ounces of alcohol (sp. gr. .850) into the stomach of a full-grown dog, which immediately uttered a loud plaintive cry and fell lifeless to the ground. Not a gasp was afterward taken, nor, after the lapse of a minute or two, could a single pulsation of the heart be felt. "Never," says Dr. Percy, "did I see every spark of vitality more effectually, and more instantaneously extinguished."† It is very probable, that the rapidity of the fatal results of such an unusually small dose of alcohol, was due to the fact that the dog had been scantily supplied with food for a day or two; so that the stomach was in a condition to favour the rapid absorption of the poison into the circulation. Death in this case, was precisely like that of poisoning by *Prussic acid*.

235. In another experiment by Dr. Percy, 6 ounces of alcohol were injected into the stomach of a large full-grown mongrel dog, which was followed almost immediately, by the entire loss of sensibility and voluntary power; the animal fell prostrate on one side, never afterwards moving a limb; but the respiratory movement continued one hour longer, gradually becoming slower and laborious; the action of the heart was prolonged a few minutes, the last pulsation taking place one hour and twenty minutes after the alcohol was introduced into the stomach. The symptoms in this case were those of poisoning by opium or other narcotic.

236. In a third experiment he injected only three ounces of alcohol into the stomach of a powerful bull-terrier bitch, which howled loudly once or twice, and then fell prostrate, with a slight convulsive extension of the trunk and limbs.

---

* Medical Dictionary.
† Dr. Percy's Thesis on the Presence of Alcohol in the Ventricles of the Brain. 1839.

237. Death appeared to have taken place as in the first experiment, but it was only apparent; for although the functions of respiration were arrested for a time, the heart still continued to beat steadily, and after the lapse of three minutes a sudden deep inspiration was taken.

238. Though the respiratory movements continued oppressed, yet they were gradually restored; but it was not until forty minutes after the introduction of the poison, that the animal gave signs of returning consciousness and voluntary power; but she soon lay down again, and did not make an effort to move, but continued to moan, as if in pain, at every respiration. Though from the first the pulse was weak and irregular, it increased in rapidity, with still greater weakness; and the poor animal gradually sank and died about eight hours after the introduction of the poison.

239. In this case the narcotic effects of the alcohol were so great for a time as to produce almost complete prostration of the vital powers. These narcotic effects were transient, and the animal had nearly recovered from them, when violent inflammation of the lining membrane of the stomach and intestines set in (as examination after death showed), and it is plain that the fatal result was due to this cause; hence the alcohol acted as an irritant poison, after its narcotic effect had in a great measure subsided.

240. It may also be well to remark, the blood was every where fluid without a trace of clot being found.

241. In the fourth and last case to be noted here, $2\frac{1}{2}$ ozs. were injected into the stomach of a full grown spaniel, when symptoms of intoxication soon appeared; the animal lost the power to stand, and on trying to raise her head, let it fall again as a dead weight; the jaws moved as if in the act of masticating, the fore-leg as in running, and the tail wagged continually, with occasional whining. About twenty-five minutes after the introduction of the alcohol, she vomited a kind of frothy mucus; and then became extremely restless, at one time writhing and contorting her body in all directions, occasionally moaning, whining and howling loudly, as if in severe pain; at another time appearing to be in a state of delirious excitement; the tail and all the extremities being affected with rapid movements, as if she was swimming, or in swift pursuit of some object of prey; and once she shook her head, as if she had grasped her imaginary victim. About nine hours afterward she was found sitting up and attempting to walk, but her hind-legs seemed to be paralyzed; a few hours after she ate food, and seemed comparatively well; but there appeared to be, for several days, a lack of voluntary power over the hind legs.

242. These experiments of Dr. Percy, on dogs, clearly prove the poisonous nature of alcohol.

ALCOHOL IS POISONOUS TO ALL ANIMALS.

243. According to Fontane, leeches, when wet with alcohol, die in two or three minutes. When partially immersed in it, the part of the body which touches it is paralyzed. Forty drops given to a frog proved fatal in forty minutes, but when injected under the skin it killed in one minute. It was fatal when applied to the spinal marrow and brain. The crural nerve of a frog being moistened with alcohol, the limb lost its power of motion. Turtles were speedily killed by injecting alcohol into the stomach or bowels, or into the cellular tissue; and fish lost their activity in water containing but a small portion of it.*

244. As early as 1679—93, Courten, Lanzoni and Baglivi showed that highly rectified spirits might prove fatal instantly when injected into the veins; after death the blood was found coagulated in the heart, lungs and other parts.

245. When VIBORG injected two drachms of whiskey into the jugular vein of a horse, there was produced all the phenomena of alcoholic intoxication. The animal became gay, the eyes were prominent and bright, the ears moved to and fro, and the pulse was full and active. The phenomena continued for three quarters of an hour, but gradually diminished, and were followed by signs of depression and debility; and it was four hours before the horse appeared the same as before the experiment.†—WERMER WIRKUNG.

246. Mitscherlich injected one ounce of absolute alcohol into the stomach of large rabbits, which produced no excitement, but great depression, and within from two to twelve minutes, there was a complete loss of sensibility and muscular power, so that the strongest mechanical excitants scarcely induced the slightest movement. The breathing was hurried, and the pulse very rapid; slight convulsions of the feet and eyes ensued; the pupils, at first contracted, became largely dilated, and death, without convulsions, took place in from one and a half to two hours. The body was immediately opened. The alcohol appeared to have exerted a chemical action upon the follicular and vascular structures of the stomach. The mucus upon its inner surface was coagulated, and in some places stained with blood. Where this had occurred, the mucous coat was softened, but elsewhere was fragile, and formed of corrugated cells; a result, undoubtedly, of the withdrawal of the water from them by the action of the alcohol.

247. The vascular and the cellular coats were thickened by an exudation, which in some cases was clear, and in others bloody. The odour of alcohol was quite perceptible in the peritoneal cavity, but not in the small intestines; the latter organ was but slightly affected, its epithelium being partly converted into mucus.

---

* Wermer Wirkung, &c., i. 90. † Lancet, 1839—40. ii. 443.

248. He found no particular alteration in any other organ. The brain was somewhat congested; the blood unchanged, and with no alcoholic odour.

249. A series of experiments were performed upon pigeons, rabbits and dogs, by Jacobi and Falck, with various mixtures of alcohol and water; the results obtained were similar to those just decribed.*

EFFECTS OF CONTINUED USE OF ALCOHOLICS.

250. The effects of continued use of alcoholic liquors upon dogs, have been described by Huss, after experiments at Dahlstrom. Three dogs of different ages and disposition, were chosen, and for a period of eight months, six ounces of potato brandy were daily given to each. The symptoms produced upon all were alike, and about as follows. The animals at first did not exhibit any aversion to the liquor; but at the end of one month, they would not swallow it unless it was administered by force.

251. During the first three months, they displayed a peculiar liveliness which approached delirium, and voracious appetites, after the alcohol had been given: they were also very thirsty. During all this period they continued to be fat, and in good condition. But in the fourth month their bark began to grow hoarse and lose its clear tone; a harsh and dry hiccough and cough accompanied it; the eyes were watery and staring, the sense of hearing less acute, the whole manner listless: the sleep was disturbed by spasms of the limbs, and the animals often uttered plaintive cries; they seemed averse to making exertions, and preferred lying upon the side. After the fourth month they were tremulous while standing. The limbs, especially the hinder ones, were weak, so that the animals ate, sitting.

252. As they lay upon their sides, twitchings were visible in the muscles of the trunks and limbs; and, although their manner was generally indifferent, the sight of other dogs excited them to violent anger, and furious attacks, in spite of their weakness. Gradually their strength declined more and more, and the cutaneous sensibility, particularly of the ears, diminished in a remarkable degree. The appetite was also impaired, and at last they showed a decided aversion to food, and could not be induced to devour raw meat.

253. Their animosity toward other dogs continued, and displayed itself when they were no longer able to make an attack. None of the dogs lost flesh; on the contrary they were fatter than when the experiments began. One of the three died at the expiration of eight months, with signs of complete exhaustion; the others were killed. Similar changes were found in the bodies of all of them. The stomach was found contracted, and its mucous membrane lead-coloured and œdematous; the intestinal mucous

---

* Brit. and For. Chirur. Rev., April, 1858, p. 530.

membrane was unaltered, but covered with thick and fetid mucus. The liver was considerably enlarged, of diminished consistence, and dark colour; the bile was also dark, thick and stringy; the heart, spleen and kidneys unchanged; the mucous membrane of the nose, trachea and bronchia was slightly inflamed; the cerebral vessels were distended with blood; the muscles pale, flaccid and atrophied, and the sub-cutaneous fat, spongy.*

254. The series of experiments by Duchek, were essentially similar to the above, but showed the different influences on nutrition of the stronger alcoholic preparation. A dog two years old, rather thin and of small species, was given about half an ounce of absolute alcohol daily, which was regularly followed by intoxication. Emaciation, and weakness in the hinder limbs also occurred. Death at length took place; the blood abounded in carbonates, and contained much sugar. Two or three spoonsful of corn brandy were given to a large setter for 93 days; he became very fat and quite well, when he was accidentally killed. The blood contained much sugar, but no other anatomical change.†

THE POISONOUS EFFECTS OF ALCOHOLICS ON MAN.

255. On man, the effects of large doses of strong alcohol are precisely the same as those described when pure alcohol was introduced in the stomachs of other animals. Prof. Christison gives the case of a man who stole a bottle of whiskey, and fearing detection, drank the whole of it. He died in four hours, with symptoms of coma.

256. Dr. Mitchell‡ mentions the case of a boy ten years old, who secretly drank from a whiskey bottle, in imitation of his father, who was at work in the field. The sudden silence of the boy attracted his father's attention, when a wild, fixed gaze was discovered, denoting something wrong. He called the boy by name, but in vain, and in less than an hour he was dead.

257. § A man, previously enjoying good health, drank by mistake about eight ounces of alcohol, 50° above proof; he dropped instantly on the floor insensible. When a physician saw him, a few minutes after, he was exceedingly cold, with respiration calm, pulse nearly gone, and lips blue. His friends would not have his stomach emptied, but gave some purgative pills. He was cold and insensible for eleven hours. He went to work the next day, apparently well. At the end of three weeks he was so unwell, that he applied to an apothecary, who gave him an emetic, and a cathartic. After their operation, he was found by Dr. Bird, with pupils dilated, with pale countenance, pulse 120,

---

* Cronische Alkohols-krankheit, 1852, p. 517.
† Philadelphia Medical Examiner, February, 1854.
‡ Therapeutics, page 109.   § London Lancet, Vol. I., for 1839-40.

good appetite, and inclined to be drowsy. There was no paralysis, and yet he was not able to follow his trade.

258. Dr. Bird thought the case bore some analogy to delirium tremens. A variety of treatment was resorted to, but without effect. Up to date of report, about five months, the man remained unwell. This presents several points of interest. 1st. The sudden effect of the alcohol. 2nd. The apparent recovery at the end of eleven hours, and the continuance of that state for three weeks. 3rd. The obvious decline of health after that time, and the apparently incurable condition of the patient. In the same report there is a case of a lad of sixteen, who, for a wager, drank a pint of gin. In spite of all medical efforts to restore him, he remained insensible for twelve hours. He still exhibited marks of feebleness and disease, and was a burden to his family, at the time of the report.

259. Orfila* mentions the case of a man who died immediately from the effects of a large dose of brandy.

260. Dr. Rösch relates three cases, in which adults died from the immediate effects of excessive drinking, in a few hours. He also relates the cases of two children, in which quite a small quantity proved fatal. Dr. Seaverns mentions the case of a child of two years, that died in about twenty-four hours, from drinking less than one ounce of New England rum. Dr. Taylor tells of a man who died in half-an-hour after swallowing a bottle of gin for a wager. A chimney-sweep drank eighteen glasses of rum (nearly a quart,) in quick succession; he soon became perfectly insensible and motionless, but his respiration and circulation continued for about six hours, when he died.†

261. Dr. Chowne relates a case of poisoning by gin, in a boy eight years old, in whom life continued for sixty-seven days and a half, though he was in a state of partial insensibility; when death seemed to take place from slow suffocation, there being found no inflammation in the stomach after death.‡

262. Dr. Taylor, in his MEDICAL JURISPRUDENCE, relates the case of a boy seven years old, who was killed by drinking two wine-glassfuls of brandy.

POISONED BY WHISKEY.—CHILDREN.

263. P. De Marmon, M. D., of King's Bridge, N. Y., in a paper read at a meeting of the New York Medical Journal Association, Feb. 18th, 1870, said: "Within a year I have seen three cases of poisoning by alcohol, in children; of those cases two died."

264. CASE 1.—Philip A., aged five years, a healthy and strong child, born of Irish parents, took on a Sunday morning at

---

* "Traite de Toxicologie."
† Lancet, Vol. X., p. 57.
‡ Lancet, Vol. I., p. 219, 1838-9.

six o'clock, a tumblerful of whiskey. * * I did not see the child until nine o'clock in the evening. He was then in a completely comatose state, respiration stertorous, and 84 in a minute; pulse full, very irregular, but rather slow; temperature taken at axilla 93½ F. * * * This child had involuntary stools and micturition, which added to the vital signs, indicated great danger. He was perfectly insensible, and had some clonic convulsions: * * died nineteen hours after the ingestion of the fatal drink. No post-mortem could be obtained."

265. CASE 2.—Sarah F., a little girl five years old, on Saturday afternoon, at four o'clock, took a tumblerful of whiskey. It had been given to her by a lad about fifteen years old. I saw her * * * two and a half hours after the ingestion of the liquid. She is a strong-looking, healthy child, of Irish and sober parents. * * * There was hyperæsthesia of the skin, principally of the lower extremities, which were cold, and anæsthesia of the cornea, which was glassy; respiration stertorious; if it had not been for the odour of the liquor exhaled, it would almost have been impossible not to think it was a case of cerebral hemorrhage or of asphyxia. The temperature in the axilla 94° F.; pulse 60, respiration 80; the finger introduced into the mouth beyond the pharynx produced no sensation; she had involuntarily soiled the bed, and she vomited a couple of times, about an hour after taking the drink. I ordered the child to be kept warm, and every half hour a tablespoonful of liq. ammon. act., to be administered. The father of the child was at my house the next morning at seven o'clock, and declared that the child was all right."

266 CASE 3.—Robert X., a boy eight years old, of Irish parents, father and mother both regular inebriates, took some whiskey at eight o'clock on Friday morning, the quantity of which could not be ascertained, still less the quality, inasmuch as the child's parents were both drunk, and denied that the boy had taken anything. Some charitable persons took upon themselves to send for a physician at about twelve o'clock. I was absent. * * * I was, however, able to see the patient at 2.30 P. M. but found a doctor from the vicinity in charge of the patient. The child died on Saturday morning at five o'clock, twenty-one hours after the ingestion of the drug. On the next day, Sunday, at twelve o'clock, I was summoned by the coroner to a post-mortem examination of the subject.

267. *Autopsy, thirty-one hours after death.*—Body thin, icteric: rigor mortis well marked in the lower limbs, but none in the arms nor in the neck; the head rolling about as if it had been dislocated in its cervical articulation. The lungs were thoroughly congested, and of a dark-blue colour, and contained a large quantity of black blood, which could be pressed out, as if from a sponge, after cutting through the texture of the organ. The internal membrane of the bronchus was livid and coated with bloody, spumous mucosities; the pericardium contained about half an ounce of serum. The right ventricle of the heart

was much distended with dark blood, and had black clots; the left ventricle was empty; the blood had a smell of whiskey. The liver was congested, of a pale yellowish colour, and the gall bladder less than half full. The above are not isolated cases. Our daily and weekly papers frequently relate similar occurrences, all over our country; indeed they have become so common, that they fail to call forth any comment.

ALCOHOLIC POISONING.

268. "Among the most urgent medical cases admitted into the Northern Hospital, Liverpool, England, during the year, there were several of acute alcohol poisoning, which during 1868 numbered thirty-six. These cases generally result from the practice of sucking new rum from casks at the docks; and not unfrequently very young boys are subjects of it. The patients are generally completely insensible, exhibit no feeling when the eye-balls are touched, while the pupils are insensible to light, and the breathing is often stertorous. They sometimes remain in this condition for several hours."*

PART V.

IS ALCOHOL FOOD?

269. ALCOHOL, the essential ingredient in all liquids, having undergone vinous fermentation, has by the universal judgment and consent of toxicologists, been classed, as already seen, as a poison when taken in large doses. Yet there are those who seem to be unable to distinguish between a poison and a food. Poisoning, it is true, may differ in degree according to the strength of the poison, or the power of the organism to resist its toxical effects. If no substances except those which produce immediately fatal effects, were classed as poisons, the number would be very limited.

270. It appears very illogical to suppose that a substance, which if given in large doses will destroy life, becomes a food when taken in smaller quantities. Two pounds of good bread or beef, are no more a poison than two drachms, while one-sixtieth of a grain of strychnia, is as much a poison in its nature as any other quantity.

271. The first inhalation of a poison, though its effects may not be noticed, is none the less injurious, for it inevitably contributes its part in producing the fatal effects which follow re-

---

* Medical Times and Gazette, 1869.

peated inhaling. The first inspiration was as poisonous as the last, though its injurious effects were not immediately apparent.

272.—If alcohol is a poison, it cannot, by any straining of logic, be a food. If it is food, it cannot be a poison. A poison is any substance "that disconcerts and disturbs life's healthy movements." and is not capable of being converted into, or becoming a part of the living organism."

273. Prof. Dalton says, "Under the term food, are included all those substances, solid and liquid, which are necessary to sustain the process of nutrition." The first act of this process is the absorption from without of those materials which enter into the composition of the living frame, or of others that may be converted into them in the interior of the body." Which of these definitions corresponds to the nature and effects of alcohol? Are not its nature and effects that of a poison? The action of alcohol, after it enters into the blood-current, is a question that has long, and is still, as already seen, agitating the scientific world.

274. The Leibigian doctrine, that though alcohol is not a tissue-forming substance, but a calorific agent, has had many supporters, who maintained its value as a respiratory, or heat-generating food, though no proof of any kind was presented by Leibig that alcohol was eliminated from the blood by a process of combustion. This doctrine had a long reign, and much was written and said about carbon, and the respiratory and heat-giving power of alcohol, without any facts to show that it was burnt up, or decomposed within the body. Professor Moleschott advanced the doctrine, that if alcohol was not food itself, it made food last longer. Afterwards it was discovered, that alcohol destroyed molecular life, by narcotizing it. and that when there was less life, there was less waste, and consequently less need for food. This error, like every other, died amid its worshippers.

275. But that the food doctrine might not yet die, Dr. Anstie steps in with another theory; labouring earnestly to prove in his book on "Stimulants and Narcotics," that alcohol in certain doses is a stimulant and a tonic, and not a poison; and by attaching other definitions to words, endeavoured to prove that food is medicine, and medicine food; and that alcohol is both food and medicine ; as by his theory stimulants are tonics, and tonics, stimulants, and as food was both stimulant and tonic, and alcohol being both a stimulant and a tonic, it must therefore be food. Dr. Anstie says (page 714)—"*One of the most deadly poisons is in small doses, an excellent tonic, namely, arsenic. Hence there seems to be a radical difference, and not one of degree, between the effects of large and small doses of alcohol.*" If arsenic is a tonic, why not use it, as well as alcohol, as a beverage, in small doses? Why not call it a food? Again he says (page 715)—"*The very fact that the 'poison-line' of alcohol can be shifted by an alteration in the state of the bodily health, is, to my mind, one of the strongest confirmations of the theory that there is a radical distinction between the effect of large and small doses. So long as*

there is any need for alcohol in the system, it will fail to intoxicate."

276. This might be applicable to the taking of a beefsteak, when the stomach was not in a condition to digest it. But as regards the need of the system for alcohol, preventing it from intoxicating, we fail to see the force of the argument. The doctor admits that in certain doses alcohol is a narcotic.

277. Every mother who has ever given her child a narcotic, knows that if it is repeated often, the dose must be increased to produce its desired effect. It has been said, that alcohol lessens the vital powers by narcotizing the system, and hence, that the system requires an increased dose of the narcotic to arouse the sensibilities blunted by the use of the poison, and not that the increased and repeated dose is required by the needs of the organism. True to the theory of supposing that the craving or needs of the system will prevent alcoholics from intoxicating or injuring the system, the following very aptly applies :—

278. "*The nervous system, the very centre and basis of the vital functions, has been drained of blood and exhausted of force, and unless it be quickly restored to its wonted activity, life must cease.*" Now, when "the vital functions have been drained of blood," etc., it would be the act of common sense to administer to the system some of the blood-making substances, to increase the force ; but instead of which Dr. Anstie says : "*Under these circumstances, the rapid absorption of a substance, which, like alcohol, has a special proclivity towards the nervous system, is precisely the best means of reviving the failing circulation in the nervous centres, and upholding the powers of life (i.e. keeping the machinery going), until the body can be supplied with its ordinary nutriment in sufficient quantity to restore the condition of healthy nutrition.*"

279. Here the doctor admits that alcohol will only keep the machinery going until it can be supplied with ordinary nutriment. Now if it is food and nutriment, why not continue its use instead of the "ordinary nutriment?"

280. If it will not supply the place of ordinary nutriment, how can it have any claim to be food? If the "vital functions have been drained of blood and exhausted of force," why lose time by waiting for alcohol to keep the machinery going? Why not give the proper nutriment at once, in the form of beef tea, milk, &c., instead of alcohol, which gives no force, but will use up the little force still remaining, in its efforts to eliminate it from the system.

281. Dr. Richardson says :* "They themselves (alcohols) supply no force at any time, but cause expenditure of force, by which means they get out of the body, and therewith lead to exhaustion and paralysis of motion. * * * The animal force which should be expended on the nutrition and sensation of

---

* Cantor Lectures, p. 30.

the body, is in part expended on the alcohol, an entire foreign expenditure."

282. Dr. Anstie says: "*If it be well understood that a glass of good wine will relieve a man's depression and fatigue sufficiently to enable him to digest his dinner, and that a pint of gin taken at once will probably kill him stone-dead, why haggle about words? On the part of the medical profession, I think I may say that we have long since begun to believe that those medicines which really do benefit our patients, act in one way or another as foods, and that some of the most decidedly poisonous substances, are those which offer, in the form of small doses, the strongest examples of a true food action. On the part of alcohol, then, I venture to claim, that though we all acknowledge it to be a poison, if taken during health, in any but quite restricted doses; it is also a valuable medicine food. I am obliged to declare that the chemical evidence is as yet insufficient to give any complete explanation of its exact manner of acting upon the system; but that the facts are as striking as they could well be, and that there can be no mistake about them.*"

283. Here we are told that medicine of value is food, and food is medicine, and alcohol must be somehow food; yet he frankly confesses a very important fact, that he is not able to tell us how alcohols act on the system. Have we arrived at the last quarter of the nineteenth century, with the experiments of English, French and German instigators before us, and still are ignorant of the action of food? If not, how can alcohol be food? But let us examine the food power of alcohol.

NUTRITION AND ALCOHOL.

284. Every substance capable of nourishing the human system, and entitled to the name of food, consists either of starch, sugar, oil, albuminous or glutinous matter, whether derived from the animal or vegetable kingdom.

285. The blood is the bearer of nutriment to the tissues of the body, to replace the waste arising from the disintegration that is constantly taking place in the organism; commencing with the first breath drawn into the lungs of the infant, yielding up, as it is carried through the circulatory system, constituents of its substance, to supply the place of those particles that have become waste, and eliminated from the body, in the different excretions.

286. Nutriment furnished by the food, is, by the various processes of digestion, assimilation, &c., gradually converted into blood, from which the tissues extract their own proper pabulum.

287. But food has another office to fulfil. It is necessary to health, nay, to life itself, that the temperature of the body be maintained at a given point, which point is the same, with little variation, by day or night, when active or at rest, at all seasons of the year, and in all climates,

288. This heat is generated in the body itself, the materials for its maintainance being found in the blood, partly from combination of the oxygen inspired by the lungs with certain elements of disintegration, but chiefly, in climates like this, by this combination with certain elements of our food. Every substance capable of being employed as food subserves at least one of these processes; the formation of tissue, or the production of heat.

289. Thus food has a double office to fulfil, namely, to furnish the blood with the materials for repairing the waste of the tissues and its fluid secretions, and with the materials for carrying on this internal combustion, the fuel for this ever burning fire.

290. Each of these processes is of vital importance to health and life, whether the food be taken consciously or unconsciously. The vital functions cannot be performed nor life itself preserved if the nutriment elements are not supplied, within a certain time, to fulfil the demands of the system's waste and supply force. And all these functions will fail, and life itself cease, if the heat of the body is allowed to fall, for any length of time, below the normal standard.

291. Dr. Pavy* classifies foods on the basis of their chemical nature, and to simplify their study, divides them into four groups: 1st, Nitrogenous principles. 2nd, Hydro-carbons, or fats. 3d, Carbo-hydrates. 4th, Inorganic materials. Dr. Pavy says: "While nitrogenous matter may be regarded as forming the essential basis of structure possessing active living properties, the non-nitrogenous principles may be looked upon as supplying the source of power. The one may be spoken of as holding the position of instruments of action, while the other supplies the motive power."

292. Nitrogenous alimentary matter may, it is true, by oxydation, contribute to the generation of the moving force; but in fulfilling this office, there is evidence before us, that it is split up into distinct portions, one containing the nitrogen, which is eliminated as useless, and a residuary non-nitrogenous portion which is retained and utilized in force production.

293. It is true also, that non-nitrogenous matter may be applied to tissue-formation, but it is probable that, in doing so, it is simply for the purpose of being stored up for subsequent appropriation to force-production, according as circumstances may require.

294. The non-nitrogenous alimentary principles comprise, according to Dr. Pavy,† "1st, Hydro-carbons, or fats; 2d, The Carbo-hydates, starch, sugar, &c.; and 3d, Principles such as alcohol, and the vegetable acids, which do not strictly fall within either of the preceding groups."

---

* A Treatise on Food and Dietetics, Physiologically and Therapeutically Considered. By F. W. Pavy, M.D., &c.
† No. 27.

295. Dr. Edmunds,† defining the term 'food,' said: "I would say that a food is that which being innocent in relation to the tissues of the body, is a digestible or absorbable substance, that can be oxydized in the body, and decomposed in such a way, as to give up to the body the forces which it contains." This definition of a food is clear, concise, logical, and based upon the physiological and chemical action of a true food; or in the words of the doctor, "brings food in relation to the body, into a perfect parallel with fuel in relation to a steam-engine." There is no doubt that that is philosophically correct in the last degree.

296. Keeping this definition in view, as its correctness cannot be doubted, let us endeavour to ascertain if alcohol be a food. Dr. Gordon said: "It would be difficult to find a more destructive poison than ardent spirits,"—dilute alcohol. We may recall the experiment of Dr. Percy who injected two ounces and a half of alcohol into the stomach of a dog, and immediately the animal uttered a loud plaintive cry, and fell dead at his feet. "Never," says Dr. Percy, "did I see every spark of vitality more instantaneously extinguished."

297. The action of alcohol in this case produces death precisely as would a large dose of Prussic acid. Is alcohol innocent in relation to the tissue? Is it not destructive to life? Would two ounces, or even two pounds of the most concentrated food have killed the dog? It is clear that in this case alcohol acted as a poison. Now what quantity would have acted as a food? Where or what is the line of demarcation? It must have some point where one action ends, and the other begins, to be both a food and a poison, at once. You may say, with Dr. Anstie, that the needs of the system will decide. How can you tell when it needs alcohol? Must we first take it, and wait to see whether it acts as a food or a poison?

298. If it acts as a poison, it will then be too late: the evil will be done; and if as food, at the best it is but a poor and unsafe one. We have seen (page 19,) that one hundred parts of cane sugar and water $C_6 H_{12} O_6 + H_2 O$) produce, after fermentation or putrefaction of the sugar, 50.3 to 50.27 parts of carbonic acid, and 52.62 parts of alcohol.

299. Now it is very clear that what is formed by the decomposition of sugar cannot contain the properties of the sugar, if they are destroyed. Look at the sugar, which is a nutritious substance. Compare it with alcohol, and you see a totally different substance from what it was when in the form of sugar. More than one-half of the elements in the sugar, that gave it nutrient value, are lost by being formed into alcohol, which we know will destroy life; so that if all the elements of the alcohol were as nutrient as when in sugar, to say nothing of the poisonous nature of alcohol, it still, as a nutriment, is less than one-half of the value of sugar.

---

* In a Lecture in New York city, Sept. 17th, 1874.

IS ALCOHOL FOOD? 73

300. Many of our English and German citizens, and even Americans, and some in the medical profession, have a notion, that because ale, stout, and foaming lager are made from barley, they must still, somehow or other, contain the nutritious elements of the barley: which is very pardonable in persons ignorant of chemistry, and its laws of composition and decomposition, and the changes that occur in the processes of fermentation. This class of persons suppose that they are taking their barley in liquid form. The same fallacy is abroad in regard to wine; for as grapes are nutritious, so must the wine be; hence the deep rooted impression in the minds of the mass of our people, that because malt liquors, wine and spirits, are made from food, or nutrient substances, they must also be food. But is this so?

301. As malt liquors are esteemed to be highly nutritious, we will take beer or ale as an example, and see how much of the nutrient properties of barley remain in the drink: or how much food material is left in the beer.

302. If three* bushels of barley, or 156 pounds, will make a barrel or 31 gallons, to make 1 gallon of beer will take 5.2 pounds. What has become of this 5.2 pounds, or 83.2 ounces of barley? Of these 83.2 ounces of barley to make a gallon of beer, there was extracted:—in malting, as "malt-cooms," 20 ounces: in mashing as "grains," 27.4 ounces; in fermenting, 13.4 ounces; in fining, as barrel-bottoms, etc., 9 ounces, or a total of 70 ounces, thus leaving in each gallon of ale, beer, etc., 13.2 ounces of the barley, being principally gum, worth little or nothing as nutriment, and scarcely deserving the name of food.† Yet this is the so-called "nutritious beverage," the "Juice of Malt," the boasted "liquid bread." Need more be said of the food value of malt liquors? Baron Liebig, the father, we may say, of the theory that alcohol is food, said:—"If a man drinks daily, eight or ten quarts of the best Bavarian beer (equal to our lager beer), in the course of twelve months he will have taken into his system the nutritive constituents contained in a five pound loaf of bread." Why, you may ask, do persons feel stronger, after drinking them, if they are not nutritious? They are not stronger. They are deceived by the "mocker" alcohol. Alcohol gives no strength. You drink beer for strength, and receive a narcotic that irritates and paralyzes the nerves, and the result is weakness; you drank to prolong life, but have used up to-day your vitality‡ that should support the system to-morrow; thus you expend, so to say, the principal instead of the interest of your vitality; and will the sooner become constitutionally bankrupt.

303. The component parts of malt-liquor are water, alcohol, a gummy extract of malt, or barley, and a little acetic acid, differing

---

* The Brewers' Congress estimate two and-a-half bushels per barrel.

† For further information on this subject, see tract by the author entitled, "Malt Liquors, their Nature and Effects," published by the National Temperance and Publication House, New York.

‡ See No. 146.

slightly in the various kinds; alcohol being an essential ingredient in all malt liquors, as well as every other intoxicating beverage. This each can prove for himself with but little cost.

304. Take a pint of ale, weighing eighteen ounces, and put it into a retort, and apply to it a gentle heat, when about an ounce, or a little less, of alcohol will be driven off, which can be preserved. By increasing the heat, the remaining water, about 15 ounces, can be evaporated, leaving at the bottom of the retort about an ounce of black gummy extract of barley and hops, that no one would take as food; yet this is all the nutriment contained in a pint of ale or beer, and the sum total of all that can impart nourishment in that foaming and "nutritious" beverage.

305. The following analysis gives the amount of ingredients contained in the liquors named:

Name.	Whiskey, per cent.	Wine, per cent.	Porter, per cent.	Ale, per cent.	Beer, per cent.	Number of ozs. in a pint of beer.
Alcohol	28 to 55	14 to 23	3.00	5.85	4.00	$\tfrac{19}{25}$ ounces.
Extract	....	....	6.09	5.00	5.66	$1\tfrac{16}{25}$ ounces.
Acetic acid	....	....	.21	.15	.17	
Water	72 to 45	86 to 76	90.70	89.00	90.17	13 ounces.
Total	....	....	100.00	100.00	100.00	16 ounces.

From the evidence presented, it must be very clear that alcohol and all its compounds, if they are food, are very poor as well as dangerous.

306. To escape from the dilemma, of alcohol being both food and a poison, some of the advocates of the doctrine tell us that:—"common salt contains an irritant poison; it is itself a poison if taken in sufficient large quantities." Let us examine the scapegoat. Common salt is found as a constituent in the different tissues of the body, and its presence is important as regulating the phenomena of endosmosis and exosmosis; besides this a certain amount of salt is found to exist naturally in the tissues of animals, and in vegetables.

307. This cannot be said of alcohol, which has never been found as a component of any animal or vegetable body; nor can it be proved that it is needed to supply any natural demand, while chloride of sodium, *common salt*, excites the digestive fluids, and aids in the solution of food; alcohol prevents the digestion of food, by coagulating the albumen, hardening the food, and destroying the solvent power of the gastric juice, as will be seen hereafter. The same advocate says: "The air we breathe contains poison, and would not be a vitalizer without its poisonous properties, * * and our Good Father, and not we, made the air, the sea, and land."

308. Is it any reason, that because a small percentage of carbonic acid—1.2500 of the whole—is mixed with the air in the lungs, that we should take another poison into our system; or because we cannot breathe without taking a small amount of this

poison, that we should call it a food? We fail to see that this can make alcohol less a poison or more a food.

309. It may be said that food consists of all substances that will aid to build up the system or to sustain the processes of nutrition. But before food is able to perform these offices, it must be digested and absorbed into the blood. The first process is to masticate and mix the food with the secretions of the mouth; it then passes into the stomach, where it is acted upon by the gastric juice, a chemical solvent containing a dilute acid, and an organic substance called *pepsin*. The gastric juice acts mainly upon the albuminous portions of the food; while sugar, starch, and fat, are principally acted upon in the intestines by the *pancreatic juice*, the bile, etc.

310. Albuminous elements are the sources of all animal structures. Alcohol, like heat, hardens albuminous substances, and prevents their transformation into fibrine, and thus interferes with the building up of the animal structure. Alcohol depresses the plastic powers of the blood, prevents nutrition, and so deteriorates the vital forces, that those who habitually use alcoholics, receiving but a very slight injury, are not so easily cured as total abstainers; and if they have used alcoholics excessively, a cure is rendered almost impossible. Every observing physician knows this fact.

311. "A copious London beer drinker," says Dr. Grindrod,* "is all one vital part; he wears his heart upon his sleeve, bare to a death-wound from the claw of a cat, or a rusty nail." Again he says, "Every medical man in London dreads a beer-drinker for a patient in a surgical case." "Among the coal-heavers," said Dr. Gordon, "who are brought to the London hospitals, the mortality is frightful!" The moment these beer-drinkers are attacked with acute disease, they die directly.

312. We learn from Dr. Edwards, that the diseases of beer-drinkers are always of a dangerous character, and that such persons can never undergo the most trifling operation with the security of the temperate.

313. It seems very improbable, if not impossible, that beer or other alcoholic beverages can act as food. It is also difficult to conceive by what wondrous alchemy, ale, beer, porter, e c., can nourish and strengthen a system already trembling in the balance between life and death, when they so destroy vitality, that those who habitually use them are unable to resist the power of disease, as those can who abstain from them.

314. Food repairs the wear and tear of the tissues of the body. Alcoholics cannot. We have no proof that alcohol is decomposed within the system: but the bulk of the evidence is, that it leaves the body the same compound it was when it entered. It goes into the body, alcohol, and comes out alcohol. It does not act in

---

* "Bacchus" an Essay by Dr. Ralph Barnes Grindrod, p. 280, 1st American edition, 1848.

the body like starch, sugar, or fat, though it is claimed by some, to belong to the same class.

315. If it was found in nature, like starch, sugar and fat, and possessed the same number and arrangement of the elements, the advocates of its use as a food might have a shadow of reason in their doctrine. True, alcohol contains carbon, hydrogen, and oxygen. But these gases are not the food of man, for it is the office of vegetation, to change unorganized and destructive gases into compounds capable of becoming food, to nourish and repair the tissues, give force and sustain animal life.

316. Alcohol cannot form a particle of tissue. The animal economy repels, and exerts all its powers to expel it from the system. Even Liebig says: "Beer, wine and spirits furnish no element capable of entering into the composition of the blood, muscular fibre, or any part which is the vital principle." "Alcohol," said Dr. Smith, F.R.S., "is not a true food, it interferes with alimentation." It is very plain that any substance capable of acting as food, must undergo in the body a chemical or vital change, to give force, or become a part of the organization. We have no proof that alcohol undergoes any such change; without which, it certainly cannot add a particle of matter to the tissue, or give force. Hence it is not food. Its effects while in the system are that of an irritant to every tissue and organ it touches."

317. Every one can prove this for himself by holding alcohol for a few minutes in his mouth, when he will find his mouth burned and inflamed. It will produce like effects upon every membrane and tissue with which it comes in contact.

318. This accords with the experience of Dr. Thomas Sewall, of Columbia College, Washington, D. C., who said:* "Alcohol is a poison, ever at war with man's nature; and in all its forms and degrees of strength, produces irritation of the stomach, which is liable to result in inflammation, ulceration, mortification, a thickening, and induration of its coats, and finally, *schirrus cancer*, and other organic affections. * * * No one who indulges habitually in the use of alcoholics, whether in the form of wine or more ardent spirits, possesses a healthy stomach." Now, is there a single article of food known, that produces such effects? Would any intelligent conscientious physician, recommend to a sick person, as a food, any article however nutritious, whose effects on the stomach were such as Dr. Sewall ascribes to alcohol?

319. It is due to the medical profession that we should mention the several Medical Declarations that have been made concerning alcohol. The first was drawn by Mr. Julius Jeffreys, in 1839, and "declared the opinion to be erroneous that wine, beer or spirits was beneficial to health; that man in ordinary health required no such stimulant, and could not be benefitted by the habitual employment of such in either large or small quantities; and even in the most moderate doses, alcoholic drinks did no

---

* Pathology of Drunkenness.

good, while large quantities (such as by many would be thought moderate) sooner or later prove injurious to the human constitution, without any exception." Signed by Sir B. Brodie, Sir James Clark, Sir J. Eyre, Dr. Marshall Hall, Dr. A. T. Thomson, Dr. A. Ure, the Queen's physician, Professor Quain, Mr. Bransby Cooper, and seventy of the leading physicians and surgeons.

320. Eight years later (1847,) the Second Medical Declaration was made and signed by 2000 of the most eminent medical gentlemen in Great Britain, including Sir B. Brodie, Sir G. Clark, Sir W. Burnett, Sir J. Forbes, Sir H. Holland, Sir A. Monroe, Sir J. M'Gregor, Sir R. Christison, Dr. W. B. Carpenter, Dr. Copland, Dr. Neil Arnott, Dr. A. Farre, Professors Guy, Allen, Thomson, Miller, McLeod, Thompson, and Simpson; which reads: "We are of the opinion: 1st, That a very large portion of human misery, including poverty, disease, and crime, is induced by the use of alcoholic or fermented liquors as a beverage. 2nd, That perfect health is compatible with total abstinence from all such intoxicating drinks, whether in the form of ardent spirits, or as wine, beer, porter, cider, &c. 3rd, That persons accustomed to such drinks, may with perfect safety discontinue them entirely, or gradually, after a short time." 4th, That total and universal abstinence from alcoholic drinks, and intoxicating beverages of all sorts, would contribute to the health, prosperity, morality and happiness of the human race." There is nothing in the testimony of the two thousand medical men, to indicate that alcohols are in any sense food; but they tell us that total abstinence from alcoholic liquors is compatible with perfect health.

321. The Third Medical Declaration in England was prepared twenty-four years later, (1871,) by Professor Parkes, on the suggestion of Mr. Ernest Hart, and Mr. Robert Rae, and reads as follows: "As it is believed that the inconsiderate prescription of large quantities of alcoholic liquids by MEDICAL MEN for their patients, has given rise, in many instances, to the formation of intemperate habits, the undersigned, while unable to abandon the use of alcohol in the treatment of certain diseases, are yet of the opinion, that no medical practitioner should prescribe it without a sense of grave responsibility. They believe that alcohol, in whatever form, should be prescribed with as much care as any powerful drug, and that the direction for its use should be so framed as not to be interpreted as a sanction for excess, or necessarily for the continuance of its use when the occasion is past.

322. "They are also of opinion that many people immensely exaggerate the value of alcohol as an article of diet, and since no class of men see so much of its ill effects, and possess such power to restrain its abuse, as members of their own profession, they hold that every MEDICAL PRACTITIONER is bound to exert his utmost influence to inculcate habits of great moderation in the use of alcoholic liquids.

323. "Being also firmly convinced that the great amount of drinking of alcoholic liquors among the working classes of this country is one of the greatest evils of the day, destroying, more than anything else, the health, happiness, and welfare of those classes, and neutralizing to a large extent the great industrial prosperity which Providence has placed within the reach of this nation, the undersigned would gladly support any wise legislation which would tend to restrict within proper limits the use of alcoholic beverages, and gradually introduce habits of temperance." Signed by George Burrows, M. D., F. R. S., President of the Royal College of Physicians, etc., George Busk, F. R. S., President of the Royal College of Surgeons; Professor Parkes and 189 of the leading physicians and surgeons of London, and 69 medical practioners, heads of medical institutions in the various cities and towns of England.

324. The medical practitioners of Montreal, seeing the widespreading evils resulting from alcoholic drinks, have also issued a Declaration, as follows:—

February, 1873.

"We the undersigned, members of the medical profession in Montreal, are of opinion—1st, That a large proportion of human misery, poverty, disease, and crime, is produced by the use of alcoholic liquors as a beverage. 2nd, That total abstinence from intoxicating liquors, whether fermented or distilled, is consistent with and conducive to, the highest degree of physical and mental health and vigour. 3rd, That abstinence from intoxicating liquors would greatly promote the health, morality and happiness of the people." G. W. Campbell, M. D., Prof. of Principles and Practice of Surgery, and Dean of Faculty of McGill College; E. H. Trudel, M. D., Prof. of Midwifery, and 25 Professors in Medical Colleges, etc., and seventy other physicians of Montreal.

325. Thus the "world moves," and though the English Declaration is non-committal on the question at issue, yet, they say that alcohol, in whatever form, should be prescribed with as much care as "any powerful drug;" this assertion alone should be enough to establish a well-defined conviction in the mind of every man and woman that any article which requires as much care in its use as "any powerful drug," must be a very unsafe "food," "and not innocent to the tissues," and one that in all cases should be avoided, when other food can be obtained, if even less nutritious, in order not to run the risk of the injury that may result from so powerful an agent.

326. The 3rd, or Montreal Declaration, like the second, charges alcohol with being the cause of misery, poverty, crime and disease; and that abstinence from it, "is consistent with, and conductive to the highest degree of physical and mental health and vigour."

327. This negatively decides the question; for if health and vigour are promoted by abstinence from an article, that article

certainly cannot be a nutriment, but must be a poison to the animal organism.

328. Dr. Lehman, in his Physiological Chemistry, says:— "We cannot believe that alcohol, theine, etc., which produce such powerful reaction on the nervous system, belong to the class of substances capable of contributing towards the maintenance of the vital functions." And Prof. Moleschott, of Erlanger, says:— "Alcohol does not effect direct restitution, nor deserve the name of an alimentary principle."

329. Dr. W. B. Carpenter says:—"Alcohol cannot supply anything which is essential to the due nutrition of the tissues."*

330. Charles A. Cameron, M. D., Professor of Hygiene in the Royal College of Surgeons in Ireland, says, "That alcohol is incapable of forming any part of the body, is admitted by all physiologists. It cannot be converted into brain, nerve, muscle, or blood. As an ordinary food, alcohol is extremely costly; and it is one which is not necessary in the case of healthy persons. Unless used in *very* moderate quantities, it injures digestion, and depresses the vital powers."

331. Alcohol does not contain the constituent elements of the body, and hence cannot build it up. It has no gluten, lime, or phosphorus, no albumen, the basis of living bodies, no iron, or salts of the blood, and hence cannot in any way perform the office of food.

332. We conclude that alcohol cannot be food from the following facts:

1st, Food nourishes, and warms the body, alcohol does not.

2nd, Food is digested. Alcohol is not. For the proof is wanting that it is ever decomposed in the animal body.

3rd, True food builds the body by assimilating with the tissues. Alcohol never does.

4th, Food makes blood. Alcohol does not; it only mixes itself with the fluids, and irritates the tissues, and destroys the plastic powers of the blood.

5th, Food feeds or improves the blood-globules or cells. Alcohol destroys them.

6th, Food produces in the animal system healthy, normal actions of all its functions. Alcohol always tends to produce disease.

7th, Food gives force and vitality. Alcohol destroys force and vitality; excites reaction, and reduces the normal powers of the whole system.

IS ALCOHOL RESPIRATORY FOOD?

333. Some advocates of the food value of alcohol still adhere to the theory of Liebig, who classed alcohol with fat, sugar,

---

* Manual of Physiology, page 327.

starch, etc., as respiratory food, which, though they do not enter into, or build up the tissues, yet keep up the heat of the body.

334. Liebig taught the doctrine that nitrogenous matter alone constitutes the source of nervous and muscular power; that the tissues were consumed in the exercise of their functional activity, and that fresh nitrogenous matter was needed to replace that which had served for the production of power. This doctrine was at once accepted, like his others, on its plausibility, without proof.

335. But experimental inquiry has thrown great doubt on the theory. So that now it is fully established, that force is not due to the destruction of the tissue, but to the oxydation of non-nitrogenous matter, the muscles merely serving as a medium for the conversion of the generated force into motor power. It is also now the opinion of some of our most learned physiologists, that starch, sugar and fats, are not any more entitled to be exclusively classed as respiratory food, than the nitrogenous alimentary substances.

NITROGENOUS SUBSTANCES ARE NOT THE ONLY SOURCES OF FORCE, ETC.

336. The Liebigan doctrine rests upon the argument, that if the force evolved by muscular action proceeds from the destruction of the muscular tissue; nitrogenous matter would be needed to replace the tissue lost; which would be equivalent to nitrogenous matter, through the medium of the muscle, being applied to the production of motor power. Now, if, by the action of muscle, there is a destruction of tissue, there must certainly be as a product of this destruction, a nitrogen-containing substance eliminated;—which is excreted in the form of urea.

337. The theory that muscular work is dependent on, and in proportion to, the destruction of muscular tissue by oxydation, received a decisive blow from Drs. Fick and Wislicenus, professors of Physiology and Chemistry respectively at Zurich.* They chose for the experiment the ascent of the Faulhorn, a mountain 6561 feet high, near the lake of Briënz in the Bernese Oberland; and being furnished with hotel accommodation on the summit, remained over night, and descended the next day. To simplify the experiment, the food consumed was solely non-nitrogenous, so that the nitrogen found in the urine might be derived exclusively from that belonging to the system.

338. On August 30th, between 10 minutes past five in the morning, and 20 minutes past 1 in the afternoon, the ascent was made. From noon of the 29th, no nitrogenous food had been eaten by them; their diet being solely of starch and fat, made in the form of small cakes, and sugar; with tea, beer, and wine—as drinks.

---

* "On the Origin of Muscular Power," by Drs. Fick and Wislicenus, Philosophical Mag., Vol. XXXI., 1866.

339. After ascending the mountain they rested, and took no other kind of food until 7 in the evening, when they partook of a meal of meat and its usual accompaniments. The secretions were collected from 6 P. M. of the 29th, six hours after the commencement of their non-nitrogenous diet. That secreted from this time till 10 minutes past 5 A. M. of the 30th, when the ascent began, was called, "before work." That during the ascent was called "work urine;" and that from 1.20 P. M. to 7 P. M. (from the completion of the ascent to the cessation of the non-nitrogenous diet) "after work." Finally the secretions during the night spent on the Faulhorn, up to half-past 5 A. M. were also collected, and denominated night urine.

340. Each specimen was measured, and the quantity of urea and the absolute amount of nitrogen contained detetermined. The following was the result:

QUANTITY OF NITROGEN EXCRETED EACH HOUR.

	FICK.	WISLICENUS.
Before work	0.63 grammes	0.61 grammes
During work	0.41 ,,	0.39 ,,
After work	0.40 ,,	0.40 ,,
Night	0.45 ,,	0.50 ,,

341. The result proved that whilst the nitrogen excreted, was related to the food ingested, it was not related to muscular action. Less nitrogen was voided during the "work," and "after work," than during the period before work, which is plainly attributable to the absence of nitrogenous food from the diet. During the night after the meal of mixed food there was increase, greater in Wislicenus's than in Fick's case; but the one meal did not bring the amount of nitrogen up to the point at which it stood shortly after the commencement of their abstinence from nitrogenous diet.

342. The conclusion to be drawn is that muscular work is not accompanied by that increased elimination of nitrogen, to be expected, if it resulted in the oxydation of the tissue of the muscle. For if work produced is the result of the oxydation (burning) of muscle, the force producible from muscle so ozydized, should be equivalent to the force expended. But the results of the experiments show that the force expended exceeded considerably the amount derivable from the nitrogenous matter consumed.

343. For further information on this subject we would refer the reader to the views of Prof. Frankland* and Dr. Parkes.†

344. By these and other experiments it has been clearly ascertained that a more or less proportion of nitrogenous matter ingested, undergoes a metamorphosis, attended by the produc-

---

* "On the Origin of Muscular Power." London Philo. Mag. Vol. XXXI. 1866.
† Proceedings of Royal Society, Jan. 1867, Vol. XV. No. 69, and Id. Vol. XVI. No. 94.

tion of urea: but as to the precise state of the metamorphosis, our present information is little more than surmise.

345. As the force produced is in proportion to the chemical action, the measure of the value of the different articles of food for force production, is the amount of oxygen they will consume in the process of complete oxydation.

346. Prof. Frankland[*] experimentally determined the actual amount of heat evolved during the oxydation of the various organic substances. The oxygen consumed by oxydation of starch, albumen, and fat is as follows:—

The amount of oxygen appropriated in oxydizing 100 parts as consumed within the body.

    Grape Sugar (Anhydrous)......................106
    Starch.......................................120
    Albumen......................................150
    Fat..293

By the above as a force-producing agent, taking capacity for oxydation as a measure, albumen is about half the value of fat, and of more value than either the starch or sugar.

347. The following results of Prof. Frankland's experiment, differ very little from the ratio representing the oxygen consumed in oxydation.

Units of heat evolved by oxydation of one gramme (15.434 grains consumed in the body.

    Grape Sugar (commercial)....................3277
    Starch (arrow-root).........................3912
    Albumen (purified)..........................4263
    Fat (beef fat)..............................9069

348. The heat evolved by the oxydation of sugar and starch, in the calorimeter, represents the heat given off when consumed in the body, every reason being in favour of the conclusion that the ultimate products in both instances are the same.

349. but in regard to the albumen, it is known that its complete oxydation does not take place in the system; for the nitrogen that escapes in the urea, carries off some of the combustible portion of the compound unconsumed.

350. Prof. Frankland says:—"The actual energy developed by the combustion of muscle in oxygen represents more than the amount of actual energy produced by its oxydation in the body, because when muscle burns in oxygen, its carbon is converted into carbonic acid, and its hydrogen into water; the nitrogen being to a great extent evolved in the elementary state; whereas when muscle is completely consumed in the body, the products are carbonic acid, water, and urea—a substance which still retains a considerable amount of potential energy."

---

[*] Philosophical Magazine, Vol. XXXII, 1866.

351. What we have said of albumen, applies to other nitrogenous substances, with slight variations for the difference in their elementary composition.

352. We arrive then to the conclusion, that while nitrogenous matter may be regarded as forming the basis of structure possessing active living properties; the non-nitrogenous principles supply the source of power; the one holding the position of the instrument of action, while the other supplies the motor power.

353. While it is true, that nitrogenous alimentary substances may, by oxydation, contribute to the generation of moving force, yet there is evidence to show that it is divided into two distinct parts, one containing the nitrogen which is eliminated as useless, and a non-nitrogenous portion that is retained utilized in the production of force, and applied to tissue formation.

354. Let us now consider the nature and use, more particularly, of the non-nitrogenous alimentary matter. Liebig classed starch, sugar, fat, etc., as simply heat-producing food, and they are yet classed as carbonaceous compounds by some writers and chemists, though, as already seen, other alimentary substances, as albumen, etc., produce heat.

355. Fat or oil is composed of carbon, hydrogen and oxygen, ($C_{10} H_{18} O$) forming a compound, which by its oxydation, produce heat and force in the body.

356. For example, take four ounces of beef fat, or tallow, and a cotton wick, and make it into a candle. If you apply a flame to the wick, the combustion or oxydation of the fat begins, and the elements that were held together by the concentrated sun-rays, are separated.

357. Then a part of the oxygen of the air, united with carbon, forms carbonic acid ($C O_2$), and another part of the oxygen, with the hydrogen, forms water ($H O_2$). Thus the elements that formed, or were absorbed in the growth of the grass and grain, on which the animal was fed, return to their original elements—carbonic acid and water; while the sun-rays that cemented them together, pass off in light and heat.

358. The same takes place when coal is consumed in a locomotive. If instead of burning the fat in the form of a candle, you had eaten and digested it; the body would be to the fat of the beef, what the wick is to the fat of the candle. The tissues of the body, and the breathing apparatus being only instruments for oxydizing the fat, and obtaining from it its force. If you would collect the breath, by letting it pass through a tube surrounded by ice, you could obtain the very water upon which the grass fed; and by passing the uncondensible gas through lime water, you can precipitate the carbonic acid gas in the form of insoluble chalk, that will settle at the bottom. In the water and the chalk you will find the same weight of four ounces that you had in the fat. The sun-rays that cemented the elements, carbon, hydrogen, and oxygen together, are not passed off, as light and heat emitted

from the candle, but as heat and force which enables you to think and act. Hence you see that food is something that can be decomposed, and can give up its force to the body, that it may be able to perform its functions and sustain its vital powers—"to live, move and have a being."

359. Starch, sugar, and fat in the body, are oxydized, or burned partially in the lungs, and partially in the circulation. In the process of breathing, by every inspiration oxygen enters the system, which is absorbed into the blood, when a chemical change takes place: carbonic acid, and watery vapour are expired, and heat is generated, which may be said to be matter in motion, a kind of force.

360. The capacity of a material for heat production depends upon the amount of unoxydized carbon and hydrogen it contains; and of all the alimentary materials, the fats, in this respect, hold the highest place. While the starchy saccharine, and such matters, contain a sufficient amount of oxygen in the compound to oxydize all the hydrogen present, leaving only the carbon in an oxydizable condition: in the fats, not only is the carbon, but also the chief portion of the hydrogen in an unoxydized state.

361. For instance, it may be stated that starch contains in round numbers 45 per cent. of carbon, and six per cent. of hydrogen, making 51 per cent. of carbon and hydrogen altogether; the remainder consist of oxygen amounting to 49 per cent. Sugar and gum contain, in round numbers, 43 per cent. of carbon, and 6 per cent. of hydrogen, making altogether 49 of carbon and hydrogen, leaving 51 per cent. to be made up with the oxygen.

362. The value of these compounds in relation to their capacity for oxydation, may be compared by their formula, that of starch consisting of $C_6 H_{10} O_5$; of sugar $C_6 H_{12} O_6$; in which, and in all other allied compounds, the hydrogen and oxygen exist in the proportion to form water, $H_2 O$.

363. While fat is represented by the formula $C_{10} H_{18} O$, in which two atoms of hydrogen only, have their combining equivalent of oxygen; the remaining sixteen atoms, and the carbon, are in a free state for oxydation.

364. The amount of oxygen consumed in oxydation in a specified amount of alimentary principle, varies with the amount of uncombined carbon and hydrogen it contains; and their relative value as heat producers may also be represented through the medium of the oxygen they have the capacity to appropriate. The following figures show the positions fat, starch, and sugar, hold with regard to each other, and the amount of oxygen required to oxydize fully 100 parts:

$$\text{Fat } (C_{10} H_{18} O.) \dots 293.$$
$$\text{Starch } (C_6 H_{10} O_5) \dots 120.$$
$$\text{Sugar } (C_6 H_{12} O_6) \dots 106.$$

Thus showing that fat will have the power of appropriating about

2.4 times as much oxygen as starch; or in other words, will develope 2.4 times as much heat in its complete oxydation, and therefore is 2.4 times the value of starch as a heat-producer.

365. As matter is indestructible, and cannot be created, so it is now understoood to be with *force*. And though force may be transmuted from one form to another (from chemical energy in heat, mechanical power and the like), this is considered all that occurs; and what holds good in the world around us, also applies within the living body. The physiologists now not only refer the chief source of heat in the living organism, to the oxydation of carbon and hydrogen, but to the same source is now ascribed the production of mechanical power; that the energy set free by chemical action manifests itself as mechanical work. Fick and Wislicenus suggested this comparison: "A bundle of muscle-fibres is a kind of machine, consisting of albuminous material, just as a steam-engine is made of steel, iron, brass, etc. Now as in the steam engine coal is burned in order to produce force, so in the muscular machine, fats or hydrate of carbon are burned for the same purpose. And in the same manner as the constructive material of the steam engine (iron, etc.,) is worn away and oxydized, the constructive material of the muscles is worn away, and this wearing away is the source of the nitrogenous constituents of the urine. This theory explains why, during muscular exertion, the excretion of nitrogenous constituents of the urine, is little, or not at all increased, while the carbonic acid is enormously augmented; for in a steam engine moderately fired, and ready for use, the oxydation of iron, etc., would go on tolerably equally, and would not be much increased by the more rapid firing necessary for working; but much more coal would be burned, when it was at work, than when it was standing idle." Viewing the evidence presented it must be admitted that the results of modern "scientific research," go to show that the non-nitrogenous foods do not produce heat only, but also other *forms* of *force;* and that nitrogenous matter which constitutes the basis of the various organs and tissues, forms the instrument of action, whilst the oxydation of non-nitrogenous matter supplies motor power; and are not, as was taught by Liebig, simply heat producers; and that nitrogenous tissues are consumed in functional activity, and that nitrogenous matter alone constitutes the source of muscular and nervous power.

366. But, "is alcohol respiratory food?" Our readers need not be told that there are two kinds of blood in the body, the *arterial* blood, which is a bright red colour, and the *venous* blood, which is dark, commonly called black blood.

367. The venous blood is incapable of supplying the organism with stimulus and nutrition, but is a poison in the fullest sense of the term. The venous blood is carried back to the heart, and thence to the lungs, where it is changed into arterial blood. During the process of respiration, the air, when drawn into the lungs,

is composed of about 21 per cent. of oxygen, and 79 per cent. of nitrogen, and somewhere about one-twentieth of one per cent. of carbonic acid, which is an impurity, and a small quantity of watery vapour, and a trace of ammonia.

368. After the air has passed through the lungs, it becomes changed. 1st, It has lost oxygen. 2nd, It has gained carbonic acid. 3rd. It has absorbed watery vapour.

369. The blood, during its circulation through the lungs, also becomes changed. 1st, Its colour is changed from a dark to a light red colour. 2nd, It has absorbed oxygen. 3rd, It has exhaled or given off carbonic acid and watery vapour. The carbonic acid existed in the blood before it passed through the lungs. The oxygen absorbed during respiration passes off in a free state with the arterial blood.

370. The oxygen and carbonic acid of the blood, are in solution principally in the blood globules; the change of the blood from purple to scarlet, in its passage through the lungs, is due to the blood globules giving up carbonic acid and absorbing oxygen. The blood may be considered a medium to convey oxygen from the lungs to the various tissues, which take it up, and it becomes a part of their substance. Carbonic acid is produced in three ways; in the lungs, in the blood, and in the tissues; the tissues being the most important source of carbonic acid in the blood.

371. Carbonic acid is not produced, as some have supposed, by a process of oxydation, or direct union of oxygen with the carbon of the tissues, but by the decomposition of the organic ingredients of the tissues, and perhaps other substances, with which we are not yet fully acquainted.

372. It may be readily inferred that the purification of the venous blood is indispensable, for death will quickly take place, if the venous blood is not arterialized, or purified. All the functions of the body are subordinate to *respiration*. If we alter the relative amount of oxygen by increasing, or by diminishing it, we do violence to the organism. If there is too much oxygen, the excitement of the system is augmented, the brain and the nervous system are stimulated, and increased in action. The converse is the case, when a number of persons are shut up in an unventilated room, where there is a diminution of oxygen, and carbon is not sufficiently eliminated from the blood; so that death sooner or later will be the result of too little or too much oxygen. Life may also be shortened not only by an increase of oxygen, but by an increased action caused by endowing the organism with a greater affinity for oxygen. In view of these chemical and physiological truths, let us see if alcohol is respiratory food. Let us suppose that Liebig's theory is true, that alcohol is oxydized in the body. What will be the result? The alcohol having a greater affinity for oxygen than for other elements of the food, the hydrogen in the alcohol will unite with the free oxygen circulating in the blood, and life is burned out too fast. Again, the

alcohol will injure the system by adding carbon to that which is already in the blood; by changing the arterial blood into venous. This is Liebig's doctrine, for he says: "The oxygen of the arterial blood, which, in the absence of alcohol would have combined with the matter of the tissues, now combines with the elements of the alcohol.

373. "The arterial blood becomes venous, without the substance of muscles having any share in the transformation."

374. Thus, by Liebig's own showing, alcohol, instead of being respiratory food, stops the changes that should take place in the blood during respiration, so that it not only prevents the natural and necessary results of respiration from being produced; and the elimination of the waste and effete matters from being expelled from the system, which are of themselves poisons to the animal organism; but adds more poisonous carbon to the body, which it is the office of the respiratory functions to eliminate from the system. These being the effects of alcohol, according to this theory, is it respiratory food? Is it not truly a respiratory poison?

375. Two-thirds of the inhabitants of the globe, from the torrid to the frigid zones, live, and are able to endure the hardships and fatigues incident to their various modes of life without alcohol.

376. Dr. Lionel Beale, F. R. S., the eminent microscopist, says: "Alcohol does not act as food, it does not nourish the tissues; it may diminish waste by altering the consistence and chemical properties of the fluids and solids. It cuts short the life of rapid growing cells, or causes them to live more slowly." If alcohol retards cell growth, it cannot form tissue, or repair waste, and hence it is not food, but poison. Alcohol cannot repair or build up the tissues, nor increase the nerve force, being destitute of nitrogen, and thus, according to Liebig's own doctrine, cannot nourish muscular and nerve tissue.

DOES ALCOHOL PRODUCE HEAT?

377. From what has been said of alcohol, is its nature such that it can be burned in the human body without injury? Alcohol is not a heat-producer; not a fuel-food in the animal economy, such as fat, starch or sugar. Alcohol, we are told, contains hydrogen, and carbon, in common with starch, fat, and sugar, and hence must act like them as fuel-food. True, alcohol contains hydrogen, and carbon, and so do some of our most deadly and corrosive poisons, and mineral acids. But would any one on that account use and recommend them as fuel-food?

378. Alcohol, when first taken, does appear to give warmth and heat to the body, but it only last for a few moments, when the temperature falls, and the system is not as able to resist the effects of cold.

379. This apparent increase of heat is really a cooling process, a quicker radiation of heat.

380. The experience of American and English navigators to the polar regions—Ross, Parry, Franklin, Kane, and others,—has clearly demonstrated the pernicious effects of alcohol in the cold latitudes, where all the powers of life are required to oppose the destructive forces of nature. Alcoholics are depressants; and whatever tends to lower vitality, or the vital activity of the system, will depress its heat-generating power; hence, to be able to resist the influence of cold, alcohol should be avoided. Sir John Richardson, M. D., a member of the English Arctic Expedition, said, "I am quite satisfied that spirituous liquors diminish the power of resisting cold. Plenty of food and sound digestion, are the best sources of heat."

381. "We found on our northern journey that tea was far more refreshing than wine or spirits, which we soon ceased to care for, while the craving for tea increased. Liebig, I believe, considers that spirits are necessary to northern nations, to diminish waste of the solids of the body; but my experience leads me to a contrary belief." (An ounce of experience is worth a ton of theory, So much for the Liebigian doctrine). "The Hudson Bay Company has for many years entirely excluded spirits from the fur countries of the north, over which they have control, to the great improvement of the health and morals of their Canadian servants and the Indian tribes."

382. Dr. McRae said at Montreal, in 1856; "The moment that a man had swallowed a drink of spirits, it was certain his day's work was nearly at an end. It was absolutely necessary that the rule of total abstinence be rigidly enforced, if we would accomplish our day's task. Whatever it could do for a sick man, its use as a beverage, when we had work on hand, in that terrific cold, was out of the question."

383. The Red River (of the North) Expedition, Captain G. L. Hugshe, of the staff of Colonel Sir G. Wolseley, in speaking of the soldiers, their sanitary condition and behaviour, says:— "Up early, hard at work all day, rowing or portaging from 5 A. M. to 8 P. M., with a short interval for breakfast and dinner, nothing to eat but salt pork and biscuit, nothing to drink but tea, yet looked as healthy as possible, and when they reached Fort Francis there was not one sick amongst them. They had no time to be sick." These men were constantly wet through, sometimes wet for days together, yet they were always well and cheerful, and never seemed to feel the absence of spirituous liquors. The captain considers this experiment of an expedition without the issue of spirit rations, an unequivocal success; and trusts the time has come when the "issue of spirit rations to a British army in the field will be forever abolished." He says the men were better without it; that "its absence was marked by an almost entire absence of crime, as well as the wonderful good health and spirits of the men."

384. The men themselves were soon reconciled to the loss, and admitted the superior value of tea as a substitute. Their good humour was invariably sustained, and the work they performed, " stands wholly unrivalled for its unusual nature, as well as its severity."

385. Though ample evidence has been presented of the evil effects of alcoholics, and their entire uselessness as means to aid the body to resist severe cold, yet the following shows its effects in various doses.

386. From an article entitled "Oinology" in the "Cincinnati Medical Repertory," by S. E. McKinley, we learn that a group of twenty-six men, some years ago travelling over a western plain, on a track dimly visible by day, lost their direction when overtaken by darkness. The weather, very cold in the afternoon, became more so as the night advanced. Though well provided with food, clothing, and plenty of whiskey, they had no wood or other fuel to make a fire.

387. The occurrences of the night are given in the language of the only physician who accompanied the expedition. He was a man of good strong, hard sense, with quite creditable medical attainments, considering the limited opportunities he had for securing them, which consisted in reading the domestic practice of Gunn, Ewell, and Thomas. He knew no more than their books could convey; but to his credit he knew *all* they could impart. He had only heard of, but had never seen a medical college.

388. Addressing the men, he said :—" As we can't get wood, boys, we must keep warm, or at least alive, through the powers of Madam vis Medicatrix Naturæ. She is all right in any weather, if we don't clog her up, and pucker her forces. If I have got any medical knowledge at all, I am going to use it to-night, and the first thing I begin with is this: I am as fond of whiskey as any man dare be, but by the gods, the man that gets drunk to-night to keep warm, won't see daylight. When the great God of the universe made man the boss work of the earth, he made all other things first, and the elements too, not to rule over him and to kill him; but to hunker down to his wants. But boys, whiskey was scored out of that bill of fare. The *vis Medicatrix Naturæ* is the highest of all other things, and if she aint *splintered* up by our own d——d folly, she will ride safe through any storm. We have got to keep stirring round or huddle up in the straw of the waggons, as many of us as can cram in together. Each one will keep the other warm; we must all eat as much as possible, but whiskey aint the thing. * * * This is what I told them all; but very few minded me. I didn't taste a drop, nor did Carter or Finley. We took off our boots and overcoats, and then got on the straw, and put our blankets over us and our overcoats on the top of them. We

were only cold, but did not suffer or freeze. Clark, Reilly, snd Tanner, were very cold, and we heard them yelling nearly all night. They suffered very much, but were not frozen; they drank very little whiskey, but they took several thin drinks in the run of the night. Seven other fellows that drank a good deal had their toes and fingers scorched, but they got over it in a few weeks. Six of the boys that drank pretty strong were badly frozen, and never got over it; and four that got very boozy were frozen so badly that they died three or four weeks afterwards. But Hutchinson, McElroy, and McAlpin were stiff dead by daylight. They got dead drunk, and as they did not make a fuss, the other boys thought the whiskey was keeping out the cold, so they drank the stronger. I tell you, sir, they all suffered just according as they took in the whiskey; those that got drunk, froze dead; those that drank less, but too much, died, after a while; those that drank only moderately will feel it as long as they live, and those that took only thin drinks were well nigh shut up. We three didn't drink any. The *vis Medicatrix Naturæ* brought us through. These men were all Americans; their ages ranged from twenty-three (McAlpin) the youngest, to forty-one (Carter) the oldest of the group. All were equally well provided, each having two blankets. All were in the bloom of life, in the best health, and ready to encounter, and able to overcome the hardships inseparable from a frontier life." Another triumph of the principles of total abstinence is witnessed in the late English Arctic Expedition. Among the crew there were a knot of noble fellows who dared to face the icy rigours of the North Pole in the well-tried armour of total abstinence. The number of total abstainers was six—Wm. Malley, Adam Ayles, Wm. Gore, Joiner, and Self, of the Ship "Alert," and Henry Petty, of the "Discovery." Ayles, Malley, Gore, and Petty, were Good Templars, and all except Gore were true to their colours to the end. Joiner had been a total abstainer for eight years, and Self for twenty-one years, but neither were Good Templars. Both took drink during the toilsome sledge journeys. The only men in the "Alert" that did any sledge work worthy of remark were Malley, Ayles, Joiner, and Self. The rest of the crew, including Gore, were severely punished for their drinking, having suffered disease and exhaustion. At the close of the sledge duties, at the end of July, the abstainers on the "Alert" found they had surpassed the remainder of the crew in the number of days' sledging done. Ayles had been out one hundred and ten days, and Malley ninety-eight. It is a fact most worthy of note, that neither of these men suffered with scurvy, but enjoyed good health, being only weakened by the arduous duties in sledging, which is said to be the hardest work ever imposed on man. Ayles was one of the only two men that was free from scurvy. He not only did one hundred and ten days of sledging, but on one occasion was out of the ship for eighty-four days, and this often in the severest and most extreme cold. One time the temperature was 104° below frost, or 72° below zero. Ayles at one time was with Commander Aldrich when five of the men were struck down with scurvy, and he, with Mr. Aldrich alone, were left to drag them back to the ship. The officer said: "Ayles for God's sake take some spirits, or we shall all be lost." "No," said Ayles, "I promised my mother when a boy never to touch it, and if I perish in this ice, I will keep my word." He did keep his word and never suffered from scurvy, frost-bite or other sickness. Another fact worthy of note is this: Each man had a design painted on canvas on his back, to attract the attention of those following, and to prevent *snow blindness*, The Good Templars had the Grand Lodge seal of the I.O.G.T. painted on theirs. The one that went the farthest was to leave his behind. Adam Ayles performed this feat, and buried the Good Templar's seal in a cavern nearer the North Pole than any other human being has yet gone. All honour and glory to Brother Adam Ayles, and Good Templarism. The evidence that alcohol is not a fuel-food is not confined to experience. Scientific research steps in to confirm the testimony; for Dr. Prout's experiment,* (1814,) more than sixty years ago, established the fact that alcoholic liquors diminished the quantity of carbonic acid eliminated, more than any other article he experimented with.

389. When porter was taken for dinner, the quantity exhaled was always reduced below the natural standard, while it was the reverse when water was taken.

390. He found that alcohol in every state or quantity, uniformly lessened in a greater or less degree the quantity of carbonic acid according to the quantity and circumstances. Taken on an empty stomach, the effects were most remarkable, depression following instantaneously; but after a time the constitution appeared to rally; the quantity increased, then sank again, and afterward rose slowly to the standard. On a full stomach, the effects of vinous liquors were slow, but no less sure and remarkable. As long as the effects of alcohol were perceptible, so long was the quantity of carbonic acid gas below the standard.

391. Dr. Prout's often repeated experiments prove:—"That alcohol enormously depresses the combustion of the carbon of the system during its existence in the body."

392. As early as 1850, Dr. N. S. Davis, of Chicago, Ill., instituted an extensive series of experiments to determine the effects of the different articles of food and drinks on the temperature of the system, when it was conclusively proven that during the digestion of all kinds of food, the temperature of the body was increased; but when alcohol was taken, either in the form of distilled spirits or fermented beverages, the temperature began to fall within a half hour, and continued to decrease for two or three

---

* London Lancet, April 1, 1843, Vol. II. p. 17; and "Annals of Philosophy," II. 328? IV. 331.

hours; and that the reduction of temperature in extent as well as duration, was in direct proportion to the amount of alcohol taken.

393. Now if alcohol prevents the combustion of the carbon in the system, it cannot produce heat. Its effects are that of closing the damper of a stove, not to increase the heat, but to prevent the generation of heat. Hence it cannot be a heat-producing food, whatever else it may be. These views of Prout, Davis and others are confirmed by later experiments of Dr. Edward Smith.* The experiments of Dr. Benjamin W. Richardson, F. R. S., show that the temperature of the body is decreased in some cases as much as eight degrees, Fah.; and requires from seven to eight hours to restore the body, under the most favourable circumstances, to the natural temperature.

394. Dr. B. W. Richardson, in a Lecture at Leamington, Eng.,† defined food as "something which supplies to the living body either matter or force."

395. Against the argument that alcohol is consumed in the body, he showed from his own experiments, that it reduces the animal temperature, reduces muscular activity, and that the especial effects it engenders depend on the amount administered, in relation to the weight of the animal's body. He maintained that an agent which reduces muscular activity, and the animal temperature, cannot be a true food; at least it is worse than useless, if it be admitted by any hypothesis, into the list of foods. He could not distinguish alcohol from chemical substances of the exciting depressing class. When it is physiologically understood that what is called stimulation or 'excitement, is in fact, relaxation, paralysis, more or less complete, of the circulation of the blood in the extreme parts of the body, we grasp the error in which we have been educated, and obtain a clear explanation of the experience that all excitement, all passion, leaves after its departure, lowness of the heart, depression of mind, sadness of spirit. We learn, in respect to alcohol, that the temporary excitement is produced at the expense of the animal matter, and animal force, and that the ideas of the necessity of resorting to it as a food, to build up the body, or to lift up the forces of the body, are ideas as solemnly false as they are widely disseminated." The experiments of Dr. Hammond also show that the temperature of the body is decreased by the use of alcohol.

396. Liebig, the highest authority for the theory that alcohol is food, lays the foundation for a comparison something like this: If it takes 100 parts of oil to produce by its combustion, a given amount of heat, it will take 240 parts of starch, 249 parts of

---

* See Philosophical Transactions, 1859.

† The Inaugural Lecture of the Tenth Session of the Leamington Philosophical Society, Nov. 14, 1873.—*Leamington Courier.*

sugar; but of alcohol it will require 260 parts to produce the same results.

397. Now, if this estimate of the heat-producing power of alcohol were true, we find it to be one of the very worst, for one pound of fat as a heat generator, is equal to three or four pints of whiskey.

EFFECTS OF ALCOHOL ON THE TEMPERATURE OF THE BODY.

398. Fatal doses of alcohol, it has been clearly demonstrated, produce a rapid fall of temperature, often amounting to 5° C.; and that even when intoxication is induced the temperature falls about 3° C.

399. Richardson's experiments show that in some cases very minute doses of alcohol decrease the temperature about $\frac{1}{2}$° F. in mammals, 1° F. in birds. Alcohol acts on man as regards heat, as upon the lower animals.

400. Recently Dr. Franz Riegal* made some original investigations of the effects of alcohol upon men; comprising about 86 experiments, from which he arrives at the following conclusions: "1st. Alcohol, even in moderate doses, in many cases, causes a lowering of the temperature of the body, amounting to some tenths of one degree. 2d. It is only in exceptional cases the elevation of temperature is noticed, and not unfrequently, after small doses, no change is observed. 3d. The diminution of temperature in convalescents is less than in healthy subjects, or altogether unnoticeable. 4th. In those who habitually use alcoholic stimulants, their depressing influence is wanting. 5th. The frequent repetition of the doses of alcohol, diminishes their lowering effects upon the temperature. 6th. The amount of diminution of temperature is directly proportional to the dose of alcohol given. 7th. The depression of temperature caused by alcohol is, for the most part, of but short duration, and the temperature soon returns to its previous grade." Dr. Tscheschechin, of Russia, in his researches on rabbits, found, that in twenty minutes the temperature sank from 39° 2′ to 37° 2″. Both respiration and pulse became quicker, and the vessels of the head were strongly injected. After an hour the temperature sank to 35° 7″."

401. Dr. Binz, who made forty-nine experiments, says: "We started with the conviction, that the stimulating influence of the alcohol was indubitable on the vital properties of the juices. * * * But the results were not in accordance with this view." All the experiments gave identical results, "Half a glass of light hock, or a small glass of cognac, caused a fall from 0.°4 to 0.°6 in a

---

* Deutsches Archiv. für klein, Medecin, 1873.

very short time." Large doses of alcohol given to a strong poodle *reduced the temperature* in 2¾ hours from 38° 4' to 36° 7', while it raised the *pulse* from 89 to 118."*

402. It is a well established physiological doctrine, or more truly a well established law of life, that elevation of temperature is always accompanied by an increased activity of the nutritive processes. Not only is carbonic acid discharged in greater quantities, but the ingredients of perspiration, and other secretions, show, according to Liebig, an increased waste or wearing out of the tissues; hence an increased supply of food is needed, as well as an increased quantity of oxygen. Now, if the alcohol is decomposed in the body, as Anstie and Dupré still contend some of it is, the oxygen will be diminished; for the hydrogen in the alcohol having a greater affinity for oxygen than for the other elements in the food, will deprive the system of the oxygen needed to repair the waste.

403. We have seen by the experiments of Drs. Prout, Smith, Richardson, Riegel, Binz, and Hammond, that the elimination of carbonic acid is diminished, and the temperature of the system lowered; hence alcohol cannot be a fuel-food. But even if it did, as it does not, act as a fuel, we have seen that for the purpose of producing heat, it is not worth one-fourth as much as fat, and is of less value than starch, besides being a very dangerous food, not "innocent as regards the tissues."

404. Alcohol is not needed in the healthy body, for normal heat can be supplied at a much cheaper rate, by a sufficient supply of ordinary food; for vegetable and animal food are not only able to supply the necessary wants of to-day, but to store up in the fatty tissues a supply for future use. Let us admit, for the sake of argument, that a part of the alcohol is decomposed, as it must be to produce heat or force, at the best it is one of a very low order, and a more expensive one than articles of ordinary diet.

405. Professor Frankland† undertook to experimentally determine the force-producing value of various articles commonly used as food. His results are claimed to represent the actual force evolved by complete oxydation, under the form of heat, measured by means of the calorimeter.

406. Heat and mechanical work are not only mutually convertible, but have a fixed quantitive relation to each other; hence it follows, that a certain amount of heat is transformable into a definite amount of mechanical work; thus by calculation, the working power of a given article of food is easily represented. The unit of heat is the amount of heat which will raise the temperature of 1 gramme (15.432 grains) of water 1° cent. (1.8°

---

* Practitioner, Sept. 1869.
† Philosophical Mag., Vol. XXXII., 1866.

Fahr.) A kilogramme of force is the representative of the power required to lift 1 kilogramme (3.2046 lbs. avoirdupois) 1 metre (3.2808 feet) high. By Helmholtz's calculations, the animal system is capable of turning one-fifth of the actual energy developed by the oxydation of food to account, as external work. Prof. Frankland has determined the *weight* and *cost* of various articles of food, that would be required to be consumed in the system to raise the body of a person weighing 140 pounds to the height of 10,000 feet.

Name of Food.	Weight in lbs. required.	At price per lb. s. d.	Cost. s. d.
Beef fat	0.555	0.10	0.5½
Butter	0.693	1.6	1.1¼
Cocoa-nibs	0.735	1.6	1.1½
Cheshire cheese	1.156	0.10	0.11½
Oatmeal	1.281	0.2¾	0.3½
Flour	1.311	0.2¾	0.3¾
Ground rice	1.341	0.4	0.4¼
Lump sugar	1.505	0.6	0.9
Commercial grape sugar	1.537	0.3½	0.5½
Hard boiled eggs	2.209	0.6½	1.2½
Bread	2.345	0.2	0.4¾
Lean ham (boiled)	2.001	1.6	4.6
Lean beef	3.532	1.0	3.6½
Potatoes	4.068	0.1	0.5¼
Apples	7.815	0.1½	0.11
		per qt.	
Milk	8.027	0.5	1.3½
White of egg	8.715	0.6	4.4½
	Bottles.	per bottle.	
Guinness's Stout (bottled)	6¾ "	0.10	5.7½
Bass's Pale ale (bottled)	9 "	0.10	7.6

407. From the above we find that little more than a half pound of fatty matter, will furnish the same amount of power as is obtainable from 1.3 lbs. of flour, 1.5 of sugar, 3.5 of lean beef, and 5 lbs. of potatoes. And furthermore that the same amount of work is obtainable from oatmeal, costing 3½d. (about 7 cents;) or flour, 3¾d. (7½ cents,) bread 4¾d. (9½ cents,) beef fat 5½d. (11 cents;) beef, 3s. 6½d., as from 9 bottles of Bass's Pale Ale, costing 7s. 6d. ($1.87,) or 6⅓ bottles of Guinness's Stout, costing 5s. 7½d. ($1.40.)

408. Thus if wine, beer, and spirits are foods, they are costly ones. This is confirmed by Liebig, whom many venerate as authority on this question. He says, "If a man drinks daily eight or ten quarts of the best Bavarian beer, in the course of a year he will have taken into his system, the constituents contained in a five pound loaf of bread, or in three pounds of flesh.

409. To be able to obtain this amount of nutriment, a man will

have to drink from 2.920 to 3.650 quarts of that beer. If Bavarian beer is as strong as lager beer, or contains 4 per cent. of alcohol, to procure the nourishment of that amount of bread, he must drink annually, from 116 to 146 quarts of *pure alcohol*. *Truly beer is nutritious; verily, Alcohol is Food!*

410. Though saccharine or oleaginous elements must enter into the composition of foods; yet it is very doubtful if they are sufficiently nutritious to alone support the animal in perfect health, for a protracted period. Professor W. A. Hammond was enabled to live for ten days on boiled starch and water. On the third day, his general health began to fail, and he became very much impaired before the close of his experiment. It is only by the use of a mixed diet, composed of all the proximate principles, that health can be very long sustained.

411. Dr. F. R. Lees states that a man who lifts his own weight, 150 lbs., up to the height of 7,560 feet, has really done work equal to raising 506 tons one foot high. As all the power to do this comes from our food, we will measure the value of various kinds of foods by this standard, or by Dr. Lees' dietary table, which is as follows:—

I. AS NUTRITION.

412. Food required to supply half an ounce of nitrogen, the minimum amount needed in health per day.

Food.	Weight in ounces.	Heat value in Foot-tons.	Cost in England. s. d.	Cost in America. $. cents.
Pea meal	15	2.194	0.3	0.02½
Oatmeal	20	3.134	0.3½	0.03¼
Wheaten bread	40	3.236	0.5	0.13
Rich cheese	10	1.627	0.6	0.10
Lean beaf	12	667	0.7½	0.14
Potatoes*	120	4.709	0.7½	0.07
Rice	50	7.304	1.0	0.22½
Milk	100	2.446	1.0	0.31

II. AS FUEL.

413. Substances required for doing 4,000 foot-tons of bodily work, by their combustion:

---

* Very valuable for supplying potash to the blood, and thus averting scurvy. Lemon and lime Juice answer the same purpose, not because of their acid, but their potash.

Food.	Pounds Weight.	Cost in London. s. d.	Cost in New York. $. cents.
Oatmeal	1⅝	0.4½	0.03
Fat of meat (dripping)	¾	0.6	0.20
Potatoes	6½	0.6½	0.06
Wheaten bread	3	0.6	0.15
Lump or dry sugar	1⅞	0.11	0.22
Butter	⅞	1.2	0.42
Good oily cheese	1½	1.3	0.33
Boiled eggs	2¾	1.6	0.25
Arrow-root	1⅝	1.8	0.57¾
Lean beef	4½	3.6	0.63

415. Now, if the alcohol and the extracts of beer and ale are really of use as food, or undergo decomposition, which, as already said, is very doubtful, they are very costly. Dr. Lyon Playfair, estimates that ale contains of nutriment only, in bulk, *one part* in sixteen hundred and sixty-six.

416. Admitting all Liebig claims for alcohol, would it not be the acme of folly, and an evidence of imbecility for a man to pour into his stomach annually, 2,920 quarts of beer, or 116 quarts of pure alcohol, at a cost of $292, in order to obtain the nutriment of a five pound loaf of bread, that he can obtain almost anywhere for less than 30 cents, and thus have to pay more than $291 a year for the delightful privilege of swallowing 29 gallons of an acid, narcotic poison? To say the least, "he pays too much for his whistle."

417. It is still an unsettled question, how sugar and fat disappear in the body; but this much we know, that starch is converted into sugar within the organism, and is absorbed in the tissues; but of the exact nature of their transformation, we are as yet ignorant; though the difference in their disappearance and that of the albuminous substances is only a matter of time. The nutritive value of a food, does not depend upon its containing any particular alimentary substance, but upon its containing many elements mixed in the requisite proportion to maintain the healthy nutrition of the body.

418. Animal heat must not be regarded as purely the result of a combustive process; for there is no proof that the mass of food is burned in the circulation for its assimilation by the substance of the tissues.

419. To arrive at a reasonable cause of animal heat, it must be considered as the result of numerous combinations and decompositions, that follow each other incessantly during the process of nutrition, and not by the decomposition of any particular article of food.

420. If all that is claimed by the advocates of the combustive

theory of sugar and fat be true, it does not prove that alcohol performs any such office; for we have no evidence that alcohol is either decomposed in the body, or adds a particle to the substances of the tissues.

421. We must therefore conclude that the warming or heat-giving power of alcohol is a deception, for it diminishes the carbonic acid exhaled and lowers the temperature of the body; and that the sensation of warmth felt on the ingestion of alcoholics is merely the effect of diminished sensibility of the nervous system by its narcotic and sedative effects. Liebig asserts that "Spirits (dilute alcohol) by their action enable the drinker to make up sufficient power at the expense of the body;" and that "He consumes his capital, instead of the interest." * * "Wine is constantly followed by the expenditure of power." Who is so dull, as not to comprehend, that an article which causes an expenditure of power, cannot impart force or power?

422. Dr. Markham, in summing up a long discussion on alcohol, in the "British Medical Journal," said: "Alcohol is not a supporter of combustion. Part, probably the whole of it, escapes from the body: and none of it, so far as we know, is assimilated. It is therefore not a food, in the eye of Science."

DOES ALCOHOL RETARD THE WASTE OF TISSUE?

423. The theory of Prof. Moleschott was, that if alcohol is not food itself, it becomes a sort of a savings bank, making food last longer by preventing the waste of tissue; for alcohol destroyed molecular activity, by narcotizing the nerve forces, and in consequence there was less activity, and less waste, and therefore less food was needed: for in the words of Dr. Beale, "It (alcohol) cuts short the life of rapidly growing cells, or causes them to live more slowly."

424. That is all that can rationally be understood by the theory that alcohol saves tissue, yet the doctrine has still its advocates, in our own and other countries. Among the advocates of this doctrine, in this country, if we rightly understand him, is Dr. Hammond of New York: for he said in his address, on assuming the Presidency of the New York Neurological Society, May 4, 1874: "We know that a certain amount of tissue is decomposed with every functional action of the organ to which it belongs. Just as steam results from the combustion of fuel, so thought results from the combustion of gray nerve tissue, motion from the combustion of muscle, and the force to secrete bile from the combustion of the substance of the liver. We know very well, that if fresh fuel is not supplied to the engine from time to time, steam ceases to be formed, and the machinery set in motion by it, no longer works. The like is true of the body, and were it not for the formative processes which are con-

tinually going on, whereby new material derived from the food is deposited, to take the place of that which is consumed, death would very soon result. It must be distinctly understood, however, that ordinary food does not directly furnish any force inherent in the body, but that it must first be converted into flesh, and brain, and heart, &c., from the destruction of which organs the force peculiar to each is evolved."*

425. He also says, "In science, however, we believe nothing which is not demonstrated, and even then we do so provisionally, with the full understanding, that if to-morrow new facts are brought forward which appear to be inconsistent with those upon which a favourite theory rests, and which are of greater weight, the hypothesis shall be abandoned without hesitation."

426. This being a clear and fair explanation of the doctrine, we will examine the theory and the hypothesis on which it rests. This we shall do without any disrespect to Dr. Hammond, whom we much esteem and admire, for his far-reaching views on most medical questions, and his painstaking and important experiments on the effect of alcohol; but we do not believe in his theory: that alcohol limits the destruction of tissue, nor in the hypothesis on which it rests.

427. All will agree that life requires food for the growth and renewal of the tissues; and matter, which shall by chemical or other transformation, give up the energy or force consumed in life work. It is also clear that the nitrogenous tissues and nitrogen containing excretions, must be derived from nitrogenous food.

428. But the doctor, notwithstanding later scientific research, if we understand him, holds on to the Liebigian theory: that the energy of muscular action is derived from the destruction or oxydation of muscle-substance itself, whereby the latter disintegrates in proportion to the work done. Or, in his own words:

429. "*It must be distinctly understood, however, that ordinary food does not directly furnish any force inherent in the body, but that must first be converted into flesh and brain and heart, etc., from the destruction of which organs, the force peculiar to each is evolved.*"

430. But is this true? If it is, then the nutritive value of food must be measured by the nitrogen it contains, and the theory of Liebig still holds good.

431. This being so, then muscular action is the result of the destruction of muscular tissues; hence there must, as a product of this destruction, be eliminated a nitrogenous excretion: as compounds that have served their office in the animal organism, are discharged from the body. It is well known that nitrogen,

---

* See Report of Lecture in Tribune Extra, No. 19.

having fulfilled its purpose in the animal economy, is eliminated in the form of *urea;* and that the nitrogen excreted in the form of *urea* is nearly equal to the sum of the nitrogen taken in the food;* hence the *urea* may represent, for all practical purposes, the whole of the nitrogen excreted.

432. Now if Dr. H's or Liebig's theory is correct, the amount of *urea* must vary with the labour performed, rising and falling as exercise or rest is taken; and that the amount excreted during exercise, or work, should be the measure of the amount of chemical action which is equivalent to the energy required to do a certain quantity of work. But unfortunately for this theory of Liebig's, and for Dr. Hammond's hypothesis, it cannot be *demonstrated*, for when put to the test it fails.

433. We have already seen (¶ 340-346) that the experiments of Drs. Fick and Wislicenus, Professor Frankland, and Dr. Parkes have clearly demonstrated that muscular work is not accompanied by the increased elimination of nitrogen to be expected, if the work resulted from the oxydation of the tissue of the muscle. If the muscular tissue does not consume itself during exercise, and the *role* of nitrogenous principles are not to repair the waste of tissues disintegrated by work; Dr. Hammond must "abandon without hesitation his favourite theory," for it cannot be "demonstrated," and in science we cannot believe it.

434. As already quoted, the Doctor said: "If fresh fuel is not supplied to the engine from time to time, steam ceases to be formed, and the machine set in motion by it, no longer works." This we are ready to admit, and also that the source of heat, and force, is the fuel. But Dr. Hammond holds a different opinion, if we understand him, by what follows: "The like is true of the body, and were it not for the formative processes which are continually going on, whereby new material, derived from the food, is deposited, to take the place of that which is consumed, death would very soon result."

435. The experiments and facts presented (¶ 340-346,) demonstrate very clearly that the "hypothesis" on which Dr. H's "favourite theory" is based, will not stand the test; that force is not produced by the "destruction of the organs by which the force peculiar to each is evolved;" that exercise does not increase the waste of nitrogenous matter any more than when at rest; that force is due to the oxydation of non-nitrogenous matter, the muscles serving merely as a medium for the conversion of the generated force into motor power.

436. Hence, as a house built on the sand must fall, the Doctor's theory of alcohol's power to preserve the waste of tissue, must fall, when the foundation on which it rested no longer

---

* Dr. Parker confidently asserts that the amount of nitrogen discharged by the kidneys and intestines is equivalent to what enters with the food.

remains; for if the tissues are not wasted by labour; or "if *thought* does not result from the combustion of the gray nerve tissue; *motion* from the combustion of muscle, and *force to secrete bile*, from the combustion of the substance of the liver;" alcohol, it is very certain, cannot preserve the waste of the tissues during labour, that is never wasted by labour, only in the imaginations of the deluded disciples of the deceived Liebig.

437. "Let us suppose," says Dr. H., "that a working-man, labouring twelve hours a day, upon a diet consisting of 10 ounces of meat, and 16 ounces of bread, finds that he loses weight at the rate of 1 ounce a day. Now in order to preserve his health, and perhaps his life, he must either take more food, or he must lessen the waste of his tissues. Meat and bread are expensive, and he finds it difficult to obtain them, or what is not at all improbable, the quantity that he eats is as much as he has any appetite for or can digest." The alternative presented to him is to work less. We have already shown that the tissues are not wasted by exercise; therefore to labour less will not prevent the waste of nitrogenous tissues; hence some other means must be adopted to "save the tissues;" this is done accordingly by Dr. Hammond's hypothesis, "by the man taking a mug of porter, or a glass of wine, or, what would be worse, a dram of whiskey after his mid-day meal." The result of which, we are told, is that "he is pleasantly exhilarated, his vigour is increased, and he labours on to the close of his task contentedly, and when it is concluded, he is more cheerful, and less fatigued, &c.; he weighs, and finds he has lost but half an ounce." He repeats his experiments the next day; like results follow, and when he weighs himself, finds that he has lost nothing. The inference therefore is that the beverage he has imbibed retarded the destruction of his tissues, or has itself aided in supplying the material for the development of the force he has expended in his labour.

438. To show that tissue is retarded by alcohol, Dr. H. tells his hearers that carbonic acid is a product of the metamorphosis of tissue; and Dr. Prout, whose experiments we have already cited, "ascertained that after the use of alcohol the amount of carbonic acid excreted by the lungs was considerably reduced." But let us examine the Doctor's hypothetical case of the man who lost an ounce a day, and to prevent this waste, he must take something to prevent the waste. This hypothetical man, we are gravely informed, not being his own master, cannot work less, and "bread and meat being expensive," he "finds it difficult to obtain them," so he takes a mug of porter "*and finds he has held his own, or gained an ounce a day.*" A query arises as to whether the increase of weight was the result of *tissue saved*, or the *increase* of *nutriment taken?* We suspect it was the intention of the doctor to infer the latter; which, if so, the man certainly paid dear for his nutriment; "for bread and meat are expensive."

439. If Bavarian beer contains the alcoholic percentage of porter, he must drink to obtain the nourishment of a five pound loaf of bread,* 5840 mugs of porter, which at five cts. a mug or pint will cost him 292 dollars, while the bread which is so "expensive and so very difficult to obtain," would cost at the highest rate not more than thirty cents.

440. The doctor infers that in addition to retarding the waste of tissues, material has been supplied by the porter "for the development of the force expended in his labour." Now we have seen (¶ 406) that by Dr. Frankland's experiments on the weight and cost of the various articles of food required to be consumed in the system, to raise the body of a person weighing 140 pounds, to a height of 10,000 feet; that $9\frac{1}{2}$ cts. worth of bread, or 11 cts. worth of beef fat, will give as much force as 9 bottles of Bass's Pale Ale, costing $1.87, or as $6\frac{1}{4}$ bottles of Guinness's Stout, costing $1.40. Wonderful economy! What a glorions *savings-box* alcohol must be! If it saves the tissue as it saves money, it is needful that mankind should learn its virtues speedily. So much for the economy of porter, *versus* bread and meat.

441. Again. How does alcohol give force, and at the same time retard the waste of tissue? By the Doctor's theory the combustion of tissue must take place to produce force. He says:— "Thought results from the combustion of the gray nerve tissue, motion from combustion of muscle, etc."

442. Now if the combustion of tissue produces force, how can force exist when the combustion of tissue is retarded? Let the Doctor get out of his own dilemma. By the following experiments of Dr. Parkes, it is evident that alcohol does not retard the waste of tissues.

DR. E. A. PARKES' EXPERIMENTS ON THE EFFECTS OF ALCOHOL AND EXERCISE ON THE BODY.

443. Dr. Parkes, in a paper presented to the Royal Society, gives the particulars of some experiments tried on a man, March, 1872. The objects of the experiments were to ascertain how far exercise caused an increased elimination of nitrogen; whether this was affected by the use of alcohol; and if the exercise caused an increased elimination, whether the nitrogen was derived from the food, or from the disintegration of the tissues of the body. A steady temperate soldier, aged thirty, five feet six inches high, forty inches around the chest, and in good health, was selected as the subject of these experiments. As the man was a Scotchman, it was decided that he should live on oatmeal, water, and milk.

444. After some inquiries it was found that he required 28

---

* See ¶ 416. Page 97.

ounces of oatmeal and two pints of milk per day, on which he subsisted and maintained his health for sixteen days. The water he took daily amounted to 135 fluid ounces, and no other food, except the brandy (if it may be called food) which he took for experiment. He remained perfectly well and vigorous. The oatmeal and milk, and the brandy were carefully analyzed, and every precaution taken against error.

445. The experiments were conducted as follows:—The man was allowed six days' rest, only walking enough to keep him in health. For three days he then worked hard at digging, from eight to nine hours daily.

446. He worked as hard as he could, making the labour as uniform as possible each day. He was then kept at rest for three days. And then he worked at digging for three days, but these latter three days, he took 12 fluid ounces of brandy—containing 5.4 fluid ounces of absolute alcohol—daily, in three doses of 4 ounces each, at ten, two, and six o'clock. After which he rested for three days. On all these days the condition of the man during rest and exercise was carefully ascertained. He was accurately weighed every morning. The excretions were analyzed daily, and the exact amount of nitrogen recorded. The pulse was taken every two hours, after the man had been in a recumbent position for fifteen minutes. The temperature of the body was taken nine times daily, at intervals of two hours. The elimination of the alcohol was also tested, and the effect of the brandy on the man's power to labour.

447. The average daily excretion in grammes,* of nitrogen during each period was found to be as follows:—

	In Urine.	In Feces.	Total.
1st, Rest	15.183	3.765	18.948
2nd, Exercise on water	16.274	4.981	21.255
3rd, Rest	15.850	3.251	19.101
4th, Exercise on brandy	15.750	4.372	20.122
5th, Rest	15.007	3.215	18.222

For the whole period, the total average of the daily discharge of nitrogen was 19.59 grammes, against 20 grammes, ingested, so that there was a loss in sixteen days of about 7 grammes (108 grains).

448. It was also found, as in the former experiments, that the brandy deranged the action of the heart, by causing it to perform an unnecessary amount of work; which, in the case of this man, caused a daily increase of 6,552 pulsations of the heart over the period of exercise with water. The man being in perfect health during the water period, we must suppose his heart properly performed its functions.

---

* A gramme is 15¼ grains, nearly.

449. The experiments in reference to alcoholic elimination, show that before the brandy was given to the man, nothing passed off by the skin, the lungs or kidneys, which produced the slightest change on bi-chromate of potassium test; but after the brandy was given, a substance which reduced at the test, passed off by all these outlets, especially the skin. It is to be very much regretted that Dr. Parkes did not take the means and trouble to ascertain the amount of alcohol eliminated through the skin; for it is impossible to estimate the quantity of alcohol that is eliminated from the system, until we know how much is passed off through the skin.

450. One noteworthy fact is this, that when the man began to take the brandy, he thought it would give a kind of spirit to do much more work, but he found he was deceived. And when he took the second and third doses their narcotic effects were strongly marked. He felt heavy, and could hardly refrain from giving up his work. At the end of the experiments, the man's judgment was that he could do the work better without the brandy; which is a corroboration of the experience of all, who within the last forty years have given total abstinence from alcoholics a fair trial.

DR. PARKES' CONCLUSIONS.

451. Dr. Parkes arrives at the following conclusions:—1st, The elimination of nitrogen during exercise was unaffected by brandy, and since the experiments led to the same results in the former series, during comparative rest, it seems certain that, in healthy men, on uniformly good diet, alcohol does not interfere with the disintegration of nitrogenous tissues. 2nd, The heat of the body, as judged of by the axilla and rectum temperature, was unaffected by the amount given. 3rd, The pulse was increased in frequency, by four ounces of brandy, and palpitation and breathlessness were brought on by larger doses, to such an extent as to greatly lessen the amount of work the man could do, and to render quick movements impossible. As the effect of labour alone is to augment the strength and frequency of the heart's action, it would appear obviously improper to act on the heart still more by alcohol. In this effect on the heart, and through it on the lungs, is perhaps to be found the trainer's rule, which prohibits alcohol during exertion. Whether in a heart exhausted by exertion, alcohol would be good or bad, is not shown by these experiments: but it can hardly be supposed that to urge a heart that requires rest, as would then be the case, can be proper. 4th, It seems clear, from the suddenness with which marked narcotic symptoms came on after the third dose was taken each day, that the eight hours, from ten to six o'clock, were not sufficient to get rid of the brandy taken at ten and at two, and that in fact the body must have been still saturated at six o'clock. The exact amount of brandy which commenced to lessen the labour

the man could perform, is not shown by these observations, and would require more careful modes of investigation. It was evidently some quantity more than four ounces, which produced effects sufficiently marked to attract attention. But I should not wish to affirm that even four ounces produced no effect in that direction. The man himself was of opinion that four ounces had no influence either way. He was quite certain it did not aid his work, but he could not see that it injured it. The second four ounces produced a decidedly bad effect. 5th, Neither exercise on the water, or on the alcohol, produced any effect on the phosphoric acid of the urine. The result is in accordance with that of the experiments recorded in No. 89 of the proceedings of the Royal Society. The effect on the free acidity of the urine was inconsiderable. The free acidity may have been a little increased in the brandy period, but the change was slight. The effect on the chlorine was not certain, as its ingress was not sufficiently constant, but it seems to be lessened in the exercise period. As the action of alcohol in dietetic doses on the elimination of nitrogen, and on the bodily temperature, is so entirely negative, it seems reasonable to doubt if alcohol can have the depressing effect on the excretion of pulmonary carbon, which is commonly attributed to it. It can hardly depress, one would think, the metamorphoses of tissues, or substances furnishing carbon, without affecting either the changes of the nitrogenous structures or bodily heat. It seems most important that fresh experiments should be made with respect to its effects on carbon elimination, as without a perfect knowledge on that point the use of alcohol as an article of diet in health cannot be fairly discussed.

452. Do not these experiments "*demonstrate*" that *alcohol does not prevent the waste* of tissue ? To be consistent with the Liebigian theory, when it enters the blood-current and passes into the lungs, the hydrogen must seize upon the oxygen and consume it, while the sugar, fat, etc., will not be completely oxydized; hence they will accumulate in the system, to its injury.

453. If alcohol had not been taken the oxygen would have oxydized or burned the waste or worn out tissues, and the elements of the food, to have produced force ; instead of which they are retained in the blood and will ultimately produce disease. For what else can we expect to be the result of retaining waste or effete matter in the body, but disease ? Nothing else, sooner or later can result.

454. D. Campbell Black, M.D., L. R. C. S., Edin., says :— "It seems to me a remarkable fallacy, that physiologists should persist in talking of the propriety of 'Sparing the tissues,' inasmuch as the proper function of the tissue is, to such an extent, their destruction, life the resultant of the change. Indeed when any tissue is unduly retained in the system, it may of itself constitute *materies morbi*.

455. Whatever may be the notions of those who believe that a glass or two of wine at dinner will lessen the wear and tear of body and mind, to the true scientist it must appear the very *acme* of fallacy. For according to this doctrine, it is by the destruction of tissue, that *force* of any kind is generated, and without the metamorphosis of the substance of the organs, *force* cannot be evolved, or work done. Yet we are told, that alcohol will retard the destruction of tissue, produce force, and enable a man to perform his labour more easily.

456. The believer must either abandon the notion that all force is derived from the destruction of tissue, or the idea that alcohol can retard the waste, give *force*, aid to promote health, increase the vigour of body or mind, and enable a person to better endure physical or mental labour. That veteran of the cause, the late Dr. Charles Jewett, very aptly put the question from the stand point, that force was developed at the expense of the tissues. The question being asked, "Did alcohol in the body prevent the waste of tissue?"* when he said:—"Prevent the waste of tissue? It does, to a certain extent. It stupefies the fellow so that he cannot use his muscles or brain. Wherever you develop power, you waste tissue. If you develop thought, you waste brains. When a fellow is dead drunk he saves his tissues. Toads have lived in rocks one hundred years. But who wants to live a toad's life for the sake of saving his tissues? I don't want to save my tissues. I want to go to my table every day, and have it well spread with substantial food, and incorporate the vegetable compounds, and make them a part of Jewett; and then I want to use up the energy in advancing the glory of God and promoting the good of mankind. This idea of saving tissues is all a humbug."

457. Dr. Hammond, in the address already referred to, said: "With reference to the moderate use of alcoholic liquors, it must be remembered that we are not living in a state of nature. We are all more or less overworked; we all have anxieties, and sorrows, and misfortunes, which gradually in some cases, suddenly in others, wear away our minds and our bodies. We have honours to achieve, learning to acquire, and perhaps wealth to attain. Honours, learning, and wealth are rarely got honestly, without hard work, and hard work exhausts all the tissues (?) of the body, and especially that of the nervous system (?) Now, when a man finds that the wear and tear of his mind and body are lessened by a glass or two of wine at his dinner, why should he not take it? The answer may be, because he sets a bad example to his neighbours. [Not so, but because there is nothing in the wine that can nourish.] But he does not. His example is a good one, for he uses in moderation and decorum one of the things, which ex-

---

* At the Sixth National Temperance Convention, Cleveland, Ohio, July 29-30, 1868.

perience has taught him are beneficial to him. Dr. Parkes says:* "When beer is taken daily in excess, it produces a state of fulness and plethora of the system, which probably arises from a continual though slight interference with elimination of both fat and nitrogenous tissues. When this reaches a certain point, appetite and the formative power of the body is impaired. The imperfect oxydation leads to excess of partially oxydized products, such as oxalic and uric acids. Hence many of the anomalous affections classed as gouty and bilious disorders, which are evidently connected with defects in the regressive metamorphosis."

458. We have not space to analyze the Doctor's sophistry, but would merely refer him to the following letter written by Sir Henry Thompson, F. R. C. S., Surgeon Extraordinary to his Majesty, the King of the Belgians, and Surgeon to the University Hospital, and addressed to His Grace, the Archbishop of Canterbury: "I have long had the conviction that there is no greater evil, moral and physical, in this country, than the use of alcoholic beverages. I do not mean by this, that extreme indulgence which produces drunkenness. The habitual use of fermented liquors to an extent far short of what is necessary to produce that condition, and such as is quite common in all ranks of society, injures the body, and diminishes the mental powers to an extent which I think few people are aware of. Such, at all events, is the result of observation during more than thirty years of professional life devoted to hospital practice, and to private practice in every rank above it. Thus I have no hesitation in attributing a very large portion of some of the most painful and dangerous maladies which come under my notice, as well as those which every medical man has to treat, to the ordinary and daily use of fermented drink, taken in the quantity which is conventionally deemed moderate.

459. "Whatever may be said in regard to its evil influences on the mental and moral faculties, as to the fact above stated, I feel that I have a right to speak with authority, and I do so solely because it appears to be a duty, especially at this moment not to be silent on a matter of such a truth, and how such a declaration brings me into painful conflict, I had almost said with national sentiments and the time-honoured and prescriptive usages of our race. Cherishing such convictions, I rejoice to observe an endeavour to organize on a large scale in the National Church, a special and systematic plan for promoting temperance, and I cannot but regard this as an event of the highest significance. I believe that no association in this country has means to influence society in a favourable direction at all comparable to that existing in the English Church; and the example and teaching of its clergy may do more than any other associations which have long laboured with the same object, to diminish the national vice. My

---

* Practical Hygiene, p. 258.

main object is to express my opinion as a professional man, in relation to the habitual employment of fermented liquor as a beverage. But if I ventured one step further, it would be to express a belief that there is no single habit in this country which so much tends to deteriorate the qualities of the race, *so much disqualifies it for endurance in that competition which in the nature of things, must exist, and in which struggle the prize of superiority must fall to the best and the strongest.*" When doctors disagree, each may claim the right to judge.

IS ALCOHOL A SOLVENT OF FOOD?

460. Alcohol coagulates and hardens albuminous substances, which are important food principles, hence it would seem not to be a solvent of food.

461. Alcohol may be very useful in the laboratory of the chemist, and to the pharmaceutist, as a solvent of gums; to extract and dissolve the medical properties from certain products of the animal and vegetable kingdoms; but the stomach of the living animal was never intended by the Creator to be made into a chemist's laboratory, and wholesale drug store.

462. Water is the medium by and through which, in the living animal, all the vital functions are carried on. No other liquid can act as a solvent of most vegetable substances. This almost universal solvent the Creator has bountifully supplied; God's chosen solvent. Water is the only true solvent of food in the living stomach, except the gastric juice, and other digestible fluids in the alimentary canal. He who drinks any other liquid, with the expectation of aiding in the solution of food, deceives himself, thwarts God's designs, violates His laws, and must suffer the penalty. A very little reflection will make it clear and self-evident to all, that water is the only drink designed by the Creator for man's use, as no other will so well quench the thirst, and never increase it. It aids to nourish the tissues, but never injures them. Water is so great a necessity, that a healthy adult requires from 1500 to 2000 lbs. annually. It will be evident that this quantity is needed, when we consider that four-fifths of the blood, three-fourths of the brain, nerves, muscles, and other semi-solid tissues, is water; and that water is the chief agent of digestion, absorption, nutrition and secretion; and aids in all the wonderful changes that takes place within the animal organism. It must be evident that so much water being in the blood, and semi-solid tissues, it must play a most important part in sustaining and building up the human system; and also that anything interfering with the natural operations of water in the body must produce abnormal and injurious results.

463. A necessity for water is sooner felt than for solid food. A person may pass eight, ten, or even twelve hours without solid

food, with but little inconvenience; but if deprived of water for a much shorter period, the system will become much exhausted, and its want greatly felt; as tens of thousands of our soldiers experienced during our late war.

464. Magendie found that dogs being supplied with water alone, lived six, eight, and even ten days longer, than when deprived at the same time of both solid food and water.

465. Alcohol, brought in contact with an animal membrane, is absorbed, and diffused into the tissues. Liebig says: that for every volume of alcohol absorbed by the tissues, three volumes of water were supplied.

466. This is easily proved by putting a piece of any kind of flesh into alcohol, when it will shrink and shrivel up. These effects are produced by the expelling of the water and coagulating of the albumen. These effects will take place in the living stomach in a greater or lesser degree, according to the alcoholic strength of the liquor.

467. Hence alcohol injures the human system, by interfering with the natural operation of water within the organism, by expelling it from the tissues, coagulating the albumen in the blood, and in the semi-solid and solid tissues.

468. It must certainly be injurious to the system, to expel the water from the tissues and coagulate the albumen. No abnormal physical or chemical change can take place in any of the vital organs without impeding their normal action and injuring them.

469. Such abnormal changes will be inevitable, if one volume of alcohol absorbs or expels three volumes of water from the tissues.

470. Every physician who knows anything of the condition of the stomach after drinking, knows that there is more or less congestion and inflammation of its mucous membrane, and other mucous tissues; and if he has practiced much among persons suffering from inebriation, or recovering from it, must have seen large quantities of undigested food ejected from the stomach during the operation of an emetic, and this undigested food was ingested, perhaps, ten or twelve hours before. These facts prove that alcohol is not a solvent of food. It is now well known that it takes from one to five hours and a quarter to digest the various articles of food, yet food will remain in the stomach four and five times as long undigested, if alcohol is taken during the process of digestion. Hence, *alcohol cannot be a solvent of food.*

DOES ALCOHOL AID DIGESTION?

471. If alcohol is not a food, nor a solvent of food, can it aid digestion? No! Alcohol in this case, as in the others already examined, will prove a *deceiver, a mocker*. Alcohol, instead of aiding digestion, retards and prevents it, by destroying the most important ingredient in the *gastric juice—Pepsin;* which is precipitated and coagulated: its power to dissolve alimentary substances is destroyed. Says Drs. Todd and Bowman—"The use of alcoholic stimulants retards digestion by coagulating the pepsin, * * * and were it not that wine, spirits, etc., are rapidly absorbed, their introduction in any quantity would be a complete bar to the digestion of food, as the pepsin would be precipitated from the solution as quickly as it is formed."

472. Dr. Dundas Thomson, corroborating the above, says:— "It is a remarkable fact, that when alcohol is added to the digestive fluid, it produces a white precipitate, so that the fluid is no longer capable of digesting animal or vegetable food."

473. A series of experiments was instituted by Dr. Monroe,[*] to establish or confirm the above, if true, or refute, if false. In order to test it, he had bottles containing finely minced meat, with gastric juice from the stomach of a calf. In one bottle gastric juice was mixed with water; another with alcohol, a third with pale ale. The temperature was maintained at 100°, and the contents were churned to imitate the movements of the stomach, during the process of digestion. The following were the results:—

Finely minced Beef.	2nd hour.	4th hour.	6th hour.	8th hour.	10th hour.
1st Bottle, Gastric juice and water.	Beef becomes opaque.	Digested and Separated.	Beef much lessened.	Broken up into shreds.	Dissolved like soap.
2nd Bottle, Gastric juise and alcohol.	No alteration perceptible.	Slightly opaque but beef unchanged.	Slight coating on beef.	No visible change.	Beef solid on cooling. Pepsin precipit'ed.
3rd Bottle, Gastric juice and pale ale.	No change.	Cloudy with fur on beef.	Beef partly loosened.	No further change.	No digestion on cooling. Pepsin precipitated.

474. From these experiments it is clearly proved that alcoholics destroy the solvent power of the gastric juice and prevent digestion; for even the pale ale, with its 5 or 6 per cent. of alcohol, does not aid digestion; and the stronger the alcoholic per centage, the more digestion will be interfered with. It scarcely need be said that if alcohol destroys the organic substance upon

---

[*] "Physiological Action of Alcohol," London, 1865.

which the solution of the food depends, digestion can only take place when the alcohol has been expelled from the stomach.

475. Is it not an exceedingly great mistake, for any man, and especially a physician, who is supposed to know something of the nature and action of various articles of food and medicine upon the body, to take as an article of food, any substance that will prevent the solution of alimentary matter?

476. As alcohol coagulates albuminoid substances, and as the gastric juice mainly acts upon albuminous alimentary substances, alcohol cannot help poisoning the blood, and consequently the tissues.

477. The gastric juice, unmixed with foreign substances, seizes at once upon the albuminous aliments, the true builders of the tissues, dissolves them, and then they are absorbed in the blood; but put alcohol in the stomach, and it becomes a kind of a "dog in the manger;" not being capable itself of building up the tissues, it prevents the solution of those substances necessary to nourish and build up the animal organism, and repair the wear and tear of the tissues.

478. Hence it must be very evident, that, *alcoholic beverages do not, and cannot aid digestion, but retard and prevent the solution of alimentary substances.*

PART VI.

DOES ALCOHOL SUSTAIN VITALITY?

479. WHATEVER may be our ideas of Life, all will agree, with Life comes action; and that all motion is necessarily attended with wear and tear, to a certain extent, of whatever produces motion. The tools and machinery of the mechanic and artizan wear more or less with use; and by continual use will finally wear out.

480. The same is the case with the mental and physical apparatus of human beings. But while the human system from the moment it receives the power to act, begins to decay, or to be destroyed, by physical and mental action, yet the organism has a power within itself, to repair the injury, providing the elements fit to build up the worn out tissues of the organs and to generate force are supplied.

481. Whatever interferes with the organism's appropriating the elements to repair the waste of the system, will proportionately impair the *vital forces*.

482. Whatever is taken into the human system, will either injure or benefit it. We do not accept the doctrine, that any substance can be taken into the body, and if it does no good, will do no harm. What is not, in relation to the human body, a food or nutriment, in a state of health, is detrimental. There exists in the animal body, a concentration of forces, that are the measure of the strength or capability of the constitution for nutrition, or excretion, for physical and mental endurance, and resistance of disease. When nutrition is impaired by bad living, or other causes; the *vital forces* are enfeebled, and the power to resist disease or decay is lessened.

483. The animal organism can only receive its sustenance from without. The wear and tear of the organs must be supplied by appropriate nutrition, for the organism has not the power to generate force independent of what it derives from without; for its powers, mechanical, chemical, and intellectual, depend upon the nutrition of the organs, and these will fail to exert their powers, to perform their various functions, unless they receive the proper elements to nourish them.

484. It is very evident that alcohol is incapable of nourishing or strengthening the organs of the body, since it cannot be assimilated, so that it may become a part of the tissues of the body. It cannot sustain the power or vitality of the system; for by the testimony of Lallemand, Perrin, and Duroy, alcohol passes

out of the body the same indentical compound it was when it entered, and no one has yet found traces of any chemical resolution or combination; hence, not being decomposed, or oxydized in the system, it can neither generate heat, nor by assimilation become a part of the tissues; and therefore can no more sustain vitality, or produce force, than the whip or spur can supply the place of oats, corn and hay, and sustain the vitality, or give strength to a jaded nag.

485. Every day's experience of thousands of men, of every profession and employment, in every condition and clime, shows that alcoholics are useless as supporters of vitality, or generators of force. As already seen, the nutrition of the tissues and organs depend upon the blood corpuscles, which are made from the food we eat, and the liquids we drink; hence, the quantity as well as the quality of the blood will depend upon what we eat and drink. The proportions, in 1,000 parts of blood, are about as follows, in health: Water 782, globules 127, fibrine 3, solid matter of serum, including albumen, fat, etc., 80. Inorganic matter of serum, including salt, potash, etc., 8. The blood also holds in solution the products of the disentegrating process on, their way to be expelled from the body by the different excretory organs.

486. The blood corpuscles are of three kinds: 1st. A few molecules, which are composed of chyle, and are generally increased in number during active digestion. 2nd. Colourless cells, which are identical with those of lymph. 3rd. Coloured corpuscles; the essential elements of the blood, appearing under the microscope of a straw-colour; but when aggregated together in mass, the colour is red. The size of these coloured corpuscles varies greatly in different animals, being in man, in breadth about $\frac{1}{3200}$ of an inch, and in thickness $\frac{1}{12400}$ of an inch.

487. Alcohol acts most perniciously upon the red corpuscles, by dissolving the iron, and devitalizing them. Drs. Virchow,* and Boecker,† agree that "alcohol poisons the blood, arrests development, and hastens the decay of red corpuscles;" there being also a loss of power, by a decrease of the vitality, in the blood discs to become red when exposed to the air in the lungs; as well as changing the red blood to purple.

488. "Alcohol," says Professor Schultz ‡ "stimulates the blood discs to an increased contraction, which hurries them to the last stage of development—that is, induces their premature decay and death. The colouring matter is dissolved out of them and the pale discs lose their vitality, whence less oxygen can be absorbed, and less carbon carried out."

489. Dr. Beale says: "It cuts short the life of rapidly growing cells, or causes them to live more slowly." Hence alcohol

---

* In 1853.   † In 1854.   ‡ In 1842.

retards the nutrition of the body. Nor is this all, for as already seen, alcohol coagulates the albumen in the stomach, and acts perniciously upon the albumen in the blood, and thus seriously impedes and prevents the reparative processes.

490. After enumerating a number of diseases caused by alcoholic drinks, Dr. Williams says: "When taken only or chiefly with food, not as a substitute for it, but as constituents of general free-living, fermented liquors contribute to the production of an abundance of ill-assimilated, over-heated blood, which either finds vent in eruptions of the surface in local hemorrhages or fluxes; or causes vertigo, stupor, bilious attacks, dyspepsia, or sometimes gout or gravel."

491. Dr. Parkes says: "That the use of alcoholics in health is not only unnecessary, but absolutely injurious."

492. These being the facts, we are unable to conceive how alcoholics can support health, sustain vitality, or in any manner aid man to perform either physical or mental labour. When disease becomes a supporter of health, we may then, on the same principle, conjecture that it may be possible for alcohol to sustain vitality.

493. Dr. Benjamin Brodie* says: "Stimulants do not create nerve power, they merely enable you, as it were, to use up that which is left." If alcohol is a stimulant (?) and if stimulants use up the nerve forces, how can they sustain them? "A gentleman travelling in Ireland was astonished to find that in his bill of daily expenses there was one frequently recurring item, 'refreshment for horse, two-pence.' 'What is the meaning of this?' he inquired. 'Oh, sir,' was the reply, 'that is for whip-cord.' If that is what you mean by stimulation, I am ready to admit that alcohol is a stimulant. If refreshment or stimulation is *whip-cord*, something to excite the force into action that is in the human system, I am prepared to admit the analogy; only however with a certain qualification."†

494. Dr. E. Smith says of alcohol:—"There is no evidence that it increases nervous influence, while there is much evidence that it lessens nervous power." Professors Lallemand and Perrin, said, "Muscular power is weakened." Dr. William Brinton says: "A moderate dose of beer or wine would in most cases at once diminish the maximum weight which a healthy person could lift. Mental acuteness, accuracy of perception, and delicacy of the senses, are all so far opposed by alcohol, as that the maximum efforts of each are incompatible with the ingestion of any moderate quantity of fermented liquors."

---

* Psychological Inquiries, I. page 143.

† Lecture by the Rev. Hugh Sinclair Paterson, M. D., of London, entitled "Stimulants and Strength."

DOES ALCOHOL SUSTAIN VITALITY?

495. Liebig said, "Wine is quite superfluous to man. * * * * It is constantly followed by expenditure of power." Will the advocates of the food power of alcohol, or of its power to retard the waste of tissue, and to generate force, still maintain the idea, when the father of the doctrine says, it "expends power?" Alcohol is an article foreign to all the normal wants of the human system. It can never give power like food, nor purify the blood like pure air; nor produce heat like the elements in bread, beef and potatoes; nor aid, like water, the circulation, the excretions and secretions of the system; but is an agent that deranges the functions of the organism and disturbs their normal actions.

496. The perpetual and inevitable effects of all alcoholic drinks, are to arrest the development of the blood-globules, to irritate the mucous membranes, and other tissues, impede digestion of food, deaden the nerve forces, create unnatural excitement of the heart, quicken its motion, and though supplying no force, expend the powers of the whole system to effect their elimination. It is therefore a physical impossibility that alcohol, in any of its compounds, can sustain life.

497. It is sometimes said by the advocates and defenders of alcohol, that by its use force is generated more abundantly. This it certainly cannot do, as it does not furnish anything to feed the blood, or to store up nourishment to replenish the expenditure. For by their own theory, the increase of action must cause an increase of wear and tear; hence alcohol, instead of sustaining life or vitality, must cause a direct waste or expenditure of *vital force*. If, as Liebig said: "Spirits, by their action on the nervous system, enable him—the poor labourer—to make up deficient power, at the expense of his body; to consume to-day that quantity which ought naturally to have been employed a day later, he draws, so to speak, a bill on his health bank, which must be always renewed, because, for want of means, he cannot take it up. He consumes his capital instead of his interest, and the result is the inevitable bankruptcy of the body."

498. Will the advocates agree with Liebig? If they do, how can alcohol be food? Dr. Hammond asks: If alcohol is no food, what is it? We answer: By his own experiments, it was shown to be a poison.

499. We cannot comprehend how alcohol can give force and sustain vitality, while the user makes up the "deficient power" at the expense of his body. It surely cannot give *force*, while it consumes to-day, what ought to be consumed to-morrow. The truth of the matter is: the action of alcohol in all its forms blunts the *nerve forces*, intended for the perfection of life, and the maintenance of the vital functions.

500. To take a practical view of it, what would we think of a merchant who would draw a note and pay a high rate of interest when he could not invest the money in any profitable venture or

make any good use of it, but expend it in fast horses? Would you not say, and justly too, that he was either a fool or a rogue? Then how far from a fool is the man, who will expend his vital capital, or life-forces, instead of the interest which is produced day by day from the nutritious food he consumes?

501. The fact that alcohol causes the premature death of the blood discs, should be a sufficient reason to cause every physician to regard it as being unable to sustain life; and as not only useless, but seriously injurious as a common beverage.

DOES ALCOHOL PROMOTE HEALTH AND PROLONG LIFE, WHEN USED AS A BEVERAGE?

502. That alcohol is a disease producer, no educated physician will attempt to deny. Dr. Hammond plainly asserts this, as well as every other physician who has ever advocated the use of alcohol in any of its forms, or in any quantity; but they become all "in a muddle," by their efforts to reconcile old exploded theories with recent scientific "demonstrations," and facts of every day's experience. Volume upon volume might be compiled of the testimony of the best scientific experimenters and physicians on both sides of the Atlantic, to show that alcohol, as a disease producer, is unequalled by any other article used by man. It may with equal truth be fully established and demonstrated that the ratio of sickness and death, all other things being equal, is in proportion to the use of, and to the facility for obtaining alcoholic beverages. It will scarcely be an exaggeration, to say, that one half* of all the sickness and premature death in the civilized world, is directly or indirectly produced by the use of alcoholic drinks.

503. By Neilson's Statistics, the mortality of the *intemperate* from twenty-one to thirty years, is five times that of the temperate; and from thirty to forty years, four times. The duration of life after the commencement of intemperate habits, among beer-drinkers, is 21.7 years; among spirit drinkers, is 16.7 years, and among drinkers of both spirits and beer is 16.1 years. Thus we find as a rule the deaths of drinkers are in proportion to the alcoholic per centage of their favourite beverage; for spirit drinkers do not live as long by five years as beer drinkers, but the drinkers of both spirits and beer live six-tenths of a year less than those who drink spirits only. This no doubt is the result of the excess of alcohol imbibed by them. For the spirits and beer drinkers are ready at all times for every kind, and never say, "no." The average mortality among beer drinkers is 4.597 per

---

* Some may think that this proportion of the sickness and death is too great, but if we consider besides the sickness and death of adults, the thousands that die in infancy and childhood, by neglect, imperfect nourishment, deprivations, etc., resulting from the use of strong drinks, the amount of disease and death given is not more than the actual amount produced directly and indirectly from the use of alcohol.

cent.; spirit drinkers, 5.995, and those who use mixed drinks, die at the rate of one per cent. per annum more than beer drinkers; showing that the increase of the death rate keeps pace with the increase of the per cent. of alcohol in the liquor used.

504. That intoxicating drinks shorten life, is well understood by Life Insurance companies, for none of the more reliable, who have intelligent and honest agents, will insure the life of an intemperate person. Dr. Carpenter said,* at the age of forty the annual rate of mortality for the whole population of England is about 13 per thousand; while among the lives insured at "Life Offices," it is 11 per 1000; and those insured in Friendly Societies, is about 10 per 1000.

505. The average mortality between fifteen and seventy years is about 20 per 1000.

506. The following table gives the number of deaths of the assured in four of the best Life Insurance companies, during the first five years of their existence, compared during the same period with the deaths in the Temperance Provident Institution. The mortality being as follows:—

A	Issued	944	policies,	had	14	deaths,	equal	15	per	1000
B	"	1907	"	"	27	"	"	14	"	1000
C	"	838	"	"	11	"	"	13	"	1000
D	"	2470	"	"	65	"	"	22	"	1000
T.P.I.	"	1596	"	"	12	"	"	7½	"	1000

During the sixth year of the existence of the Temperance Provident Institution, there were only two deaths out of the whole number insured, making the rate of general mortality still lower. By these figures it is seen that total abstinence from alcoholics reduces the death rate at least one-half.

507. It must be remembered, that this is not the difference between the rate of mortality of total abstainers and the intemperate; but between the moderate drinkers of intoxicating drinks and the teetotalers. Life Assurance Institutions, do not, if they know it, insure lives of intemperate persons. The difference between the rate of mortality of the whole population of England (13 per 1000) at forty years, and among those insured in Life Assurance companies (11 per 1000) and the Beneficial Societies (10 per 1000) we may justly attribute to the more temperate habits of the former; while in the former are included teetotalers, moderate drinkers and drunkards. If we class the policy holders of Insurance Offices and members of Friendly Societies as nonabstainers, and compare them with the members of Beneficial Total Abstinence societies, the difference is in favour of teetotalers; for while the average mortality among the Friendly, or non-abstaining Beneficial Societies is 10 per 1000, among the

---

* "Use and Abuse of Alcoholic Liquors." Philadelphia Ed., 1869. P. 72.

Rechabites, who are abstainers, the mortality is only 7½ per 1000.

508. The average duration of life, of all ages in England, is about 42 years, while among the Society of Friends it is 55 years; the fact that many are total abstainers, and the remainder generally regular and temperate in their habits, may account for this difference.

509. In London the ratio of deaths from alcohol is 1 in 12,800 of the population, while in the whole kingdom the ratio from this cause is 1 in 26,000 of the population; and the sickness rate is about 1 in 800, varying with the greater or less opportunity to obtain intoxicating liquors, as the following statistics clearly show:

510. In England, in 1729, an enactment was passed facilitating the sale of liquors, when the mortality in London alone reached 29,722. The government, in order to remedy the evil, increased the duty on liquors; when their consumption was diminished, and the mortality decreased, in 1730, to 26,761, or 2,961, less; and in 1732, to 23,358, or 6,364 less deaths than in 1729.

511. But the act having been repealed, intemperance again increased, and the mortality reached 29,258. But in 1757-8, there being a scarcity of grain, distillation was stopped for 3 years, when the mortality decreased in 1758, 3,793 deaths.

512. In 1760, distillation was resumed, when the deaths increased in one year 1,230. In 1792, the increased consumption of spirits was attended by an increase of 1,453 deaths. In 1796, there being another scarcity of grain, distillation was suspended, when the mortality in London sank 1,891. The mortality that had risen in 1800, to 23,068, in 1801 there being another scarcity, sank to 19,378, or a decrease of 3,692 deaths; and an advance of duty in 1803 occasioned a decline both in the consumption of spirits and mortality.

513. These statistics of the rise and fall of the number of deaths in London, establish the fact that the mortality of a people will increase or decrease in proportion as the consumption of alcoholic liquors is augmented or diminished. Neilson says: "A temperate person, at the age of 20, has a chance to live 44 years; at 30, 36 years; at 40, 28 years; at 50, 22 years; at 60, 14 years. While an intemperate person's chance of life at 20, is 15 years; at 30, 13 years; at 40, 11 years; at 50, 10 years; and at 60, 9 years. The average duration of life, after commencing habits of intemperance, among mechanics and labourers 18 years; among store-keepers and gentlemen, 15 years; and among females, 14 years. Among the usages of society calculated to destroy life, the most powerful is certainly the inordinate use of intoxicating drinks."

514. Dr. Cheyne, an eminent Dublin physican, said: "The observation of 20 years had convinced him, that were ten young men on their 21st birth-day to begin to drink one glass of ardent spirits (alcohol and water), or a pint of sherry, and were to continue this daily, eight out of the ten would abridge their lives by 10 or 15 years."

515. It may be said that many men and women drink moderately of some kind of liquor all their lives, and to a good old age. This may be true; but how many more have been carried to their graves in early life?

516. The advanced age of a moderate drinker depends upon the strength of his constitution, to enable him to resist, in a measure, the poisonous effects of the drink, and in some degree on his occupation and habits.

517. A gentleman well advanced in years, a moderate drinker, one of your "*Devil decoy ducks,*" on one occasion boasted that he had drank two or three bottles of wine every day for fifty years, and he was hale and hearty as ever. "Pray," remarked a bystander, "where are your boon companions?" "Ah," he quickly said, "*that's another affair; if the truth must be told, I have buried three entire generations of them!*"

LONGEVITY AND TOTAL ABSTINENCE.

518. The Temperance Provident Institution was established in 1840, in London, to insure the lives of total abstainers only; and in 1849 the directors reported that up to that date 135 deaths might have occurred by the lowest average calculation, and 219 by the highest, but the actual deaths had only been 73. In 1850 a change was made, when respectable moderate drinkers, or non-abstainers, were admitted into a distinct section, other conditions being equal since that time; and the fact that the profits of each section are determined by the rates of mortality, and the comparative bonus allotted to the members insured on corresponding amounts in each section, the comparative health and longevity in the two classes is clearly shown. What is the difference between the two sections? The following is the answer:

519. In a paper, read in the Health Section of the Social Science Congress, held at Plymouth, England, September, 1873, Edward Vivian, Esq., said:—"When total abstainers from alcohol urge the importance, on social or moral grounds, of avoiding the principal cause of pauperism and crime, and the drain of £100,000,000, upon the national resources, which may be devoted to the amelioration of the condition of the industrial

classes, they are naturally met with the reply, that this can only be effected by the surrender of an article of diet which, if taken in moderation, tends to raise the general standard of health and strength.

520. From the following statistics, I think I shall be able to show that these impressions are in a great measure, if not wholly, unfounded. That as a general rule alcohol is not only unnecessary, but positively injurious to persons in health; and that the chemist's phial, and not the decanter, is its proper place.

521. In deducing a law on a subject of such varied experience as this, it is indispensable that there should be a broad basis of fact, both in regard to time and numbers. The experience of the United Kingdom Temperance and General Provident Association, which was founded in 1840, and of which I have been, from almost the commencement, one of the directors, affords the most trustworthy evidence which has yet been accumulated; having been in existence more than thirty years, with a steadily increasing body of insurers, which now amounts to 40,000, divided into two sections, under precisely the same management, rates of premium, and tests on admission, with the single exception, that one is confined to total abstainers from alcohol, and the other open to the general public, the funds in each section being kept distinct.

522. During the first five quinquennial periods, I shall be able to refer to the pecuniary results, and these are of course open to doubt whether the difference has not arisen from policies of comparatively greater value, having become payable in the general section. In order to test this, although the uniform character of the results render it highly improbable, the full investigation of vital, as distinguished from pecuniary statistics, and the expected as well as the actual mortality at definite periods of life, was intrusted to Mr. Brown, an eminent actuary, wholly unconnected with the temperance movement, who has furnished the following returns, for the five years ending in December, 1870:

523.   TOTAL ABSTINENCE SECTION.

Year.	Expected claims.			Actual claims.		
1866	100	for	£18,014	85	for	£15,420
1867	105	,,	18,936	71	,,	8,830
1868	109	,,	20,024	95	,,	16,526
1869	115	,,	21,136	73	,,	16,505
1870	120	,,	22,336	87	,,	15,395
Totals,	549		£100,446	411		£72,676

General Section.

Year.	Expected claims.			Actual claims.		
1866	180	for	£34,732	186	for	£39,129
1867	191	,,	37,003	169	,,	32,200
1868	202	,,	39,515	179	,,	50,320
1869	212	,,	41,583	201	,,	50,320
1870	223	,,	43,519	209	,,	57,593
Totals,	1,008		£196,352	944		£230,297

From the figures it appears that the mortality among total abstainers insured in our office during the last five years was 26 per cent. below the averages upon which the tables are calculated, whilst in the 'General Section,' which is open to the public, it is only 7 per cent.

524. "The pecuniary results during the previous quinquennial periods, as shown by the reversionary bonus declared on the premiums, had been as follows:

Year.	Section.	Per cent.	Mean per cent.
1860	Total abstinence	35 to 86	60
,,	General	25 to 57	41
1865	Total abstinence	23 to 56	39
,,	General	17 to 42	29
1870	Total abstinence	34 to 84	59
,,	General	20 to 49	34

525. The general average, as shown in this table, is 53 per cent., returnable from the amount of premiums paid in the Total Abstinence Section, and 34 in the General; an advantage of nearly one-third in favour of teetotalism, as compared with moderate drinking. The great majority of those who become members even of the General Section, are favourably disposed to temperance, and many are practically abstainers."

526. In corroboration of these returns, Mr. Vivian read extracts from Mr. Neilson's last unpublished paper before the Statistical Society, showing that innkeepers and publicans, with their male servants, die at a rate far exceeding that in any other occupation. Their annual mortality is 25 out of every 1000 living, whilst the average is only 16.2 amongst the general population. Comparing this with the experience of the Temperance Provident Association, he shows that nearly two deaths out of three amongst publicans, as compared with total abstainers, were attributable to their vocation, and constant tippling, generally short of intoxication.

527. The following were the expected and actual claims amongst the whole term Policies from 1871 to 1875 inclusive, insured in the Temperance and General Provident Institution.

	Total Abstinence Section.				General Section.			
	Expected.		Actual.		Expected.		Actual.	
	No.	Amount.	No.	Amount.	No.	Amount.	No.	Amount.
1871	127	£24,051	72	£13,065	233	£46,105	217	£40,158
1872	137	26,058	90	13,005	244	48,883	282	50,575
1873	144	28,052	118	22,860	253	51,463	246	49,840
1874	153	29,648	110	24,683	263	54,092	288	57,006
1875	162	32,010	121	24,160	273	56,907	297	57,483
5 y'rs	723	£139,819	511	£97,773	1266	£257,450	1330	£255,062

528. In Department 1, Whole Life Policies in the Total Abstinence Section, the Reversionary Bonus will range, according to the age of the assured, from 35 to 114 per cent. on the amount of premiums, since 1870.

529. In Department 9, Whole Life Policies in the General Section, the Reversionary Bonus will range from 20 to 64 per cent. The following table of comparative results cannot fail to be understood:

Year.	Temp. Section Claims.		General Section Claims.	
	Expected.	Actual.	Expected.	Actual.
1866	100	80	180	186
1867	105	71	191	169
1868	109	95	202	179
1869	115	73	212	201
1870	120	87	223	209
1871	127	73	234	217
1872	137	90	244	232
1873	144	118	253	240
1874	153	110	263	288
Totals	1,110	797	2,002	1,971

530. In the Temperance Section, during these nine years, there were 313 less deaths than expected, or only 72 died out of every 100 expected. In the General Section there were only 31 deaths less than expected, while in three years out of nine, the actual deaths exceeded the expected. The Temperance Section therefore shows a superiority over the General of 26½ per cent. for the whole nine years. One of the members, at an annual meeting, asked: "How is this, that the bonus is so large in the Temperance Section as compared to that of the General Section?" Mr. Hardy, the Actuary, replied, by saying, "the Bonus is a matter of fact. *I cannot help people dying.* THOSE WHO DON'T DRINK DON'T DIE SO FAST."

531. Dr. Ogston, of Aberdeen, who was appointed by the English Government to examine all the cases of homicide and sudden death occurring in his district, has recently published some pathological observations on the bodies of one hundred and twenty-two known drinkers. The observation deduced from the appearance of chronic or fixed habits of drinking, met in individuals who had perished suddenly, while apparently in ordinary health, in Dr. Ogston's summary is as follows: 1st. Abnormal appearance in the head, 65 cases or 89 per cent. 2nd. Within the chest, disease of the heart, 30 cases (41 per cent). of the chest, 48 cases, (or 65 per cent.) 3rd, Within the abdomen, stomach, etc., 20 cases; liver 30, or 41 per cent. Spleen and pancreas, 15 or 20 per cent. Kidneys etc., 24 cases, or 32 per cent. Retenus etc., 8 cases, or 33 per cent. of the sex.

532. If the day before these persons died, the question had been put, "How are you?" every one of them would have answered, "All right." Had the physicians been asked if these men were diseased, they would have said, "By no means; they have very good health." Thus a disorder that may bring upon you sudden death, is going on silently, to you unconsciously, but yet most surely to a fatal termination.

533. How, day by day, can an agent like alcohol be irritating, inflaming and hardening delicate tissues of our *frame, without increasing disease?**

534. Dr. Willard Parker, of New York, an eminent medical authority, said not long ago, in a public address:—"That 33½ per cent. of all the deaths in the city of New York, were occasioned directly or indirectly by the use of alcoholic drinks, and that 190,000 persons had died in that city during the last thirty-eight years from that cause." Dr. Trotter says:—"Of all the evils of human life, no cause of disease had so wide a range, or so large a share, as the use of spirituous liquors; that more than half the sudden deaths are caused by them. When mankind was presented with the art of distilling, no more fatal gift was ever presented, either by men or devils."

535. Dr. Frank says:—"The use of spirituous liquors ought to be entirely dispensed with, on account of their tendency to induce disease, premature old age, and death, even when taken in small doses."

536. Dr. Cheyne says of spirituous liquors:—"They are most like opium in their nature and operation, and most like arsenic in their deleterious and poisonous effects."

---

* "Lectures for the Million." By F. R. Lees. Page 89.

MORTALITY OF LIQUOR SELLERS AND ABSTAINERS.

537. At the annual meeting of the Manchester and Salford, (England) Licensed Victuallers' Association, the twenty-second annual report of the committee stated that: "The past year has been troublesome and expensive," and that, "the death-rate continues high." To substantiate this statement, a table of the mortality is given, extending over a period of fourteen years, introduced with the remark that, "the heavy death-rate which has affected this society so many years in succession still continues, as set forth in the following table:

Date.	No. of members.	Deaths.	Cost to the Society.		
			£	s.	d.
1856	215	5	62	10	0
1857	254	4	50	10	0
1858	290	4	50	0	0
1859	320	5	62	10	0
1860	334	4	50	0	0
1861	305	5	62	10	0
1862	297	8	100	0	0
1863	399	6	75	0	0
1864	449	5	62	10	0
1865	481	18	225	0	0
1866	371	12	150	0	0
1867	427	12	150	0	0
1868	481	11	137	0	0
1869	452	12	150	0	0

538. That the effect of alcoholic liquors may be more clearly seen, we will compare the mortality of persons engaged in the liquor trades with those engaged in other occupations in England, as follows:

Deaths Per cent.	Ages. 25 to 35.	Ages. 35 to 45.	Ages. 45 to 55.	Ages. 55 to 65.
Farmers and Graziers	.871	1.244	2.307	5.750
Grocers	.923	1.280	2.053	4.334
Carpenters	.980	1.542	2.803	6.951
Shoemakers	1.113	1.577	3.024	6.911
Labourers	.997	1.398	2.617	5.949
Inn and Hotel keepers, Publicans and Beer sellers	1.881	2.810	4.104	7.242
Inn and Hotel keepers, Publicans, Beer sellers, and wine and spirit merchants.	1.912	2.793	4.105	7.446
All England	1.228	1.767	3.110	6.225

539. The above table from the supplement to the Twenty-fifth Annual Report of the Registrar-General of England, shows that the mortality of persons in the liquor traffic from twenty-five years

of age to forty-five, is twice as great as that of farmers, or graziers, and more at all ages than with farmers, grocers, carpenters, shoemakers, labourers, and all the males of England.

540. Dr. Richardson, in his lecture on "Unhealthy Trades," Jan. 21, 1876, at Society of Arts, presents the mortality of all males in England, in stages of ten years' duration, extending from fifteen to seventy-five years, is shown reduced to 100 as a standard at each age, as compared with those of publicans.

Deaths of males, age fifteen years and upwards, and at seven groups of ages, in the year 1861, 1862, and 1871, engaged as publicans, to 100 deaths of males of all occupations at the same ages during the corresponding periods:

Occupation.	All ages	15	25	35	45	55	65	75
All males in England 15 years and upwards,	100	100	100	100	100	100	100	100
Publicans,	138	129	147	157	154	134	112	131

Thus we learn that whilst at twenty-five years of age, of a given number of the male population of England, 100 died, from the same number of publicans 147 died; and at the age of thirty-five, 157 publicans died. To corroborate the foregoing figures, and to simplify the subject, the following is extracted from the Insurance Guide (England): "The mortality of the inn and beer-shop keepers is in excess of the mortality of all other classes. Thus, for instance, during the year, at a given age:

		Died.
Out of every	1,000 farmers	12.
"	1,000 shoemakers	15.
"	1,000 weavers	15.
"	1,000 blacksmiths	16.
"	1,000 tailors and carpenters	17.
"	1,000 miners	20.
"	1,000 bakers	21.
"	1,000 butchers	23.
"	1,000 inn and beer-shop keepers	28.

The general mortality, at the same age, among the whole population of England being eighteen per 1000." Thus we find that more than two liquor sellers die for one farmer; and nearly two for one shoemaker, weaver, tailor, and carpenter. How can this be accounted for? The liquor-sellers are better fed, clothed, and housed, and less exposed to accidents and casualties than all other trades; and hence we should expect that the liquor-sellers would live much longer than others. And so they would, but for alcoholic drinks. Though they are not generally drunkards, yet they are more or less under the influence of the drink, all the time, which damages their whole organism. Hence this great mortality.

541. Dr. Monroe, comparing the sickness and death of two large societies under his charge, one composed of abstainers, and the other of non-abstainers, says: "The total abstainers have much better health, and fewer deaths, than the moderate drinkers. In the non-abstaining society, the average amount of sickness the last year, was 11 days 21 hours per member, and the number of deaths was about ½ per cent. In the total abstinence society, the amount of sickness last year did not amount to more than one and three-quarter days per member, and the number of deaths was only two in five years, or less than one-quarter per cent. per annum. I ought, perhaps, in justice to myself, to add, that, in the treatment of various diseases, in both societies, no alcoholic liquor was administered.

542. The reports of the Temperance Mutual Benefit Association of Pennsylvania, also directly prove the advantages of total abstinence: For five years the Temperance M. B. Association has had but 12 deaths, or less than 4½ per 1000 members. To show the fact still further, we will compare the T. M. B. A. with three other companies in Pennsylvania, doing business on the same plan, except that the membership is not confined exclusively to total abstainers, though all are supposed to be temperate and sober in their habits.

543. By the Pennsylvania Insurance Report for the year ending Dec. 31, 1874, we find that the membership and deaths of the following named companies were:

Western Masonic R. A. had 1098 members, 15 deaths, about 14 per 1,000
Odd Fellows   had 1,688 members, 11 deaths, about 6 per 1,000
United Brethren, (M.) "   7,033   "   58   "   "   8 " 1,000
Tem. M. B. Associa'n "   929   "   4   "   "   4 " 1,000

Thus we find that the ratio of death between total abstainers and moderate drinkers, etc., is as 4 of the former class to 6, 8 and 14, of the latter. It must also be remembered that there are many total abstainers among the latter class, which is still more in favour of total abstinence.

EFFECTS OF ALCOHOL ON THE MEDICAL PROFESSION.

544. The members of the medical profession, with all their knowledge of the nature of alcoholic liquors, are not always free from the terrible results following from their use as a beverage

and as a medicine. Dr. Cartwright, of New Orleans, gave a few years ago, in the Boston Medical Journal, some startling statistics on the effect of intoxicating drinks upon his medical brethren. The writer of the article referred to, one of the three physicians located at Natchez 30 years previous to the time of writing, says: " The new comers found only *one* practitioner in the city belonging to the same temperance school with themselves. The country and villages within fifteen miles around afforded only three more. All the rest believed in the hygienic virtues of alcoholic drinks, and taught the doctrine by precept and example.

545. Besides the practising physicians, there were ten others in the city and adjacent country, who had retired from the profession. They were all temperate. Thus, including the new comers, the total number of temperance physicians, in and near Natchez, thirty years ago, consisted of seventeen. Of these, five have died. Dr. Henry Tooley, aged about 75 years; Dr. Andrew McCreary, 70; Dr. J. Kerr, 60; Dr. Wm. Dunbar, 60; Dr. James A. McPheeter, 45. In 1823, the average age of the 17 was about 34 years.

546. According to Carlisle's tables of mortality, and those of the Equitable Insurance Company of London, seven instead of five, would have been the ratio of mortality in England. Those at present living are Drs. D. Lattimore, W. Wren, Stephen Duncan, James Metcalf, W. N. Mercer, G. W. Grant, J Sanderson, Benj. F. Young, F. G. Elliot, — Phœnix, Professor A. P. Merrill, and the writer. On the other hand every physican in Natchez and its vicinity, thirty years ago, whether practising or retired, who was in the habit of tippling, as the practise of drinking alcoholic liquors is called, has long been numbered with the dead. Only two or them, who were comparatively temperate, lived to be gray. Their average term of life did not exceed thirty-five years, and those in the habit of taking alcoholic drinks between meals, and on an empty stomach, did not reach thirty years. In less than ten years after they commenced practice, the most of them died, and the whole of them have subsequently fallen, leaving not one behind in the city, country or villages within twenty miles round. To fill the place of those who died or retired from the profession, sixty-two more men settled in Natchez and its vicinity between the years 1824 and 1835, embracing a period of ten years, not counting those of 1823, already mentioned.

547. Of the sixty-two new-comers, thirty-seven were temperate, and twenty-five used alcoholic beverages between meals, though not often to the extent of intoxication. Of the thirty-seven who trusted to the hygienic virtues of nature's beverage—plain unadulterated water—nine have died, and twenty-eight are living. Of the twenty-five who trusted to the supposed hygienic virtues of ardent spirits, all are dead except three, and they have moved to distant parts of the country. Peace be to their ashes ! Though

mostly noble fellows, misled by the deceitful siren, singing the praises of alcoholic drinks, to live too fast and to be cut off in the outset of useful manhood, it is to be hoped they have not lived in vain ; as by their sacrifice science has gained additional and important proof of the fallacy of the theory which attributes health preserving properties in a southern climate, to alcoholic bevereges in any shape or form.

STATE BOARD OF HEALTH, MASSACHUSETTS.

548. The law under which the above named Board of Health is established, requires the board to examine into and report "what, in their best judgment, is the effect of intoxicating liquors as a beverage, upon the industry, prosperity, happiness, health and lives of the citizens of the State." To carry out the enactment, the Board of Health sent a circular to the American ministers to foreign courts and the consuls of all the principal parts of the globe.

549. The reply from Netherlands contained a statement signed by six hundred physicians, which says: "The moderate use of strong drinks is always unhealthy, even when the body is in a healthy condition. It does not do any good to the digestion, but even interferes with that process; for strong drinks can only temporarily increase the feeling of hunger, but not in favour of digestion; after which, strong reaction must follow, and evils which are usually attributed to 'other causes, often result from their habitual use with moderate drinkers.

550. "2. The assertions that intoxicating drinks used moderately are naturally innocent means of cheering up; that they are useful in severe cold; or, that they are with labouring men equivalents for insufficient nourishment, or useful in misty and humid air; or for people obliged to work in water; or protection against contagious disease; are without any foundation, and contradictory to experience and to human reason; and the habitual use of the same has therefore an unhealthy effect, and an influence unlike what people expect from them."

551. "3. The habitual use of strong drinks work perniciously on all diseases, and especially on consumption.

552. "4. Regarded as the usual drink of all classes, they are not only improper on account of the above reasons, but also against moral development and material prosperity, in such measure as to be considered, and to be stamped as the greatest underminers of the actual welfare of mankind."

553. The "Board of Health" also sent circulars to the different parts of Massachusetts. To the question: What has been

the effect of the use of intoxicating liquor as a beverage, upon the health and lives of the people in your town, or in the region in which you practice?—one hundred and sixty-four medical men sent answers, which have been classified as follows:

"Very destructive to life and health.....................48
Injurious in a greater or less degree.......................49
Public health not affected by their use in their towns........16
The people of their towns very temperate..................27
Intoxicating drinks not used in their town................. 5
The effect bad upon the foreigners in their towns, but not upon
    the natives.. 4
Useful in the decline of life............................. 1
Use promotes longevity................................... 1
Indefinite replies.......................................13
                                                        ———
                                                        164

554. One only holds the opinion that they are useful in old age, or the decline of life, and another, a poor Rip Van Winkle, who is not yet wide awake, still thinks, poor man, that the "use" of liquors "promotes longevity." Though some of the answers to the questions are not up to the scientific standard of the period, yet very many of the replies were evidently the result of much serious thought and extensive observation, as the following brief extracts will show;

555. "Observation has satisfied me that the use of intoxicating liquors as a beverage does not improve the physical and mental system, but is adverse to the best condition of both."

556. "Intoxicating liquor has invariably proved a curse to those who use it as a beverage."

557. "Injurious whenever habitually used. Has destroyed many lives in the fifty years of my observation."

558. "The use of intoxicating drinks has been, so far as I can judge, only productive of evil, and he who uses them has to say often the prayer of St. Chrysostom: God keep my body from the doctors, my money from the lawyers, and my soul from the devil."

559. "The effect of the use of intoxicating liquor is here, as everywhere, injurious to health, and destructive to life. Never useful as a beverage, and seldom if ever as a medicine."

560. "Intoxicating drinks have injured health and shortened life in proportion to their use."

561. "Intoxicating drinks have decidedly injurious effect upon life and health, and are far too much used in the treatment of disease."

562. "The effect of the use of intoxicating liquor has been to ruin health and shorten the lives of the people."

563. "Predisposes to fever, rheumatism, and shortens life very decidedly."

564. "Injurious always, from first to last."

565. "Impairs health, shortens life, enfeebles offspring,"

566. "The cause of much debility and disease."

567 "Better health and longer life would have been secured had the population abstained entirely from the use of intoxicating liquors as a beverage."

568. "It has been and is still injurious to the health of the individual, to the health and happiness of his family, and to the treasury of the town."

569. "Intoxicating drinks kill more than all diseases."

570. "My impression is, that the use of intoxicating liquor as a beverage, not only exercises a very pernicious influence on the moral and social condition of the people, but undermines health and shortens life."

571. "We have little intemperance, but it is found to be invariably destructive to health and life. Moderate drinkers suffer from the habit when attacked by ordinary diseases."

572. "All cases of *gangrene senile*, which have come under my observation, have been persons accustomed to indulge in strong drink."

573. Those testimonies of the medical profession of Massachusetts show that they are generally alive to the evil results of alcoholic liquors, though some of them still cling to old fallacies and worn out theories. Yet all are agreed in the main, that intoxicaing drinks are injurious to health, destructive to life, and subversive of their pecuniary prosperity.

THE DEATH RATE OF LIVERPOOL.

574. The mortality of the cities of Liverpool, Manchester, and Glasgow, present the highest death-rate of any other towns and cities in the United Kingdom. Of these three cities, Liverpool has shown a death-rate, that has struck a deep concern into the minds of the magistrates and thoughtful citizens. The Liverpool corporation, in December, 1870, requested two of the foremost scientific men in England, Dr. Parkes and Dr. Sanderson, to inquire into the sanitary condition of the town.

575. The Doctors, on the 1st of March, 1871, proceeded to

Liverpool. The results of their investigations were presented to the magistrates in two parts, the first in June and the second in August. In the second part they deal directly with the death-rate, from the census returns, to which they had access. The mortality of Liverpool is given for ten years, 1861-1871, during which it was never lower than 32.4 per thousand, and has been as high as 50.7. In the same ten years the mean mortality per thousand, calculated upon the mean annual population of 1861-1871, was, in the following towns named:—Bristol, 22.5; London, 24.3; Hull, 24.9; Bradford, 26.2; Sheffield, 27.2; Leeds, 28; Manchester, 30.2.

576. The average is 35 per thousand in non-epidemic times, but in epidemic periods it arrives at 50 per thousand.

578. The contrast presented by the different streets is frightful; some of which, as Addison, and Sawney Pope streets, have a death-rate as high as 45.4 and 55.86 per thousand. These are worse than St. Giles, London, though many streets in Liverpool are as healthy as any in London. On the subject of infant mortality, due consideration is given to the many cases of innocents overlaid and smothered by drunken mothers. It is a most telling fact, that the greatest number of such cases is at the beginning of the week, as the fruits of Saturday's and Sunday's drinking.

579. Among the specific diseases that have swelled the mortality of Liverpool, are *bronchitis* and *phthisis*, which are not peculiar to Liverpool. For independent of climatic condition, as shown by Dr. Gairdner, they are far more common in Glasgow, than in Aberdeen or Perth.

580. By Dr. Gairdner's researches the causes are rooted in the vicious habitudes of heads of families; and especially in the source of all other vices, and of some of the many miseries—intemperance.

581. Drs. Parkes and Sanderson testify to this fact, and show that the drunkard consumes by his debasing and selfish lust, a large portion of his weekly income, depriving his family of the means of proper food, clothing and housing: so that they are forced into the lowest dens, into crowded, fetid sleeping rooms, and suffocating beds, or pallets of straw, and chilled with cold and starved with want. "This increased dirtiness (of house and person, which is said to be lamentably on the increase) is attributed to a great extent to increasing poverty and intemperance." That this is the case no one can doubt.

582. Yet this double-headed destroyer has really but one cause, intemperance. The Doctors say—"We were not at all prepared for the wretched appearance of the people, or for the terrible aspect of poverty disclosed." * * * "In many rooms there was literally almost nothing but the bare walls, a heap of

straw, covered by dirty rags, and possibly the remains of a broken chair or table. There were no cooking utensils of any kind, or only an old sauce-pan. In some cases of both men and women, we made out that the clothes had not been removed for weeks.

583. "In our visits at night we sometimes found that the clothes had been partially removed, and were then drawn over the person. Some men, indeed, were in bed quite naked, lying on the straw and covered with their clothes.

584. "What admirable hot-beds of typhus and other epidemics these places must be." They also say of the cause of all this misery:—"All to whom we have spoken attribute it to three circumstances; the irregularity of the labour market; the improvidence and careless habits of the people, especially of the Irish; and the great intemperance." The last two coalesce in one—intemperance.

585. They further say: "Following our course of independent inquiry, we endeavoured to make out what part intemperance had in producing this poverty and all its attendant evils. We cannot doubt that it plays a very large part. We have in our note book the replies given by many of the poor people whose rooms were entered. Many of them at once attributed their condition to drink; others owned it, on being pressed on the matter. Several women gave an exact statement of what their husbands earned, and what they brought home. We select two examples of workmen, in whose cases there was no irregularity of employment.

586. A tin-plate worker, in constant employment, earns 22s. a week. He has a wife, evidently a careful, respectable woman, and four children. In reply to questions she said he drank a little, and then owned, "he drank very heavy." Sometimes he brought home 18s., sometimes 16s., sometimes 12s.. Last week he drank nothing at all. If he would bring 22s. a week, she should be 'happy as the day is long.' This family (six persons) were living in one back room, for which they paid 1s. 6d. a week. It was ten and a half feet long, nine feet broad, and eight and three-fourths feet high. The furniture was a bed, a table, and two rickety chairs. Two of the four children were sick. In the front room of the same house, the rent of which was 2s. a week, a man and wife, a daughter aged seventeen, and a son of fifteen lived; the man earned 24s. a week, and passed his time in drinking hard, repenting and saving, and then drinking again: the wife drank all she could get. The son and daughter earned next to nothing."

587. Here we have two cases of constant employment and good wages, associated with utter poverty, to end no doubt in relief from rates, and death in the workhouse.

588. When the occupation is uncertain, like that of the dockyard labourers, the case is nearly the same: the temperance which is enforced from time to time by destitution, is compensated for at the first opportunity on the return of plenty.

589. "Instances of this kind seem to occur so frequently in all the poor districts of Liverpool, that we question if 20 per cent. of the labouring class in these streets are leading lives of ordinary restraint and decency.

590. "It does not appear that the bad trade of the last few years has lessened the amount of drinking: all agree that there is much more than formerly. In order to form as correct an estimate as possible of the amount of drunkenness, in certain parts of Liverpool, we applied to a source, on the accuracy of which we place the greatest confidence, although we are not permitted to name it. Data connected with most of the houses in one of the apparently most destitute streets, were submitted to us: the large wages which can be earned with comparative regularity, and the amount which is spent in drink, are astonishing. One or two instances of the worst kind (if there is really any distinction) occurring in the same street, may be cited.

591. "A man earns 27s. regularly, and spends as regularly, 21s. His four children in rags. In another instance the wages are 30s. a week regularly; the father and mother are both drunken, and three childen are half starved and in rags. In another house is a copper-ore worker, earning 27s. a week, all of which is spent in drink by himself and wife. The children are in rags and filth and look idiotic. In the same street there are sober men earning only 20s. and 23s. a week who are living in comfort.

592. "It is not surprising that our informants, who, as we stated, have the fullest information on the habits of the people, say decidedly that drink and immorality are the two great causes of mortality.

593. "We have then a population, who are living in houses originally badly planned, and very closely crowded together, and who are placed partly by their own faults, partly by circumstances, in conditions which necessitate their breathing an atmosphere which is highly fetid, from several causes.

594. "The unhappy people seem to know none of the comforts, and few of the decencies of life; and wide-spread habits of drunkenness, and consequent want of good food, aid their wretched homes in destroying their health."

THE MORBID EFFECTS OF ALCOHOL.

595. Dr. W. Dickinson, in a paper* on this subject, gives the general conclusions as follows: "Alcohol causes fatty infiltration and fibroid encroachment; it engenders tubercles; encourages suppuration, and retards healing: it produces untimely atheroma, invites hemorrhage, and anticipates age. The most constant fatty changes, replacement by oil of the material of epithelial cells and muscular fibres, though probably nearly universal, is most noticeable in the liver, the heart, and the kidneys. The fibroid increase occurs about vascular channels and superficial investments of the viscera, where it causes atrophy, cirrhosis and granulation. Of this change the liver has the largest share; the lungs are often similarly but less simply affected, the change being variously complicated with, or simulative of tubercle; the kidneys suffer in a more remote degree.

596. "Alcohol also causes vascular deteriorations, which are akin both to the fatty and the fibroid. Besides tangible atheroma, there are minute changes in the arterial walls, which of themselves, induce cardiac hypertrophy and cerebral hemorrhage. Drink causes tuberculosis, which is evident not only in the lungs, but in every amenable organ. Drink promotes the suppurative at the expense of the adhesive process, as seen in the results of pneumonia, of serous inflammations and of accidental injuries. Descending from general conditions to the individual organs, the effect of alcohol upon the nervous system must be looked upon as special and taken by itself. Apart from the changes which, like delirium tremens, are more evident during life than after death, the brain pays a large reckoning in the shape of inflammation, atrophy, and hemorrhage. With regard to the other organs, they are damaged by alcohol, much as they stand in its line of absorption.

597. Next to the stomach, the liver suffers, by way of cirrhosis, and fatty impregnation. Next the stress falls upon the lungs, taking every shape of phthisis. A large share in the pathology of intemperance, is also taken by the arterial system, as seen in its results; atheroma, cardiac hypertrophy and hemorrhage. Lastly the kidneys, more remotely exposed, have small participation in the common damage of alcoholism. They undergo congestive enlargement, fatty and fibroid change, but they do not suffer commensurately with the blood-vessels, or as frequently as the other viscera.

598. "So far, we have seen only the ills which alcohol produces. It may be asked, is there none which it obviates? Apart from its medicinal action, which the evidence before us does not

---

* Read before the Royal Medical and Chirurgical Society, Oct. 22nd, 1872.

touch, has it no per contra of prevention? It is not easy to answer this question. Some active inflammation, such as pneumonia and endocarditis, are diminished in the alcoholic trades; but it must at once be seen that the increase of the alcoholic disorders, necessarily cause an apparent diminution in all which are apparently unaffected by this agent. A man may be saved from pneumonia or acute rheumatism, not because alcohol is antagonistic, but because it kills him prematurely in another way. He can die but once. Therefore, though under alcohol, some forms of disease are comparatively unfrequent, we must use much caution in concluding that it has a directly preventive influence.

599. Nevertheless it must be laid down as an axiom, that any drug which can do no harm can do no good. Disease is most various, and may or rather *must* represent contrary conditions. It may be positive or negative, plus or minus. Too much or too little of any of the shapes of heat, food, and work, may spoil the equipoise of health. If a drug promotes one change, it may prevent its opposite. Alcohol certainly gives an asthenic type of disease. Although we cannot, as yet, say that it defibrinates, yet it retards adhesive and plastic processes. This influence may be beneficent if it hinders the development of acute inflammation, and obviates the formation of coagula, where, as in acute rheumatism, the process is harmful. It is possible that by some antagonism, we may explain the remarkable paucity of endocarditis in the alcohol series. But at the best, the protecting is less certain, and less effective than the deteriorating influence. In brief and final enumeration, alcohol replaces more actively vital materials by fat and fibrous tissue; it substitutes suppuration for new growth; it promotes caseous and earthy change; it helps time to produce the effects of age: and in a word, it is the genius of degeneration." Dr. Norman Kerr, M.D., F.L.S., said,* "I was compelled to admit that at least 120,000 of our population annually lose there lives through alcoholic excess— 40,500 dying from their own intemperance, and 79,500 from accident, violence, poverty or disease arising from intemperance of others. In one year I testified * * to the deaths of 55 persons; 13 of these died either from personal intemperance or from disease or accident arising through the intemperance of others. * * If each practitioner, on an average, had a similar experience to myself, there would have been, as the result of intemperance, 160,000 deaths. But as I have had a large number of the poor under my care, and as the poorer classes are generally believed to be more intemperate (I give no opinion myself on this point at present) than the richer, it seems to me only fair to deduct one-fifth, or 32,000 from this last number, leaving an annual total mortality from intemperance of 128,000 About a year ago, from a preliminary inquiry into the vital statistics of drinking, I formed the opinion that at least 100,000 persons

---

* "Mortality from Intemperance," by Norman Kerr, M. D., F.L.S.. London, 1880.

were yearly killed in this country either directly or indirectly by intemperance, and the reasonableness of that estimate was then publicly endorsed by a well known London physician. I have a record of 270 fatal cases, spread over 17 years, and in 60 of these, I am satisfied alcoholic indulgence was the leading factor. As there are, from official returns, over 680,000 every year in the United Kingdom; if the proportion of 60 to 270 be taken, more than 151,000 yearly deaths would be the result. But, for the same reason as before * * let us deduct a fifth, and there remains over 120,000. Thus while a single year's experience give 128,000, the mean of 17 years showed 120,800."

WILL ALCOHOLICS PREVENT DISEASE?

600. If alcoholics have any prophylactic virtues, we should certainly expect that they would be found to prevent *cholera;* as was claimed by the Brewers' Congress for lager beer.

601. Dr. Jameson, in his Treatise on Cholera, says:—"Let us seek for his haunt, and we shall find that although his chariots are aerial, and their course erratic, the poison of his nostrils is seen to come and go; and in his rambles he had preference for mud and mire, crowded houses, and low places. His great love is for drunkards and the high fed. * * He has his times to do, and not to do; but when he holds his gala days, nought but a guarded moderation in all things will turn aside his swift-flighted chariot of desolation and death. * * He comes with power of the vampire to suck out your blood; he exerts the art of the collier and fills your veins with charcoal; he shuts up the normal outlets, and makes sluices of those that should be shut. * * * Amid all the riot, amid all the conflicting abnormal strife, there comes a heavy dream, the incubus of death, and stuffs your brain with unvitalized blood, and sits sullen upon your powers of thought."

602. This we have seen is also the action of alcohol, in a great degree: for we have seen (¶ 337) that alcohol prevents the normal changes of the blood; that it plies like cholera, the art of the collier, "by changing the arterial blood into venous without the substance of the tissues having taken any share in the tranformation." Hence alcoholics tend to produce a condition in the system resembling cholera. The alcohol in lager beer is essentially the same as in whiskey, or brandy, and many ingredients of which malt liquors are composed, added to the injurious effects of alcohol, make beer, ale, and porter, really more deleterious than distilled spirits; as we have already seen (¶311) by its effects on coal-heavers in London, and others who are copious beer-drinkers.

603. A Warsaw physician writes: "The cholera does not seize on its victims at hazard, as we may say. This contagion, up to the present period, has respected all persons who led regular lives * * and has struck without pity, every man worn out by excess and weakened by dissipation." It has been ascertained that out of every hundred individuals who die of this disease, ninety were in the habit of drinking alcoholics.

604. As women are rarely addicted to strong drink, fewer women than men are attacked by cholera. Prof. Mackintosh says:—"The drunkards are persons generally attacked. It has been computed that five-sixths of all who have fallen by cholera in England, were persons of intemperate and dissolute habits."

605. Mr. Bronson, of Montreal, said:—"The habitual use of ardent spirits in the smallest quantity seldom fails to invite cholera, and to render it incurable when it takes place." Beer will be productive of injury from its alcoholic per centage, as well as from the other drugs it contains. Beer-drinkers in England are the major part of drinkers, yet it spared none who drank to excess in many places.

606. The Morning Herald (England) said:—"Intemperance is a qualification which it (cholera) never overlooks." Often has it been known to pass harmless over a wide population of temperate country people, and pour down as an overflowing scourge upon the drunkards of some distant town. In 1832, a Montreal Journal said:—"Not a drunkard who had been attacked has recovered, and almost all the victims have been moderate drinkers."

607. Dr. Rhinelander, who visited Montreal in 1832, said:— "The victims of the disease are the intemperate." Dr. Sewall said:—"Of 204 cases of cholera in the Park Hospital, New York, there were only six temperate persons, and they had recovered, and the facts were similar in other hospitals." Mr. Huber, who saw in one town in Russia, 2160 persons perish in the period of 20 days, said:—"It is a most remarkable circumstance that persons given to drink have been swept away like flies. In Tiflis, containing 20,000 inhabitants, every drunkard has fallen; all are dead, not one remaining." Dr. Adams, of Dublin, said:—"Our Foreign Reports testify, that drunkards are carried off at once by this dire disease."

608. Those who daily use but a moderate quantity of any kind of alcoholic drinks, debilitate the tone of their stomachs and digestive organs generally, and hence become easy victims of cholera and every other disease that may be prevalent at the time; for it is a physical impossibility for any person to daily use intoxicating drinks, and not be injured thereby.

609. Dr. G. K. Paterson, of Dundee, said:—"There cannot

be a doubt held on the subject, that low and intemperate habits are strong inducements in the favour of disease at any time; but far more so when an epidemic is prevalent." Nor is this the case with spirit drinkers only, for the moderate use of even malt liquors is a sufficient cause of physical deterioration to counterbalance the good effects of temperance in every other respect. The persons who drink beer or other fermented liquors, with the expectation of not being mentally and physically injured, are very much deceived.

610. It will be seen hereafter (¶ 725) that malt-liquor drinkers are very prone to apoplexy and palsy.

611. Dr. Mussy, said:—"If I must drink any quantity of alcohol, in a specified time, I should think it best to take it in distilled liquors, rather than in cider, wine, or beer." A liquor dealer in Glasgow, lamented that the cholera had cut off half his customers. Brandy was said at one time to prevent cholera, but experience has fully demonstrated that it is a conductor and a promoter of the disease. Dr. Mussy, said:—"Upon boats on the river (Ohio) the increase of brandy drinking, consequent on the approach of cholera, has been frightful, and the mortality on board those vessels has been terrible and unprecedented. One boat lost 43, another 47, and a third 59 of its passengers and crew."

612. Brandy is not a prophylactic. To the temperate it is an active, exciting cause. It is well known that a single act of intemperance during the prevalence of cholera, will often produce a fatal attack. After the 25th of September, 1832, when the jubilee of the Reform Bill took place in England; and again in Scotland, after January 1st, 1849, there was a great increase of the number and severity of the cases of cholera in consequence of the drunkenness that occurred on those days in the large cities. In Glasgow, there were only 15 new cases and 10 deaths on New Year's day, but on the day following, from the drunkenness of the previous day, there were 25 new cases and 20 deaths. In a day or two more there were 58 cases, and 27 deaths.

613. In the opinion of medical men, the Reform Bill Jubilee, or the intemperance resulting from it, caused the cholera of 1832 to be very much prolonged in the United Kingdom.

614. Dr. Adams, Professor of the Institutes of Medicine in the Anderson University of Glasgow, made a classification of 225 cholera patients treated by him. $19\frac{1}{2}$ per cent. only were of temperate habits. Of those of intemperate habits, $91\frac{1}{2}$ per cent. died. Says he:—"I have found the use of alcoholic drinks to be a great predisposing cause of malignant cholera. So strong is my opinion on this point, that were I one of the authorities, and had the power, I would placard every spirit-shop in town with these words: 'CHOLERA SOLD HERE.'"

615. When we consider the change that the blood undergoes in the case of death from cholera, and the change that Prof. Liebig says alcohol produces on the blood, and the disorganization that occurs in the vital fluid, and all the tissues of the body by the use of alcoholics, every one must perceive that no greater mistake could be made by any one than to use intoxicating drinks, of any kind or of any quantity, with the expectation that they will prevent cholera, or any other disease.

616. In Newcastle, Eng., on Christmas day, 1848, in the lower part of the town, men and women were staggering in a state of intoxication. That night and the two following days, no less than ninety-eight were attacked by cholera, and a very large proportion of them died in a few days. From December 25th, to January 5th, 325 cases were reported, and 102 deaths. In one street parallel with the river Tyne, it swept off almost every drunkard from one end of the street to the other.

617. The nurses of the cholera hospital of Manchester, Eng., at first were worked only six hours, and then allowed to go home; and so great was the mortality among them that it was feared the supply of nurses would give out. It was discovered that the nurses spent their leisure hours in drink. They were then confined to the hospital, when not another case occurred among them.

618. The Dean of Westminster, (London,) said:—"God works no miracle to save the uncleanly and intemperate. It was solemn mockery to pray to God to preserve us from disease, if we took no pains of preservation after all our warning." Between the 1st of July, and the 15th of August, in St. John's, New Brunswick, seventeen hundred persons died of cholera.

619. In Portland district, the deaths for ten days averaged one per cent. of the whole population per day. Says Mr. Charles Everett: " I have yet to learn of the recovery in a single instance of an intemperate man."

620. Rev. Dr. Lee, of St. Luke's Church, Rochester, in a Thanksgiving sermon, when speaking of five hundred that were swept away by the cholera, said:—"Most of the adults were victims of intemperance. * * * Never did I more heartily deprecate the vice of drunkenness, than when, on some occasions, I was not only forced to think of the ghastly tenant of the coffin as having as it were reeled and staggered into eternity; but was also forced to see living drunkards my attendants at the place of burial; and so under the influence of intoxication at the very grave as to unfit them to render the needed aid to those who bury the dead. On one occasion, I remonstrated with the only persons—four in number—who constituted the company at the

grave, all of whom were partially intoxicated; and within three days they had all died of cholera, and were in their graves, near the spot where I had forewarned them of their danger."

621. The sense of warmth and irritation (called stimulation) produced by alcoholic liquors, has led to the erroneous notion that they may prevent cholera. But the contrary we have seen is the truth, for the effects of alcoholics are to reduce the temperature of the body, and instead of stimulating, they narcotize, and reduce the life-forces, and predispose the system to all kinds of disease.

622. On the 2nd of July, 1866, Dr. French, the Medical Officer of Health of Liverpool, received information that a death from cholera had occurred on the previous night. This was the first case of cholera in 1866, the victim being an Irish woman. The friends resolved on 'waking' the corpse. The body was laid on a board, and in the apartment scores of persons (men, women and children) ate, drank, and slept, the orgies being kept amid drunken and profane revelry during day and night. The whole place reeked with loathsome and disgusting emanations of drunken and unwashed bacchanals. Drunken women squatted thickly on the flags of the court before the open doors of the crowded room, where the corpse lay. The husband of the woman, before a week was past, was among the dead; and before the end of July, forty-eight persons died from cholera within a radius of a hundred and fifty yards from the court which had been the scene of the ill-timed revelry.

TOTAL ABSTINENCE PREVENTS CHOLERA.

623. We have seen that alcoholics are conductors of cholera. Let us now see the effects of total abstinence. From the statistics of cholera we find that in Albany, in 1832, the fatal cases of cholera in persons over 16 years of age, were as follows: Intemperate 140, free drinkers 55, moderate drinkers 31, strictly temperate 5, members of temperance societies 2, idiot 1, unknown 2, total 333; population, 26,000; members of temperance societies, 5,000.

624. Thus while only one out of every 2500 members of temperance societies died of cholera in Albany; of those not members of such societies, one died for every sixty of the whole population. The premonitory symptoms of 282 of those who died were diarrhea; the remaining 51 unknown. Of the 5 strictly temperate, one, previous to the attack, ate stale and sour preserves; the second, after recovering from an attack, went out and got wet and had a relapse; the third eat two pineapples, which produced the attack; the fourth neglected a diarrhea; in the fifth, the cause is

unknown. Of the two members of temperance societies, one was much distressed with fear, having often told his wife, that he should die of cholera; this mental depression occasioned loss of appetite, and he had also a diarrhea, which he neglected; the other was in ill-health for sometime previous to the attack, having laboured hard, and exerted himself after diarrhea.

625. In New York, of 5.000 members of temperance societies, only 2 died. Of the Hibernian Temperance Society, numbering 123 members, and of the African Temperance Society, with 193 members, not one died. Showing that neither the Irish labouring classes nor the coloured race, providing they do not invite the disease by using alcoholics, are more liable to cholera than any other class or race.

626. Of all the persons dying of cholera in New Orleans, only three were temperance men, out of a temperance society membership of 1243; of these three, one had been a member but a week, another less than a month; consequently neither of them could be said to have recovered entirely from the effects of the injuries received from the pernicious use of intoxicating drinks; and the third was a watchman, subject to much exposure. The proportions of all the deaths from cholera in New Orleans to the population was 15 per 1000, whilst among the Sons of Temperance it was only $2\frac{1}{2}$ in a 1000.

627. When the cholera was in Edinburgh during the winter of 1848-9, not a single teetotaler was attacked with it. There were in Paisley, Scotland, 60,963 inhabitants, and 337 cases of cholera, or one to every 181 of the population. Whilst among total abstainers only one died out of a membership of 2000. The returns of the mortality among the European troops at Madras for 1849 show that the ratio of deaths among the teetotalers was 11.11 per 1000, whilst among the intemperate, 43.15 per 1000, showing that four times as many intemperate soldiers die as teetotalers.

628. In the town of Newark, Ohio, in the summer of 1854, from thirty to forty persons died of what was called cholera, in about 36 hours. The physicians and people were completely stunned at the fearful mortality, but after a little investigation, it was discovered to be caused by drinking beer. All those who resorted to beer to quench thirst caused by the fever, died.

629. In the year 1847, the 84th regiment marched from Madras to Secunderabad, a distance of near five hundred miles, and were 47 days on the road, through a country noted for the prevalence of cholera and dysentery, a route always dreaded on account of the sickness and death which usually occurred both during the march and after. Nearly the whole regiment adopted the strict rule of abstinence, and passed through several marshy districts,

in which the men were often knee deep in water. During the whole march there was not a case of either cholera, fever, or dysentery; except two cases of chronic dysentery that were taken out of the hospital at Madras. The 63rd regiment, passing through the same country, at the same time, lost a considerable number of men, and had so many sick, that when the regiments met it was obliged to borrow the dhoolies (sick palanquins) of the 84th.

630. The first nine months, the 84th was quartered at Secunderabad, a station the most unhealthy in the presidency. Its mortality was 34.9 per 1000, less than half the number lost by the 63rd regiment in the nine months preceding its removal.

631. By later accounts from India there was admitted to the hospital one in every 9.8 intemperate, while of temperate soldiers there was only 1 in 27.1. The deaths for 1865 among these troops were in the proportion of 1 to 16.4 temperate and one to 7.2 intemperate.

632. In Bengal, it is reported that out of 34,287 men, divided into abstainers, temperate, and intemperate, the percentage of daily sick in each class was represented by three, five and eight; the deaths of total abstainers, one; of temperate, two; and of intemperate, four per cent. Which is the same old story of the effects of alcohol everywhere, in all climates, and under all circumstances, that *there is " death in the cup."*

633. In Newcastle, already mentioned, one in fifty-six of the population died of cholera, among which there were only eight total abstainers out of a membership of 5000, or only one in six hundred and twenty-five teetotalers.

634. These figures need no comment. The position of the advocates that beer, brandy, or other intoxicating drink, will prevent cholera or any other disease, is like that of the old woman's, who met a physician in London, and asked him, " Which he liked best, gin, rum, or brandy?" He replied " that he was not in the habit of taking either." " What!" said she. " Not drink gin? I like gin best of everything; for I have been in the hospital, and I know all about it. *Gin only eats the skin of the liver, rum fills it up like a sponge,* but *brandy eats holes into it that I could put my finger in."*

635. There is not a disease, we are entirely satisfied, but what may be aggravated by alcohol; and we are equally satisfied that total abstinence from alcoholics, and temperance in all other things, *are the only preventives of disease.*

PART VII.

DISEASES CAUSED BY ALCOHOL.

636. THE diseases produced by intoxicating drink are legion. Thousands, aye, tens of thousands die annually whose deaths are ascribed to diseases that would not seriously have affected them, or proved fatal, if alcohol had not laid the foundation for the disease, by lowering the tone of the system, undermining the vital forces, and the conservative energies of the organism. Many diseases and deaths result from the use of alcohol, and no mention is made of this drug as the predisposing cause; yet they would not have existed without it.

637. If only a small portion of the truth respecting alcohol as a predisposing and exciting cause were known, our people would be dismayed; but as it is, hundreds are daily dying by it, and no cry is raised, no horror expressed.

638. We cannot be surprised at the comparatively large mortality among the users of alcoholics, when the numerous diseases that are produced by them are considered.

639. That all the organs of the body are more or less damaged by alcohol, we will endeavour to show. In the language of Shakespeare, the stomach:

> "Is the store-house, and the shop of
> The whole body." True it is
> "That it receives the general food at first,
> But all the cranks and offices of man,
> The strongest nerves, and small inferior veins
> From it receives that natural competence
> Whereby they live."

THE EFFECTS OF ALCOHOL ON THE STOMACH.

640. The unnatural and irritating action of alcohol upon any of the tissues, is injurious; but it is more especially so upon a tender and vascular part, like the mucous membrane of the stomach, and hence the results of its use are dyspepsia, congestion, inflammation and ulceration of the stomach; of this we have ample evidence from cases of debauch, or by its prolonged and continued use.

641. Once and only once in the record of medicine, or in the life-time of man, has a human eye been able to look into the human stomach and observe the processes of digestion. This occurred just at the time when good men began to look for some remedy to cure the evils flowing from intemperance. At the United States military post of Michilimackinac, in 1822, Alexis St. Martin, a French Canadian, received accidentally a heavy charge of buck shot in his side, while standing one yard from the muzzle of the gun. One of the lungs protruded, and the food recently taken, was oozing from the aperture. Dr. William Beaumont, U. S. A., Surgeon of the post, dressed the wound, when in one year St. Martin was able to walk about the fort, and continued to improve in health and strength until he became strong and hearty. He married and became a father of a large family, and performed for many years the duties of servant to an officer of the post; but the aperture in the stomach never closed. The doctor arranged a compress to keep his food in his stomach.

642. Dr. Beaumont perceived the value of this opportunity, and set about to improve it. He took St. Martin into his service, and at intervals, for eight years, Dr. Beaumont experimented upon him. Through the aperture (two and a half inches in circumference) he watched the entire process of digestion; and saw the liquid flow into a human stomach, while yet the cup pressed the drinker's lips. Did his stomach ache, he could look into it and see what was the matter, and place the rectifying dose in the stomach. He ascertained the time required to digest the various articles of food, and the effects of the errors of eating and drinking. He saw that a glass of brandy caused the coats of the stomach to assume an inflamed appearance. Nor did it make any material difference whether St. Martin drank brandy, whiskey, wine, cider, or beer, except so far as one was stronger than the other. Says Dr. Beaumont, "Simple water is perhaps the only fluid that is called for by the wants of the economy. * * The whole class of alcoholic liquors may be considered as narcotics, producing very little difference in their ultimate effects upon the system."

643. In 1833 Dr. Beaumont published a volume,* which contained thousands of his experiments and observations at Plattsburg, on Lake Champlain, from which we shall quote some of his observations. Let it be remembered that though he confirms the teaching of total abstainers, yet, he does not appear to have ever heard the name of teetotaler, for his work was published about the time the total abstinence societies were first formed in England; hence what he says cannot be looked upon as being the extravagant assertions of some tee-

---

* Experiments and Observations on the Gastric Juice and the Physiology of Digestion. Wm. Beaumont, M. D. 1833.

totaler, but the "demonstrations of *scientific research.*" On page 237 of his work is the following: "*July* 28*th*, 9 o'clock, A.M. Stomach empty; not healthy; *some inflammation, with ulcerous patches on the mucous surface,*

644. "St. Martin has been drinking ardent spirits freely for eight or ten days; complains of no pain, nor shows symptoms of any general indisposition; says he feels well, and has a good appetite. *August* 1, 8 o'clock, A.M. Examined stomach before eating anything; *inner membrane morbid, considerable inflammation, and some ulcerous patches on the exposed surface, secretions vitiated.* Extracted about an ounce of gastric juice, *not clear and pure as in health;* quite viscid. *August* 2nd, 8 o'clock, A.M. Circumstances and appearances very similar to those of yesterday morning. Extracted an ounce of gastric juice, consisting of unusual proportion of *vitiated mucus, saliva,* and *some bile,* tinged slightly with blood, appearing to exude from the surface of the inflammation and ulcerous patches, which were more tender and irritable than usual. St. Martin complains of no pain.

645. "*August* 3rd, 7 o'clock, A.M. Inner membrane of stomach unusually morbid; inflammatory appearance more extensive, and (ulcerous) spots more livid; from the surface of some of which, exuded small drops of grumous (or thick clotty) blood.

646. "The ulcerous patches *larger* and numerous; the mucous covering (the thin, sensitive, lining membrane) thicker than common; and the gastric secretion much more vitiated. The gastric fluids extracted this morning were mixed with large proportions of thick, ropy mucus, and considerable muco-purulent matter, slightly tinged with blood, and resembling the discharge from the bowels in some cases of chronic dysentery. St. Martin complains of no symptoms indicating any general derangement of the system, except an uneasy sensation and a tenderness at the pit of the stomach, and some vertigo, with dimness and yellowness of vision, on stooping and rising again; has a thin yellowish brown coat on his tongue, and the countenance is rather sallow.

647. "*August* 4th, 8 o'clock, A.M. — Stomach empty; less of those ulcerous patches than yesterday; inflammatory appearances more extensively diffused over the inner coats, and the surface inclined to bleed: secretions vitiated. Extracted about an ounce of gastric fluids, consisting of ropy mucus, some bile and less of muco-purulent matter than yesterday: odour peculiarly fetid and disagreeable."

648. "*August* 5th, 8 o'clock, A.M.—Stomach empty; coats less morbid than yesterday, mucus more uniform, soft, and

nearly of the natural healthy colour; secretions less vitiated, Extracted about an ounce of gastric fluids; more clear and pure than that taken four or five days past, and slightly acid, but containing a larger quantity of mucus and more opaque than usual in a healthy condition."

649. "*August* 6th, 8 o'clock, A.M.—Stomach empty : *coats clear and healthy as usual;* secretions less vitiated. Extracted two ounces of gastric fluids of more natural and healthy appearance, with the usual gastric acid flavour; complains of no uneasy sensations or the slightest symptoms of indisposition; says he feels well, and has a voracious appetite; but not permitted to indulge it to satiety. He has been restricted from full, and confined to low diet, and simple diluent drinks for the last four days, and has not been allowed to take any *stimulating liquors*, or to indulge in excesses of any kind." Dr. Beaumont remarks:

650. "These morbid changes and conditions are seldom indicated by any ordinary symptoms, or particular sensations described or complained of, unless when in considerable excess. It is interesting to observe, to what extent the stomach, perhaps the most important organ of the animal system, may become diseased without manifesting any external symptoms of such disease. Vitiated secretions may also take place, and continue for some time without affecting the health in a sensible degree.

651. Too high a value cannot be placed upon these observations of Dr. Beaumont, as they are ocular demonstrations; "actual views of the stomach, from day to day, for years; the actual observations in health and disease; the effects of the various foods and drinks upon the stomach." He says clearly and distinctly :

652. "The free use of ardent spirits, wine, beer, or any of the intoxicating liquors, when continued for some days, has constantly produced morbid changes." It is not "*ardent spirits*" alone that produces these morbid changes: but even "*wine and beer.*" Nor are these *changes indicated by any ordinary symptoms, or particular sensations described or complained of, unless when in considerable excess.* They could not, in fact, have been *anticipated* by any *external symptoms*, and their *existence* was only ascertained by *ocular demonstrat.ons.*"

653. How important for those who use alcoholic liquors, to bear this in mind; for the stomach may be extensively diseased by alcoholics, and they not be aware of its morbid condition.

654. It also shows how fallacious and dangerous is the new philosophy which teaches that a man should judge by his feelings of the effects upon his system of a virulent poison like alcohol, when under its narcotizing influences. There can be no doubt

that the moderately regular use of alcoholics produces upon the stomach results similar to those produced in the case of St. Martin, to a greater or less extent, according to the quantity and the frequency of taking the poison; yet by its narcotic influence upon the nerves, it gives no sign or signal of distress. And the drinker, while he is sipping his wine, or brandy and water, or foaming ale, may be unaware that fatal and extensive disease already exists, and the foundation is laid for premature decay and death.

655. As a proof of the injurious effects of alcohol on the stomach, next to ocular demonstration, or seeing into the stomach during life, is the *pathological* condition of that organ after death. This condition is illustrated by the plates of the stomach prepared by the late Dr. Sewall, Professor of Pathology and Practice of Medicine in the Columbian College, District of Columbia, U. S.; being the result of a professional career of upwards of thirty years. During these years, he was more or less engaged in pathological researches, and having many opportunities of inspecting the stomachs of drunkards, after death, in the various stages and degree of drunkenness, he had these plates prepared, which present the accurate condition of some of the morbid changes that take place in the stomach by intemperance, and the use of alcoholics.

656. Dr. Sewall,[*] in a letter to E. C. Delavan, Esq., said: "If the effects of intemperance are in some degree various in different individuals: if they are not developed with the same degree of power and rapidity in one case as in another, it is nevertheless true, that alcohol is a poison, forever at war with man's nature, and in all its forms and degrees of strength produces irritation of the stomach, which is liable to result in inflammation, ulceration and mortification: a thickening and undurating of its coats, and finally scirrhus, cancer, and other organic affections: and it may be asserted with confidence, that no one who indulges habitually in alcoholic drinks, whether in the form of wine, beer, or more ardent spirits, possesses a healthy stomach.

657. The first illustration, (see Frontispiece) represents the internal surface of the stomach in a healthy condition, taken from an individual entirely temperate in his habits, and copied from a sketch furnished by Professor Horner, of Philadelphia, one of the ablest anatomists of his age and country. The subject from which it was originally drawn came under Professor Horner's own observation, and the dissection was by his own hand: and he says that the individual was not only healthy, but remarkably temperate and regular in all his habits: he therefore considers the case invaluable, as furnishing a standard of

---

[*] Pathology of Drunkenness, &c., by Professor Sewall, of Columbian College, D. C. (Ill. Hist. of Alcohol. Dr. F. R. Lees, London.) National Temperance Society, &c., New York.

observation. It is of a colour slightly reddish, tinged with yellow, and exhibits something of a mottled appearance. Although supplied with a multitude of blood vessels, none of them are so large as to be seen by the naked eye. This healthy and natural appearance of the stomach would doubtless continue from the period of childhood to that of old age, if it were acted upon only by appropriate food and drink.

658. The second illustration exhibits the internal surface of the stomach of the temperate drinker, the man who takes his glass of mint-julip or gin-sling in the morning, or his toddy on going to bed; or of him who takes his two or three glasses of Madeira at his dinner. And here the work of destruction begins. That beautiful net-work of blood-vessels which was invisible in the healthy stomach, being excited by the stimulus (irritation) of alcohol, becomes dilated and distended with blood, visible and distinct. It is a well-known law of the animal economy, that an irritant applied to a sensitive texture of the body, induces an increased flow of blood to the part. The mucous or inner coat of the stomach is a sensitive membrane, and is subject to this law. A practical illustration of this principle is shown by reference to the human eye. If a few drops of alcohol, or any other irritating substance be brought in contact with the delicate coats of the eye, the net-work of fine vessels which were before invisible become distended with blood, and are easily seen. If this operation be repeated daily, as the temperate drinker takes his alcohol, the vessels become habitually increased in size, and distended with blood,

659. Besides this injected and distended state of the vessels of the stomach, the mucous coat of the organ always becomes thickened and softened; and these changes occur in the (so called) temperate drinker as well as in the confirmed drunkard. It is by this temperate drinking that the appetite of the inebriate is first acquired; for by nature man has no taste or desire for alcohol; it is as unnatural and averse to his constitution, as to that of the horse or the ox; nor is there any apology for its use by man that does not equally apply to the brute.

660. The third illustration represents the stomach of the confirmed drunkard; the man who has become habitually accustomed to the use of alcoholic drinks. And here we find the blood vessels of the inner coat, which in the temperate (rather moderate) drinker, were only *slightly enlarged, so fully developed*, as to render the most minute branches visible to the eye, like the rum blossoms on the drunkard's face; and this enlargement does not depend upon the perpetual presence of alcohol, as in the temperate (moderate) drinker, but it has become so permanent and fixed that they retain their natural size even after death; unless indeed the inebriate has for some time previous to this event, abandoned the use of alcohol, and given nature time to restore them to their

natural size. The mucous coat becomes thickened and softened, which often results in ulceration.

661. It happens, after this state has continued for some time, that all the coats of the stomach become implicated, and are found in a very thickened and indurated state ; and thus the way is prepared for *scirrhus, cancer, and other organic affections*. In this state the inebriate is never easy or satisfied, unless his stomach is excited by the presence of this or some other narcotic poison.

662. Whenever these are withheld, he is afflicted with loss of appetite, nausea, gnawing pain, and a sinking sensation at the stomach, lassitude, debility, and temporary disturbance of all the functions of the body. It is under these circumstances, and in this condition of the stomach, that the drunkard finds it so difficult to resist the craving of his appetite, and to reform his habits. Difficult, but not impossible. Thousands, thus far sunk to ruin, have reformed, and thousands are now undergoing the experiment. But it is only by total abstinence, that reformation can be accomplished.

663. No one may hope to reform by degrees, or to be cured by substituting one form of alcohol for another. So long as he indulges in the smallest degree, so long will his propensity to drink be perpetuated, and his stomach exhibit traces of disease.

664. If the reformed drunkard, abandons the use of all intoxicating drinks, his stomach, by that extraordinary power of self-restoration with which it is endowed, gradually resumes its natural appearance. Its engorged blood-vessels becoming reduced to their original size, their natural colour and healthy sensibility returns. A few weeks, or months, according to the extent of the injury done, will accomplish this renovation; after which the individual has no longer any suffering, or desire for alcohol. This process is greatly facilitated, and rendered more easy to the sufferer, by the use of cooling medicine, and vegetable diet. It is nevertheless true, and should be ever borne in mind, that such is the susceptibility of the stomach of the *reformed drunkard*, that a repetition of the use of alcohol in the *slightest degree, and in any form, under any circumstance, revives the appetite:* the blood-vessels again become dilated, and the morbid sensibility of the organ is reproduced. Abstinence, therefore, total abstinence, at once, and forever, must be the pledge of him who means to stand." Hence intemperance is a physical as well as a mental disease.

665. The fourth illustration presents a view of the ulcerated, or aphthous condition of the drunkard's stomach; a state which frequently exists, but is not readily apprehended, on account of the obscurity of the attendant symptoms. It consists in numerous small ulcerations extending over the internal coat, and which

are usually covered with a white crust, producing the aphthous (ulcerated) appearance. Upon wiping off the crust, the mucous surface is found broken and covered with small corroding sores, of greater or less size and depth, with ragged and inflamed edges; and sometimes the inflammation extends over the intervening space.

666. The fifth illustration represents the state of the drunkard's stomach after a debauch. It was drawn from the case of one who had been for several days in a state of inebriation, but who came to his death suddenly from another cause. It shows the internal coat of the organ to have been in a high state of inflammation, and presents several livid spots, with dark grumous blood oozing from the surface. I have had several opportunities of inspecting the stomach under similar circumstances, and I believe that the plate presents about the ordinary appearance of the organ when excited to a state of inflammation by excessive indulgence in the use of alcoholic drinks. It has been remarked, that the symptoms attendant upon the ulcerated state of the stomach, and especially if unaccompanied by much inflammation, are often obscure, and such as not to denote much constitutional derangement.

667. But in this condition of the organ, the whole system suffers. There is a loss of appetite, nausea, vomiting, ardent thirst, pain in the head, red eyes, bloated face, coated and red tongue, frequent pulse and symptomatic fever. The symptoms are more or less intense according to the duration of the debauch and the quantity of liquor drank; being modified in some degree, by the condition and habits of the individual. They are in some respects, such as attend the ordinary inflammation of the stomach, produced by other causes, and the appropriate treatment in both is found to be nearly the same. It consists in total abstinence from all stimulating drink, and the use of cooling and mucilaginous drinks, with entire rest.

668. The following case fully confirms the principles here laid down, and, at the same time furnishes valuable admonitions: "A gentleman equally distinguished for the powers of his mind, and the influence which he wielded in the councils of the nation, unfortunately acquired in early life, the habit of intemperance; but it was not that intemperance which is perpetual; it only came upon him at distant periods, not oftener than once or twice in the year. In the intervals he practiced entire abstinence, while at these periods he wholly abandoned himself to his propensity, and would continue drinking, until the stomach was wrought up to a high state of inflammation. I was called to attend him in at least twelve of these paroxysms during as many years, and conducted him safely through the storm. It was done upon the principle of withholding at once all stimulants, and allowing free use of ice-water, and other cooling drinks, with cupping and

blistering over the stomach. In ten or twelve days he usually became well and able to attend to his business. Unfortunately, in his last paroxysm, he came under the care of those who advised that he should not abandon his cup at once, but wind up his debauch by degrees. The advice was followed, and he fell a victim to the experiment. He died suddenly in the vigour of his day, and in the height of his usefulness; lamented and wept over by all who knew him." No one may hope to be weaned from the love of alcoholic drinks, or to be cured of a fit of intoxication, by diminishing the quantity; or by substituting one form of the poison for another. As well might the culprit who receives his fifty lashes to-day, expect palliation of his sufferings by the infliction of forty lashes to-morrow, and thirty the day after; or by substituting the cowhide for the cat-o'-nine-tails. The practice is opposed to all experience and to every principle of man's constitution. The stomach is inflamed, and must be cured, like inflammation produced by other causes, by withholding stimulants and instituting a cooling antiphlogistic treatment.

669. We here introduce to our readers a plate representing a specimen of the cancerous stomach. It was drawn from the stomach of a gentleman who had for many years followed a seafaring life. *He was not regarded as intemperate, but used his grog daily*, and was in the habit of taking a glass of brandy in the morning, unadulterated, to excite an appetite for his breakfast. At length dyspepsia came on, with pain, a burning sensation in the region of the stomach; vomiting his food an hour or two after his meals, followed by extreme emaciation and death. Upon examination of the body, the whole of the stomach, except a small portion at the left extremity, was found in a scirrhus state; its coats thickened to the extent of about two inches, and the cavity of the organ so far obliterated, as scarcely to admit the passage of a probe from the left to the right extremity; so that for considerable time before his death, none of the nutriment derived from food and drink, could have passed into the intestines. Near the right extremity of the stomach was a cancerous ulcer, of the size and appearance represented in the drawing.

670. Since the foregoing case occurred, two others of the same character, and produced by the same cause, have fallen under my observation. In both of these cases, the one a male and the other a female, the stomach was thickened, scirrhus and cancerous, and so extensively disorganized as not to admit the passage of the chyme out of the pyloric orifice.

671. The prominent symptoms in these two cases, also, were excruciating pain, a vomiting of the food in a half digested state, followed by extreme emaciation. Upon opening the body of a moderate drinker after death, about three inches of the lower portion of the œsophagus was found in a thickened and scirrhus state, the disease extending to the stomach, and so involving the

cardiac orifice, as nearly to obliterate the opening and prevent the passage of food and drink. The mucous coat of the stomach exhibited strong traces of the effects of intemperance, and the pyloric portion of the organ was found in a scirrhus state.

672. Here, you see, the stomach is represented as shrivelled up as a fire would shrivel a blown up bladder. The stomach had ceased to be a digester, except a small part at the cardiac orifice. Dr. Lees informs us that the man was never drunk in his life, in the vulgar sense of the term; he took his drams, but only "just a little;" he drank only by the rule of moderation. "He took a drink in the morning to give an appetite for his breakfast, and another dram of bitters before dinner, to improve his appetite for it, and another to help to digest it; and a glass or two at night for friendship, and not to appear odd in company, and a final glass for a night-cap." At the end of thirty years he died of an incurable disease of the stomach—cancer.

673. This is not a very rare disease in these days of light, knowledge and "scientific research," for at a late meeting of the Pathological Society in London, three cases of this disease were presented. Such cases are not rare, if the truth was known. A case of this kind occurred in Philadelphia during this year to the author's certain knowledge, and others with similar symptoms, but examination after death was not allowed. The case already given of St. Martin, was but the incipient state of this disease; for though St. Martin felt no pain, yet Dr. Beaumont saw ulcerous patches on the mucous surface of his stomach: showing that a stomach may be ulcerated and yet give no warning. The drinker feels well.

674. In the last illustration, (see Frontispiece) represents the appearance of the stomach of the drunkard who dies in a state of mania a potu, or *delirium tremens*. The history of the case from which this drawing was made, will illustrate the character of the disease, and the morbid condition of the stomach. The subject was a man amiable in disposition, courteous in manner, high in public life. By degrees he became intemperate, and although he drank daily, his excessive indulgence was confined to paroxysms of greater or less duration. Several times during the continuance of these paroxysms, he was thrown into a state of delirium; from which, however, he soon recovered. At length one of his paroxysms of drink came upon him, which was of longer duration than usual, and of greater severity; for more than two weeks his mind was entirely deranged, and it required two persons to confine him to his room. He imagined that his nearest friends were his greatest enemies and persecutors, and were constantly laying plans for his destruction. He fancied that he saw spectres and devils, and files of armed soldiers entering his apartments; deadly serpents crawling over his bed, and wild beasts ready to devour him. * * * * * His

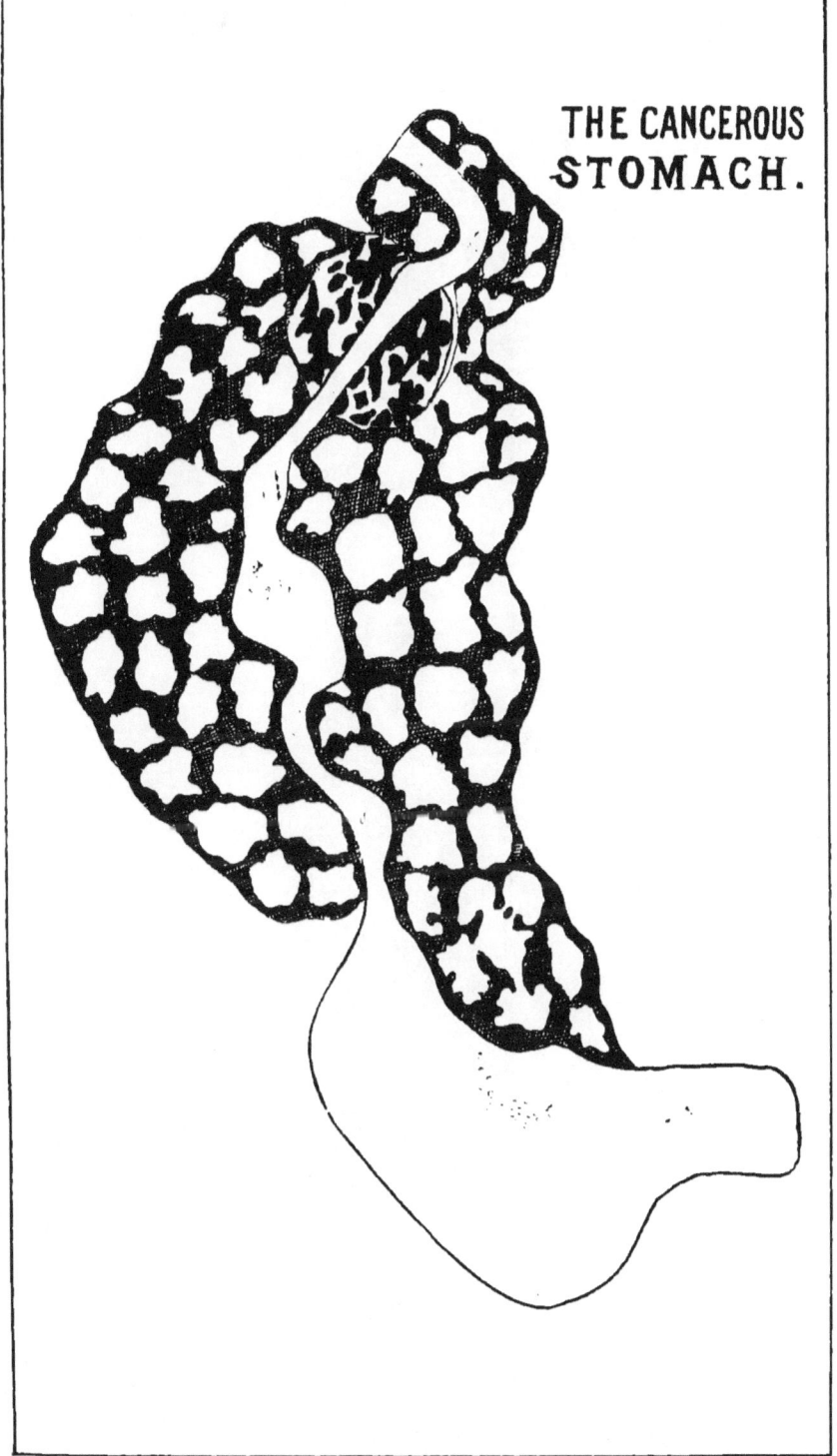

bodily functions became more disturbed, accompanied with great debility; a cold, profuse clammy sweat, and sinking pulse. These symptoms were followed by general spasms, which soon closed the scene."

675. After death the body was examined. Upon laying open the stomach it presented the appearance exhibited in the plate. It contained a considerable quantity of dark fluid, resembling coffee-grounds: the inner surface was covered with a dark brown flaky substance, upon removing which, it exhibited marks of having been in a high state of inflammation; some portion appearing of a deep red or mahogany colour, and others quite black, as if in a state of incipient mortification. It was obvious that the dark flaky matter which lined the outer coat, as well as that lying loosely in the cavity of the organ, was blood which had exuded from the vessels of the inflamed surface, and had been acted upon by gastric juice, converting it into black vomit."

676. "I have had several opportunities of inspecting, after death, the bodies of those who have fallen by intemperance, in a state of *delirium tremens:* and have found not only the symptoms attending the affection, but the morbid appearance upon dissection to be extremely uniform; and my observation fully confirms the opinion entertained by most modern pathologists, that the disease has its seat originally in the stomach, and that the affection of the brain is purely sympathetic and secondary: an opinion sustained also by the course found most successful in the treatment of the disease. * * * * The similarity in the effects produced in the body and mind by the habitual use of opium among the Chinese, and those which follow the use of intoxicating drinks among other nations, affords a fair inference that the stomach, in both cases, suffers from the same morbid changes, and would exhibit, upon dissection, the same pathological conditions."

677. It should be borne in mind that while alcoholic drinks make their first impression upon the stomach, their morbid effects are not limited to this organ: the whole of the intestine canal, and more especially the small intestines suffer more or less under their influence. The internal coat becomes irritated, inflamed, softened, and ulcerated, and occasionally affected with the organic changes, delineated in the drawing of the stomach. Nor are the consequences of intemperance confined to the digestive canal alone. The distant parts of the body became in time affected also. The liver, the brain, the heart, the lungs, and the kidneys, become the seat of alcoholic influence, an influence which is transmitted to them in two ways. The first is upon the principle of sympathy: the second is through the medium of the circulation, and the immediate action of the alcoholic principle upon the organs as it passes through them, mingled with blood. Both may be illustrated by familiar examples.

678. A person who has become exhausted by labour and fasting, finds his muscular power diminished, and his whole system enfeebled; upon partaking of food, his strength is immediately restored—restored long before his food is digested, or any nourishment can have been derived from it. This effect is produced by the stimulus of the food upon the stomach, which impression is transmitted to all the other organs of the body, through the medium of the nervous system, upon the principle of sympathy.

679. The second, through the medium of the circulation, may be shown by two facts. The odour of the drunkard's breath furnishes us with one of the earliest indications of intemperance. This is occasioned by exhalations of the alcoholic principle from the bronchial vessels and air cells of the lungs; not of pure alcohol, as taken into the stomach, but as it has been absorbed and mingled with the blood, and subjected to the action of the different organs of the body, and not containing any principle which contributes to the nourishment or renovation of the system, is cast out with other excretions, as poisonous and hurtful. It is upon these two principles that alcoholic drinks produce their morbid effects upon the different organs."

680. Thus the living and the dead present the facts to our very eyes. Need we other evidence to convince us that alcohol is a poison, a destroyer of vitality, and agent of death?

THE EFFECTS OF ALCOHOL ON THE LIVER.

681. Dr. Percy obtained alcohol from the *liver* after it had been ingested; hence it may reasonably be inferred, that it accumulated in that organ: that its presence must interfere with the performance of its functions, and injure its substance.

682. The first illustration in the plate opposite represents the colour of the liver when in a healthy condition. It is a dark coloured organ, being composed of a vast number of fine vessels containing venous blood, from which the bile is separated.

683. The office of the *liver* is to take up new substances, having not yet become blood, as well as the portions of integrated matter that can be worked over, and brought again into use. It is in fact the ECONOMIST of the animal system. It excretes *bile* and liver-sugar, and *renews* the *blood*. When the liver is disordered, the whole body is more or less deranged, and the proper nutrition of its parts arrested. Almost every one has seen the whole, or at least a portion of the liver of an animal.

684. Though when cut it appears to be uniform and homogeneous in its structure, yet if examined with the microscope, it will

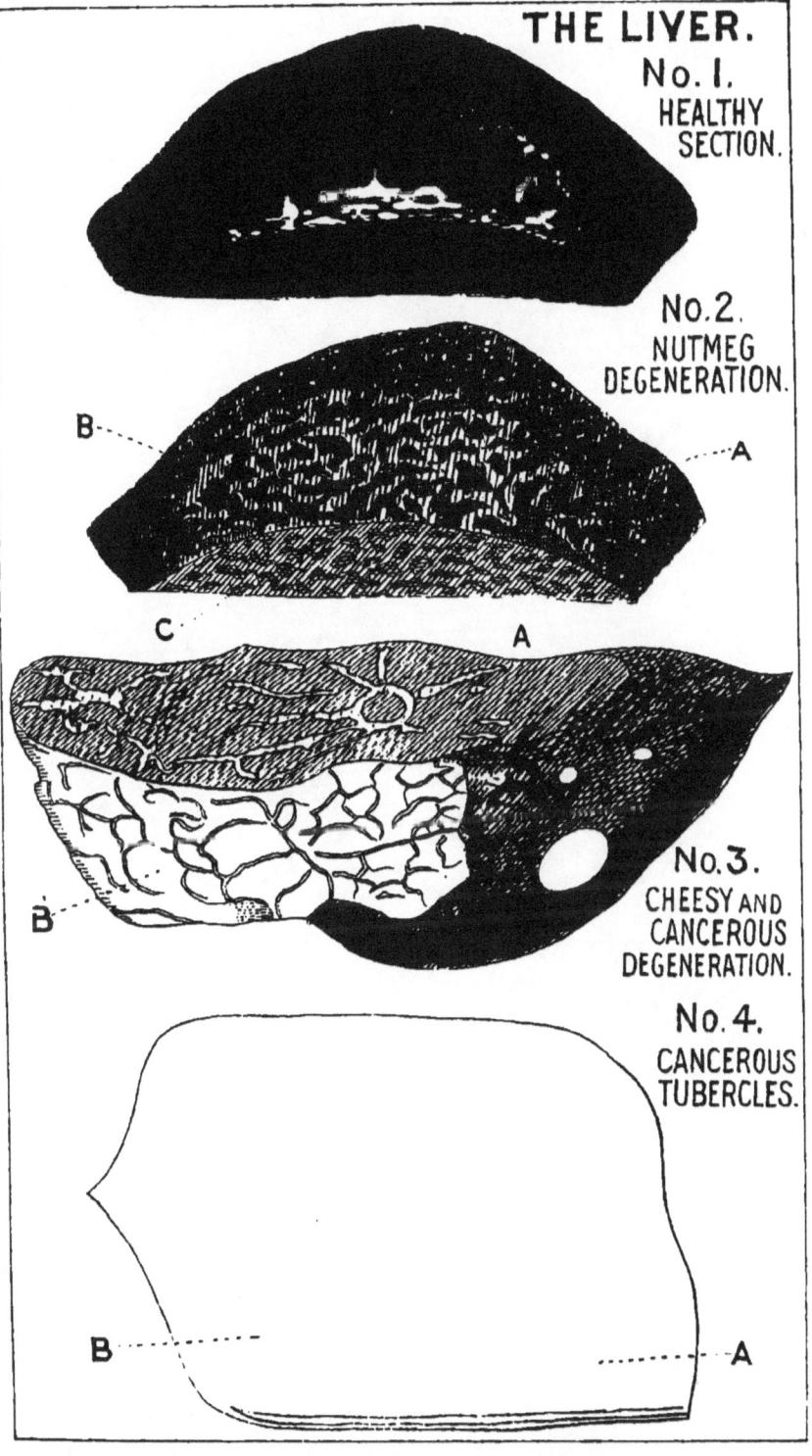

be seen that it is composed of millions of cells, small tubes and vessels, forming a most wondrous network.

685. *Alcohol* does for the *liver*, what we have seen that it does for the stomach,—irritates, inflames, narcotizes, and destroys. Almost the first result of this agent, is to change its secretion from a bright yellow colour, to a green, and sometimes to a black; and from a thin fluid, to a substance the consistency of tar, which not unfrequently causes the formation of biliary culculi (gall-stones.) Alcohol mixing with the bile and liver tissue hardens it, so that it becomes, as it were, dead matter. The liver sometimes becomes full of unabsorbed matter, which forms in spots, and consists of a kind of consolidated pus, such as is seen formed under a scab, or when an ulcer is opened. These spots at first, when seen under the microscope, may not be larger than a pin's head, as only two or three cells are ruptured, but they soon become aggregated.

686. The little spots are then more plainly seen, and as the inflammation increases, two or more unite to form a larger spot; these grow larger and larger, until eventually the whole liver is changed in colour. Hypertrophy, or enlargement of the liver, is a very common result of the use of alcoholics, sometimes increasing it to even double is natural size; accompanied very often with complete disorganization of its structure.

687. Aware that alcohol will produce the enlargement of this organ, poultry dealers in England, and some other countries, mix spirits with the food of the fowls, in order to increase the size of the liver, to enable them to supply the epicure with a greater amount of that part of the bird, which they esteem as very delicious.

688. Dr. Sewall met with a case in which the liver had become so enlarged as to weigh from eight to twelve pounds, in place of four or five, its usual weight.

689. The inflammation of this organ not unfrequently terminates in suppuration, and the formation of extensive abscesses. I once met with the case of a German butcher, who said he drank from three to four quarts of lager beer daily. He died, and upon making a post-mortem examination, the liver was found to be in a complete state of *cirrhosis*, the hepatic lobes almost entirely obliterated, and their places occupied by organized lymph. Granular degeneration had also occurred in the kidneys; the left one presented a high state of congestion, while there was nothing remaining of the right, except the cortical portion, which contained nothing but pus. The spleen was extensively hypertrophied, with the appearance of softening.

690. The second illustration in the plate represents the *gin*, or *nutmeg* liver degeneration (hypertrophy of the white substance) which Dr. Hope says, is the ordinary organic affection of the organ, and is generally attended with enlargement and lacerability. This disease is said to be common among the coal-heavers of London, a class of persons who drink almost incredible quantities of porter, and seldom attain an advanced age. A. B. on the plate indicate spots on the exterior; C. convoluted tracts in the interior.

691. George Frederick Cooke, who was not only distinguished as a tragedian, but for the drunkenness of his life, when he died in New York, was opened by Dr. Hosack, who found that the liver, while it was rather diminished in size, was in a state of induration, and surprisingly hard; that it made considerable resistance to the knife, and its colour was lighter than natural.

692. The whole substance was covered with tubercles, and the blood-vessels, *which are numerous and large in a healthy liver, were entirely obliterated,* showing that the circulation had nearly ceased long before his death.

693. The third illustration in the plate represents another disease, to which the users of alcohol are liable: the *cheesy* and *tuberous* liver. The plate gives at A. an interior view of tubera coalescing into one large mass, not unlike the section of a lemon. —B. displays many irregular elevations, while several tumours are seen throughout the organ.

694. The fourth illustration in the plate represents a section of cancerous tubera of the liver. It is taken from (fig. 94) in DR. HOPE'S MORBID ANATOMY. It is the case of a cab-driver, addicted to drinking. "The tubercles first appeared as individual *grains* or points of disease (acini), then they coalesced as at B, and finally formed large compact masses, as at A. The *liver* is enormous—five times its natural size, crammed with thousands of tubera, varying from this size o, to that of an egg. There was also 'fungoid excrescence' of the size of a bean, in the stomach, near the pylorus." The diseases of this organ at first commence with slight irritation, and end, as we have seen, in complete destruction. By a little reflection it may be easily comprehended that an organ of such size and importance, cannot safely be tampered with day by day, without seriously injuring it, marring its functions, and working injury to the whole animal economy.

695. Drs. Peters, Goldsmith and Moses, examined conjointly, some years ago, upwards of seventy bodies, to observe the pathology of intemperance; and found that the livers of moderate drinkers were a little larger than natural, and somewhat *softened*,

and their external surface spotted with fatty infiltration, extending two or three lines into the parenchyma, or texture of the organ. The colour of the rest of the liver was nearly natural, and the edges retained their normal sharpness. In old drunkards, the liver was very large, weighing from six to eight pounds, often ten or twelve. The edges were thick and much rounded, the parenchyma almost white, fat, soft and fragile, and the peritoneal covering could be torn off, in very large pieces.*

696. In his "Hygeia,"† Dr. Beddoes says: "By persons in any degree debauched, and by the drinkers of fermented liquors in general, the faintest standing sign of indigestion may serve to indicate that there is *something* amiss with the liver. Organs so intimately connected (as the stomach and liver) have sometimes been found indurated (hardened) after death, without any symptom but that of indigestion."

697. Speaking of diseases of the liver, Dr. Trotter says: "The chronic species is not a painful disease; it is slow in its progress, and frequently gives no alarm, till some incurable affection is the consequence."‡ Hence, the fallacy and danger of a man judging merely by his feelings of the beneficial effects of the use of intoxicating drinks; for his liver and stomach may be seriously diseased, while he imagines himself in moderate health."

698. Dr. Richardson says: ('Diseases of Modern Life,' p. 256-7-8), "The liver of the confirmed alcoholic is probably never free from the influence of the poison; it is too often saturated with it. * * The organ at first becomes enlarged from the distension of its vessels, the surcharge of fluid matter, and the thickening of tissue. After a time there follows contraction of membrane, and slow shrinking of the whole mass of the organ in its cellular parts. Then the shrunken, hardened, roughened mass is said to be 'hobnailed.' * * The body of him in whom it is developed is usually dropsical in its lower parts, owing to the obstruction offered to the returning blood by the veins, and death is certain.

699. " * * From the blood rendered preternaturally fluid by alcohol there may transude through the investing membrane, plastic matter which may remain interfering with natural functions, if not creating active mischief. Again, under an increase of fatty substance, the structure of the liver may be charged with fatty cells, and undergo what is technically designated fatty degeneration. I touch with the lightest hand upon these deteri-

---

* New York Journal of Medicine.
† Hygeia. Thomas Beddoes, M. D., Bristol, (Eng.) 1802.
‡ Essay on Drunkenness. Thomas Trotter, M. D., London. 1804.

orations, and I omit many others. My object is gained if I but impress the mind of the reader with the serious nature of the changes that in this one organ alone follow an excessive use of alcohol."

THE EFFECTS OF ALCOHOL UPON THE KIDNEYS.

700. The first illustration in the plate opposite represents the interior of the kidney in its healthy condition. Its function, as already seen, is to excrete nitrogen from the blood circulating in its vessels, (in the form of urea,) whence the well-known colour of this organ. W, is the ureter; P, the bowl, (or pelvis), laid open, showing how the papillæ P, project into this cavity. B, the cortical substance.

701. These organs are seldom found in a healthy condition, after death, in the drunkard, or the moderate but regular drinker of alcoholics; for even their temperate use leads to most difficult and fatal diseases. Dr. Christison states that from three-fourths to four-fifths of the cases of the disease of the kidneys which he met with in Edinburgh, were in persons who were habitual drunkards, or who, without deserving this appellation, were in the constant habit of using spirits several times a day. The experience in English hospital practice, by the testimony of Dr. Carpenter, is precisely the same.

702. The second illustration in the plate shows the granulated kidney of the drinker, which is pale, softened and enlarged. A, the pelvis, with three branches, B, C, D, leading to the cones; E, one branch open; F, the cones; G, a cone cut across.

703. That the kidneys should become thus diseased is not surprising. These organs are excited to action, to eliminate the alcohol from the circulation. But the effects of this agent do not fall so directly upon the kidneys as on the liver; as the blood of the kidneys is derived from the arteries in which the alcohol is diluted by the whole of the blood. The habitual use of alcohol produces irritation, which will certainly pass on to chronic inflammation, and to an alteration of the structure.

704. Hence, we find it to be the origin usually of Bright's disease, or granular degeneration of the kidneys, as shown in the plate. This disease we believe is rarely met with in private practice, unless the patient has been in the habit of regularly using fermented liquors, gin or whiskey; for these drinks, by having a strong diuretic tendency, produce a greater temporary activity of the kidneys, and thus have a greater tendency to produce chronic irritation. If they should escape this form of renal disease, the

long and continued excitement produced upon them will impair their functions; for we find that persons advanced in life, who have habitually used these drinks, are very apt to be afflicted with gout, rheumatism and other diseases arising from the insufficient elimination of the morbid matter from the system. The over-excitement of any organ will be regularly followed, sooner or later, by depression of its functional power, and the irritating tendency of alcohol to produce perverted nutrition will have the effect of rendering the kidneys unable to rightly perform their functions.

705. Dr. George Johnson, F. R. S., Physician to King's College Hospital, London, England, read a paper to the Royal Medical and Chirurgical Society, May 27th, 1873, in which he stated: "About ten years ago he made a tabular analysis of nearly three hundred cases of albuminaria or Bright's disease of the kidneys. Some recent discussions on the influence of alcohol in that disease led him to refer to his analysis of cases for evidence bearing on the question. Nine-tenths of the cases belong to the class of hospital or dispensary cases. It is shown that scarlet fever, intemperance, cold, wet and gout, either singly or combined, account for 120 cases out of 200, or 60 per cent. Thus albuminaria was probably the result of scarlet fever in 24 out of 200 cases, or 12 per cent.; of intemperance, in 28, or 14 per cent.; of intemperance and gout, in 12, or 6 per cent.; of intemperance and cold, in 12, or 6 per cent.; in 4 with syphilis; and in 2 with lead; of gout in 8, or 4 per cent.; of cold and wet in 23, or 11.5 per cent.; of cold in 13, or 6.5 per cent. Thus showing that intemperance, either alone or combined with other influences, was the probable cause of albuminaria in 52 cases out of 200, or 25 per cent. Of these 52 cases, in 28, intemperance was believed to be the sole cause.

706. Of the 58 intemperate cases, 11 were women and 47 men. Of the 47 men, the occupation of 5 are not recorded; of the 42 whose occupation was noted, 5 were waiters. The remaining 37 intemperate men had no fewer than 30 occupations, not one of them connected with liquor trades. Hence it is not right to assume, as Dr. Dickinson has done, that men in the class of hospital patients, who are not engaged in the liquor trades, and not notorious drunkards, may be placed in a non-alcoholic class. It is also shown that the excess of Bright's disease is amongst males, because, as a rule, men are more intemperate and more exposed to cold and wet, than women.

EFFECTS OF ALCOHOL ON THE STOMACH, LIVER, HEART AND KIDNEYS.

707. Dr. N. S. Davis, of Chicago, in a recent clinical lecture on Delirium Tremens,* exhibited the stomach, duodenum, liver, and kidneys of a hospital patient who was a victim of alcoholism. The subject was a man of intelligence, between twenty-five and thirty years of age, naturally strong and well formed, but had accustomed himself to the use of alcoholic drinks for many years. Three weeks before his admission into the hospital, he had been almost constantly intoxicated, taking from one to two pints of brandy daily, which finally resulted in his death.

708. Dr. Davis said in his lecture: "A *post mortem* examination revealed no important morbid appearance visible to the unassisted eye, except in the stomach, duodenum, liver, and kidneys. These organs are before you, fresh as they were taken from the body. The stomach and duodenum are laid open; you see the mucous membrane, in its whole extent, presenting an *intensely red and tumefied condition.* In some places, where most intensely injected with blood, the surface is dark brown, and apparently softened. These appearances are the result of severe inflammation in the gastro-duodenal mucous membrane. And this inflammation was probably the direct cause of death.

709. "The *kidney is seen to be moderately enlarged*, rather soft or flabby to the touch; and, on being laid open, the cortical or secreting structure, is pale, and several small masses of fatty tissues at different points are observable. No analysis of the urine was made. "The *liver is seen to be greatly enlarged, being more than twice its natural size.* Its colour is light olive, both internally and externally, and its increased bulk is plainly owing to infiltration, or deposit of fat globules, constituting the most common form of *fatty* liver. *The heart is also loaded with fat,* and its muscular tissue paler than natural. These morbid specimens fully illustrate the two leading effects of alcoholic drinks on the physical organization of the human body. The fatty degenerations of the liver, heart, kidneys, etc., *are the result of the slow, long continued moderate influence* of alcohol, in retarding the oxydation of the carbonaceous matters of the system, and allowing it to accumulate in the form of inert fat: while the acute gastroduodenitis is the result of the direct irritating influences of strong distilled spirits, taken in large quantities, without ordinary food.

710. "Some have expressed doubts as to whether alcoholic drinks were capable of producing direct inflammation of the

---

* In "Medical Examiner."

THE KIDNEYS.

No. 1. HEALTHY STATE.

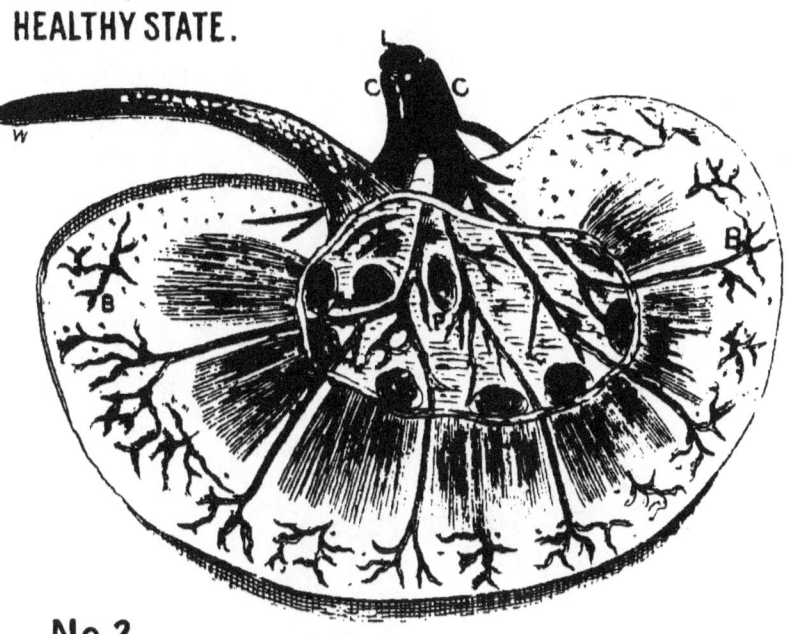

No. 2. DISEASED FROM INTEMPERANCE.

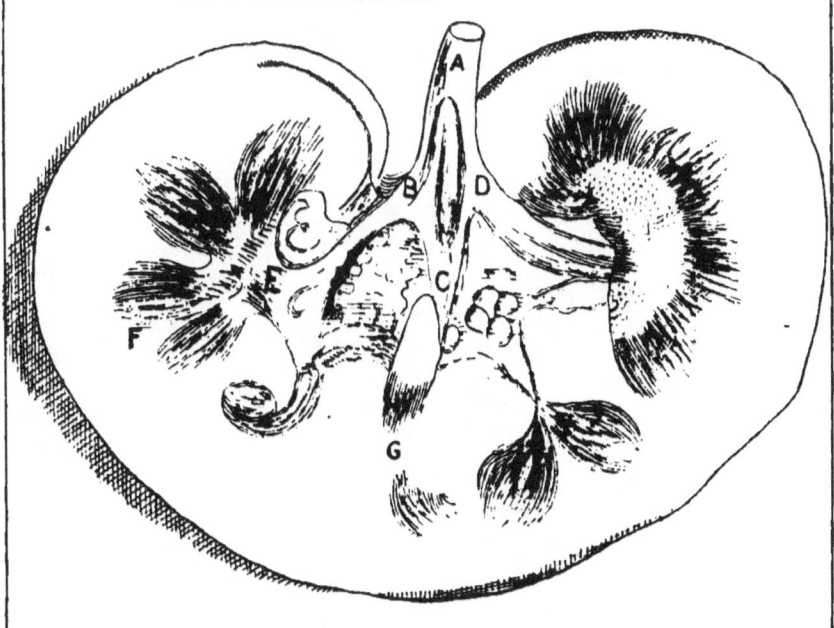

mucous membrane of the stomach; but such inflammation is certainly a frequent complication of delirium tremens, and adds greatly to the danger of that disease. It is very generally supposed that the delirium and trembling results from the sudden withdrawal of the so-called stimulating drink, and the consequent anæmic condition of the brain. And it is certainly true that, in many cases, the first indications of delirium occur from one to five days after the inebriant has been discontinued. But it is equally certain that in two-thirds of all the cases that have come under my observation, the symptoms supervened while the patients were still in the full supply of their accustomed drink. Whenever the alcoholic beverage is kept in contact with the brain structures, constantly retarding the molecular changes for a considerable time, while the supply of nutritive matter through the digestive organs is suspended or greatly deficient, that perversion of function which is styled delirium tremens ensues, whether the drink is continued or not."

711. Dr. Richardson says (Diseases of Modern Life, p. 259-60): "These deteriorations of structure in the kidney, from alcohol, give rise to those varied condition of disease known by the public under the general name of 'Bright's disease.' The same morbid states of the kidney may truly be induced by other causes than alcohol. * * * But my experience is to the effect that seven out of every eight instances of kidney disease are attributable to alcohol.

712. Another disease connected with a modified condition of the secretion of the kidneys is intimately related to excessive use of alcoholic drinks. I refer to the disease calculus, or stone in the bladder. Excessive indulgence in *malt* liquors, is, I believe, a common cause of this disease. No one who indulges, even temporarily, in alcohol, can fail to observe how soon the indulgence gives rise to an unnatural renal secretion, to a fine deposit of pinkish sedimentary matter, and to occasional production of a fine film of fatty or iridescent substance on the surface of the fluid, after it has stood for a short period. This is a condition of the secretion favourable to calculus; and whenever it is present, the prudent man, who knows he is suffering from it, will largely or altogether debar himself of the pleasure of his enemy."

PART VIII.

NERVOUS DISEASES FROM ALCOHOL.

713. FROM what has been said of the nature and action of Alcohol, it may readily be conceived that the brain and spinal cord, and all the nervous substance, will become deteriorated under its influence. These deteriorations give rise to the very worst forms of nervous derangements, among which are cerebral congestions, cerebral hemorrhage with apoplexy, and paralysis, meningeal apoplexy, cerebral thrombosis, softening of the brain, aphasia, acute cerebral meningitis, chronic meningitis, and all kinds of insanity; and among the diseases of the spinal cord are spinal congestion, anterolateral spinal sclerosis, and posterior spinal sclerosis; epilepsy, palsy, neuralgia, chorea; and many other affections of the brain and spinal cord.

ALCOHOL DRINKS CAUSE PARALYSIS.

714. It is well established that general paralysis is very often caused by intemperate habits, and the use of alcoholic drinks. Guislan attributes it mainly to the combined action of drink and study, drink and trouble. Tobacco and opium, must also be added to alcohol, as a cause of insanity, though to a much less extent.

715. Apoplexy, epilepsy, and hysteria, are among the diseases which are sometimes either caused or induced by alcoholics. Nor are they the result of the use of ardent spirits and wine alone; for Dr. Macnish says that "In seven cases out of ten, malt-liquor drunkards die of apoplexy or palsy.* Nor need they be really entitled to the appellation of being drunkards, as commonly used; but to drink large quantities of beer, ale, &c., daily, is sufficient to produce these diseases; as every physician can satisfy himself, by a little investigation and inquiry into the habits of his patients. Many persons of both sexes are paralyzed by the use of strong drinks. Their limbs become useless: you can see them every day in our streets.

ALCOHOLIC PARESIS AND PARAPLEGIA.

716. Dr. J. Lockhart Clark, believes that alcoholic paraplegia (palsy of the lower half of the body,) is generally preceded by

---

* Macnish, "Anatomy of Drunkenness."

various nervous symptoms; giddiness, a sensation of being lifted from the ground, a sensation of choking on going to sleep; numbness, various pains, chronic tremulousness, fibrillar quivering of the muscles, unsteadiness of gait, and general uncertain control of voluntary motion; imperfect articulation, loss of energy, &c.

717. Dr. Samuel Wilkes also bears testimony to the existence of alcoholic paraplegia, and states that the most important part of the treatment is the sudden and complete withdrawal of the stimulus; that delirium tremens, in his experence, never results from such withdrawal, althongh he has had numerous and very bad cases.

718. Dr. Wilks says:* "I have now seen so many cases of persons, especially of "ladies," who have entirely given themselves up to the pleasures of brandy-drinking and have become paraplegic, that I have become pretty familiar with the symptoms. From what we hear from our continental neighbours, it would seem that the compound styled *absinthe*, is productive of exhaustion of nervous power, in even a more marked degree. * * * Of course drunkards of all descriptions, suffer from muscular and nervous weakness; but as I have said, it is more especially in the legs, that the effect is most striking. * * I am now seeing a young married woman, who for some time past, has been addicted to 'drink.' She first of all had engorgement of the liver, followed by an all but fatal hematemis (vomiting of blood). She recovered of this, but continued her evil habits; she began to get feeble in mind, and tottering of limbs. She appeared at times almost lost, and spoke thickly. She had difficulty in rising from her chair, and then by a great effort staggered across the room. She now appears gradually recovering.

719. "I occasionally see * * a publican's wife, who commenced business two years ago, previous to which time she was temperate and well. Since this, the constant presence of gin before her eyes has been too much for her, and she has drunk the burning liquid in enormous quantities. This could not continue long, and now she has been confined to her bed for six months. She is almost paralyzed, having very little power to move her limbs, not being able to raise the heel from the bed, and having no power to grasp with the hands: the muscles flabby, and she has almost complete anæsthesia (privation of feeling). The mind is also somewhat enfeebled.

720. "Such cases I could multiply to almost any extent. Several I have seen end fatally, and in some a partial recovery has taken place."

---

* "Lectures on Diseases of the Nervous System," Medical Times and Gazette.

721. Dr. Sewall,* gives several cases of this disease, that came under his examination. The first, an active business man, of forty-five, who had gradually acquired the habit of tippling, *though he never drank to intoxication.* His practice was to take small quantities of brandy, gin, wine, &c., at short intervals. He at length complained of debility, a sense of numbness in his lower limbs, and inability to walk, &c., &c. The complaint increased till he could neither walk nor stand, and for months before his death, he was lifted from his bed to his chair. Several times during the progress of the case, he partially recovered, but it was only in proportion as he suspended the use of alcoholic drinks.

722. Upon examination after death, the mucous coat of the stomach was found in a state of irritation, such as is usually met with in the case of confirmed drunkards. The small intestines had participated in the irritation of the stomach.

723. In another case: Mr.——, a man of thirty, of fine, robust constitution, having acquired a habit of tippling, but not of ardent spirits, was never drunk; and no one suspected him of being intemperate. He consulted Dr. Sewall several times for numbness and loss of power in the lower limbs: and it was only after a considerable time that the doctor discovered the difficulty, so carefully did he conceal his habits. The doctor at length discovered that he kept in his grocery a pipe of wine for his own use, of which he drank frequently through the day; and would visit his grocery early in the morning, and late at night to renew his potations. The doctor informed him that the wine was the cause of the trouble; when he abandoned the traffic and the habit at once, his limbs regained their accustomed energy, and six years after, he was a sober and healthy man."

THROMBOSIS OF THE CEREBRAL ARTERIES.

724. The occlusion of the cerebral arteries with plugs of fibrine, or clots of blood in the current of the circulation from the left chambers of the heart, the pulmonary veins, or some other distant part; or in other words cerebral *embolism*, is an accident which frequently occurs, and has attracted much notice. But the cerebral may also become stopped up with clots of blood or fibrine, which have been formed from the blood itself at the place of obstruction. This is usually denominated *thrombosis*. It is met with less frequently than embolism of these arteries. Thrombosis doubtless occurs much oftener than is commonly supposed, for the relation which the cerebral arteries bear to these results is in most instances overlooked, unless the arteries are carefully examined after death.

---

* "Pathology of Drunkenness," a letter to Mr. E. Delevan. Published by the National Temperance Society.

725. Among the exciting causes of this disease, may be vaso-motary paralysis of certain of the celebral arteries, resulting from alcoholic intemperance. Dr. W. H. Dickinson,* records the case of a woman, 26 years old, who habitually used beer and gin to excess, and who, after drinking freely for two weeks, was seized with giddiness, followed in four days by loss of speech, and a feeling as of pins and needles sticking in the right arm, but without loss of consciousness. Later still hemiplegia of the right side came on, nocturnal delirium, coma, and death eight days after the first symptoms appeared. The predisposing cause, in this case, was the abnormal tendency of the blood to coagulate, which it had acquired by the intemperance of the patient; the exciting cause being probably vaso-motor *paralysis* of the basilar and vertebral arteries, due to chronic alcoholism. Hence chronic alcoholism, and intemperate habits, may be placed as an occasional, if not a frequent cause of *thrombosis*.

ALCOHOL THE CAUSE OF INSANITY.

726. That insanity should result from the use of intoxicating drinks is not surprising: nor could we reasonably anticipate other effects when we consider the poisonous and destructive action of alcohol upon all the tissues and organs of the body; and particularly when we remember the special affinity it has for the brain substance. We are strongly impressed with the belief that the intemperate, and the (so-called) temperate use of alcoholic drinks produce *more insanity than all else combined!* excepting hereditary predisposition; and hereditary predisposition is often a result of the same cause. The first or simplest form of the mental disease produced by alcoholics is:

727. DELIRIUM TREMENS, which is the result of continuous and prolonged alcoholic poisoning by ardent spirits, or other intoxicating beverages. It is a fierce though brief delirium. In the first stage of *delirium tremens*, the patient hears abusive language and provocations: he sees thieves, armed persons, animals; or he may hear the voice of his friends warning him of danger, or appealing for his help, &c. Stimulated by these excitements, the patient answers inquiries, quarrels, runs, rushes off, becomes furious, &c., all of which acts tend to develop in him a boisterous mania. At other times, he believes that his wife is unfaithful to him; that he is perhaps confined in prison, or before a court of justice, on account of various crimes; or that he is present at the funeral of his parents. Under these distressing circumstances or impressions, he is dull, suspicious; he laments, becomes terified, and attempts to escape: sometimes he attempts homicide or suicide, and presents a most melancholy aspect.

---

* St. George's Hospital Reports, pages 261, 262.

728. Magnus Huss, after describing the symptoms and causes of alcoholism, said: "If the use of alcohol is continued the convulsion may degenerate into epilepsy. Alcoholic epilepsy may degenerate into general paralysis, or it may be cured, if the use of the liquor be stopped."

729. Similar experience is repeated, and may be witnessed in every hospital and in almost every poor-house in the United States, and in the private practice in our cities; and though not so frequent in the rural districts, yet many cases are met by the physician. Cases of delirium tremens are not confined to men alone. The rational and physiological treatment of this disease, we have long held to be a total withdrawal of the alcoholic poison that produced the injury, which we have always known to be successful, never having used alcoholics in delirium tremens, nor lost a single case of that disease, when seen twenty-four hours before death.

730. Dr. Anstie said, before the English Parliamentary Habitual Drunkards' Committee:—"There is one thing which I would like to put on record very particularly, namely, that there need be no fears of the result upon intemperate individuals, of immediately depriving them of every kind of alcoholic stimulant; it would be a question which would be complicated by letting them down by degrees: the only way of letting such a man down, is by cutting him off drink altogether, and it is perfectly and absolutely safe, and the only thing which is calculated to do good."

731. "The phenomena of intoxication," says Dr. Bucknell, "presents us with another example of impairment and irregularity of the mental functions, probably referable to cerebral congestion. * * *

732. "The phenomena of intoxication are unfortunately familiar to every one: they vary however, greatly, according to the form and vehicle in which the alcohol has been imbibed. The sottish, swinish drunkenness of an English ploughman, with his stomach full of sour beer, is quite a different thing from the mad inebriation of an excitable Frenchman on fire with *eau de vie*. The former drunkenness consists more in partial palsy of the muscles and oppression of the brain, than anything deserving the name of excitement. In the latter, exalted and perverted sensations, flighty imagination, blind passion, giving way to maudlin sentiment, a general and violent stimulation (rather congestion) of the mental facuties, are the obvious characteristics of the condition; and they so closely resemble the phenomena of insanity, that while they last they may be said to be almost identical therewith."*

---

* "Psychological Medicine," Bucknell & Tuke, pp. 500, 501.

733. Besides *delirium tremens* as the result of alcohol, there is the *transient acute mania*, which takes place in some constitutions. This disease is usually the consequence of a brain exhausted by continued excitation and irritation from intoxicating drinks, until it can no longer stand the poisoning, and though continually spurred on by the drink, it finally gives way. This disease is characterized by the symptoms commencing in general paralysis, which is fortunately brief and curable, if the poison be immediately abandoned. Otherwise the mania may run in other forms of mental disease.

734. Unhappily for those who have once been victims of the intoxicating cup, there is another type of insanity due to the too free use of alcoholics, which may attack them though they have discontinued the use for a number of years. It usually follows some exciting moral or physical cause, as reversion in business, or the death of a near relative, which upsets the brain, producing a melancholy often permanent.

735. It is this form of insanity, though indirectly caused by intoxicating drinks, of which a vast number of cases are set down in the reports of insanity, as being caused by *ill-health, reverse of fortune, loss of friends*, &c., &c., which really should be ascribed to intemperance, and the use of alcoholic drinks.

736. By Drs. Bucknell and Tuke,[*] the first among the physical exciting causes of insanity, and for the most part in their order of frequency, are the following : " Intemperance, Epilepsy, and affection of Head and Spine."

737. Lord Shaftesbury, in his evidence before the Select Committee on Lunatics, in 1859, expressed his opinion that 50 per cent of the cases admitted into the English Asylum, are due to drink. It will be seen from the following that the authorities differ in their estimates of the amount of insanity caused by intemperance. Dr. Poole, estimates that 25 per cent is caused by intemperance. Dr. Needham, at the New York Lunatic Asylum, on the total number of 102, admitted the per cent for both sexes was 16; for men alone, 22 per cent. Dr. Clouston gives 16 per cent. of both sexes, 22.50 for men, for Cumberland, Westmoreland, England. Dr. Kirkbride, in his report for 1871, says that of 3,599 patients admitted in 31 years, of whom he was able to obtain information, 13.42 per cent (22.52 males, 2.39 females) had become insane through drink. Dr. Lee (1868), states that of 14,941 patients treated in 16 asylums of America, 11.97 per cent. were due to the same cause. For Northampton Asylum, Dr. Pliny Earle's statistics show 11 per cent. on the total number admitted of both sexes, and 20 per cent for men.

---

[*] Psychological Medicine," 3rd edition, page 99.

738. Of the remarkable influence of alcohol in producing *insanity* in Paris during the late war, M. Lunier has given abundant proof. During May, 1871, 55 per cent. of the admissions were due to alcohol alone. Persons in whom the nutrition of the brain is disordered by the use of alcoholic beverages, are more liable than others, to the moral and physical causes to which insanity is attributed.

739. The greater facilities in civilized countries for obtaining a knowledge of the number of *insane*, and the increased ability to recognize it, render it difficult to make anything like a just comparison. These also tend to show a greater proportion than is actually the case, yet, after making all the allowance for this source of error, we are forced to allow that insanity attains its highest development in civilized nations, while it remains at the lowest among the barbarous.

740. Dr. Pliny Earle, Superintendent of the Northampton Lunatic Hospital, Mass., speaking of the results of modern civilization, which are injurious, said:—"Where these effects will end no prophet can tell. But unless the race adapts itself more consistently and wisely to the change of circumstances, the prospect is anything but cheering to him who would wish to see a diminution, rather than an augmentation of mental disease."

741. There cannot be a reasonable doubt, that the main causes of insanity outweigh the conditions which should be supposed to favour normal mental states. Undoubtedly the unfavourable causes are the higher development of the brain, and the nervous system generally, which increases the mental susceptibility to slight impressions: the overwork that the brain is subjected to, the irrational, forcing, cramming system of education, and especially the use and abuse of alcoholic liquors, weakening the mental stamina of parents, transmitting still weaker mental and physical organizations to their offspring."

742. Of the moral causes of insanity, domestic troubles and grief are undoubtedly the most frequent. But it must be remembered that the drunkenness of the subject, or of some member of the family, in a vast number of cases is the real cause of domestic trouble; hence intemperance is remotely the cause of insanity, as well as directly.

743. * "If men took careful thought of the best use they could make of their bodies, they would probably never take alcohol, except as they would take a dose of medicine, in order to serve some special purpose. It is idle to say that there is any real necessity for persons who are in good health to indulge in any

---

* "Responsibility in Mental Diseases," by H. Maudsley, M. D., pages 285-6.

kind of intoxicating drinks. At the best it is an indulgence which is unnecessary; at the worst, it is a vice which occasions infinite misery, sin, crime, madness and disease. That of the patent and undeniable ills which it is admitted on all hands, to produce, it is at the bottom of manifold mischiefs that are never brought directly home to it.

744. "How much ill work would not be done, how much good work would be better, but for its baneful inspiration! Each act of crime, each suicide, each outbreak of madness; each disease occasioned by it, means an infinite amount of suffering endured and inflicted before matters have reached that climax. It may of course be said, that a moderate consumption of alcoholic liquors can do no harm; must on the contrary do good when exhausted nature feels the need of some stimulant.*

745. "I am not prepared to say that it always does demonstrable harm, but at the same time it is not wise to have recourse to alcoholic stimulant, (sedative, not stimulant) when recourse ought to be had to food and rest: and it is a serious harm to gain, as is sometimes done, by the factitious aid of a stimulant, the energy which should come from the calm resolution of a developed will. * * * There are persons of anxious and susceptible temperament who, having some strain in their work, or some trial in their lives, are prone to take a stimulant, in order to give themselves the necessary nerve; they fly to an artifical aid, which fails not in time to exact the penalty for temporary help which it yields; instead of deliberately exerting their will and gaining thereby advantage which such exertion would give them on another occasion. Like the pawnbroker or usurer, it is a present help at the cost of a frightful interest; and if the habit of recurring to it be formed, the end must be a bankruptcy of health. It is not possible to escape the penalties of weakening the will; sooner or later they are exacted in one way or another, to the uttermost farthing; it is not possible, on the other hand, to overrate the advantages of strengthening the will by a wise exercise; the fruits of such culture are an unfailing help in the time of need.

746. "There are at least five distinct varieties of mental derangement which own alcoholic intemperance as their direct and efficient cause. Nor do other kinds of intemperance fail to play their part in the causation of mental disorders.

747. "Were men and women with one consent to give up alcohol and other excesses, were they to live temperately, soberly and chastely, or what is fundamentally the same thing, holily, that is healthily, there can be no doubt that there would soon be

---

* It would be more correct to say nutriment, as stimulation gives no strength or force,

a diminution in the amount of insanity in the world. It would be lessened in this generation, but still more so in the next generation: a part of which, as matters stand, will be begotten and bred under the pernicious auspices of parental excesses, and the infirmities and diseases engendered by them."

DIFFERENT ALCOHOLIC LIQUORS, AND INSANITY.

748. It may not be amiss to examine the effects of the different intoxicating drinks as producers of insanity. It is very well known that the use of *absinthe* has been most injurious in *France*. Dr. Decaisne says:* "That absinthe in the same dose and strength as alcohol, or *eau de vie*, has the most disastrous influence on the system, and more rapidly produces intoxication."

749. M. Lunier, from the results of his inquiries, has arrived mainly at these conclusions :† 1st. That spirituous liquors, and particularly those made from beet-root and grain, tend in all parts of France, to take the place of wine and cider. 2nd. That while the consumption of alcohol has nearly doubled between 1849 and 1869, the cases of insanity from intemperance have risen 59 per cent. with men, and 52 per cent. with women. 3rd. That in those departments that do not cultivate either wine or cider, but produce alcohol, and where the annual consumption has increased in twenty years from about 7 pints to 12 pints 9 ounces per head, insanity from this cause has risen from 9.72 to 22.31 per cent. with men, and from 2.77 to 4.14 with women. 4th. M. Lunier also says that the alcohol from cider is more pernicious than that from beet-root or grain; that in the DEPARTMENT OF CALVADOS, where the largest proportion of cases of alcoholic insanity exists (56 per cent., men, 10 per cent., women,) a large quantity of alcohol from cider, is produced and consumed. The relative frequency of alcoholic insanity among women who were previously almost exempt from it, has increased fearfully. 5th. In the departments where neither wine, cider nor alcohol were comparatively known, and where the consumption has increased from 3⅛ pints to 5¾ pints, insanity from alcohol has risen from 7.37, to 12.25 per cent. 6th. The departments which cultivate wine and manufacture spirits of wine, but where the consumption, which was 0.53 litre‡ in 1849, and is now but 1 litre per head, alcoholic insanity has only increased from 7.63 to 11.40 per cent. and is comparatively rare among women. In Somme only little alcohol is drank, and scarcely as much in 1869, as in 1849: the number of cases of alcoholic insanity has remained almost stationary among the men, and quite so among the

---

* "Annales Medicoé-psychologiques," for 1872.
† "Gazette Des Hôpiteaux," 1869.
‡ A Litre is equal to about 34¼ fluid ounces.

women. 7th. In the departments where the people drank relatively much white wine, very slightly alcoholized, and little spirit, as in the Vendée, Loire, Inférieure, Côte d'or, alcoholic insanity appears about as common as in those in which they mainly consume alcohol; but in the former, contrary to what happens in the others, the cases of insanity from drink are comparatively rare among women.

750. M. Lunier considers these white wines almost as pernicious as spirits produced from beet-root or grain, as they contain but little tannin. He also concludes that other natural wines, particularly red wines, which have not been *suralcoolises*, rarely determine in chronic alcoholism. 8th. Increase in the number of suicides everywhere in France has followed the increased consumption of alcohol. 9th. As regards the relative effects of *beer* and alcohol, in the North, while the consumption per capita of alcohol has nearly doubled in 20 years (1849 to 1869,) cases of insanity from alcohol have quadrupled among the men, while among the women, who drink a great deal of *beer* and little alcohol, the cases of insanity from drink remain the same.

751. From these observations we learn that the pernicious effects of intoxicating drinks relative to insanity, are in the following order: Alcohol from cider, alcohol from beet-root and grain; cider, wine, beer: that the white wines referred to are much more injurious than the red.

752. Some liquors have an injurious effect, independent of the alcohol they contain. Ale, beer and porter, have their stupefying and narcotic powers much increased by the noxious compounds of bitters, hops, &c., which injure the nerves of the stomach, and sooner or later will extend their effects to the whole nervous system.

753. Every medical man, who has had much practice among malt liquor drinkers, knows, that as a class, they are very prone to palsy and apoplexy from this cause.

THE INCREASE AND NUMBER OF THE INSANE.

754. From a paper read by Dr. Herman, before the St. Petersburg Medical Society, we learn that in St. Petersburg, brandy-shops have increased seven-fold since 1859, and are now in the proportion of one to every 293 persons. In the budget for 1866, the brandy-tax for the entire empire was 115,500,000 silver roubles. The government and individuals made attempts to limit the use of brandy: but they have hitherto yielded to the resistance of the masses, and the danger of damaging the revenue.

One consequence of this increased consumption of brandy, is the increase in the number of acute cases of *delirium tremens* admitted into the St. Petersburg hospitals.

755. During the five years 1861-5, there were treated, in five hospitals, 3,141 cases of *delirium tremens*, 2,721 males and 420 females; the mortality from this disease, in the different hospitals, was from 7.73 to 16.62 per cent. After the trade in liquors was thrown open, in 1863, *delirium tremens* became double in some hospitals, and in others three and four-fold.

756. Of 286 persons in the Lunatic Asylum of Dublin, 115 were known to have been intemperate, and alcoholic drinks the cause of their afflictions.

757. There were admitted into the Lunatic Asylum of Liverpool, in four years, 495 patients; 257 were known to have been made insane by drinking. In the Pauper Lunatic Asylum of Middlesex, England, the patients in one year increased from 825 to between 1100 and 1200, this increase being chiefly caused by gin. Dr. Ellis,* resident physician of the County Lunatic Asylum, Middlesex, said that out of 38 individuals admitted in 1833, and reported as *recent cases*, 19 were known to be drunkards.

758. Boyle attributes to the abuse of ardent spirits, one-third of the mental diseases he had observed. Of the 1,079 insane admitted at Becêtre from 1808 to 1813, he finds 126 cases were caused by the habit of drinking: of 264 cases of insanity observed in "SALPETRIERE," in women, 26 were caused, according to ESQUIROL, by the abuse of wine. Casper says, "That one-third of the insanity of the lower classes is caused by the use of brandy." M. M. Deboutville and Parchappe found, that for the period of 18 years, between the 11th of July, 1825, and December 31st, 1843, 28 per cent. of insanity was from the same cause. M. Morel gives 200 cases out of 1000 whose mental disease was caused by intemperance. Of 12,007 cases in England, 1,799, or nearly twenty per cent., was from the use of liquors.

759. Dr. Sheppard, Superintendent of Colney Hatch Asylum, said in a letter to the LONDON TIMES, that 35 to 40 per cent. of insanity resulted directly or indirectly from intoxicating drinks.

760. The following statistics will serve to shows the progress of *Alcoholism:* from 1826 to 1835, of the 1,557 inmates in Charenten Insane Asylum, 134 cases, or 8 per cent. was caused by ardent spirits; from 1857 to 1864, of the 1,146 patients admitted to the same asylum, 277, or 24 per cent., were drunkards. M. Contesse,

---

* Parliamentary Evidence, 1834, p. 46.

at Bicêtre, found 1,000 cases of alcoholism, out of the 5238 cases of insanity. That from 1855 to 1862, the proportion of inebriates increased from 12.78 per cent. to 25.24 per cent. Dr. W. A. F. Browne, examined into 57,520 cases of insanity in various countries: of this grand total, 10,717 cases, or nearly one-fifth of the whole, were the result of intoxication. Of 5,721 cases admitted into the asylums of Scotland, in ten years, from 1840-49, 923 were also caused by intemperance. During the same period, of 9,033 admitted into the English asylums, 937 were due to the same cause.

761. Thus we find that more than one-fifth of the cases of insanity reported in the asylums of England and Scotland, were due to intoxicating drinks.

762. By the returns of the Pennsylvania Hospital for the Insane, during a period of 28 years, of the 5,315 cases admitted into that institution, 389 cases, or 13.9 per cent., were caused by intemperance; 357 cases were males, and 22 females.

763. By the United States Census report of 1870, there were 37,432 insane persons: or an average of one insane person for every 1,032 of the population.

764. This we may safely say does not comprise all the insane in the United States. Insanity being considered by some persons more than a misfortune—a disgrace, many insane persons are only known to exist by their relatives, and a very few intimate friends. Hence the difficulty of obtaining the number of insane, by the government.

765. The State that makes the nearest approximation to an accurate census of its insane population, is Massachusetts.

766. In 1854 the commissioners whose duty it was to collect the statistics, requested every physician to give the name of every insane person, within his knowledge. There are few or no families, whose domestic condition is not known to some physician; so that few or none failed to be reported, and the names enabled the commissioners to avoid duplicating.

767. The report of the two State censuses of 1855 and 1865, and the three United States censuses of 1850, 1860, and 1870, gave as the average number of insane, one in five hundred and seventy-two of the population. The commissioners' report was 2,375 in one million, and the census reported 1750 in the same number of people.

768. The commissioners found 28.14 per cent. more than the families revealed to the officers of the State or nation.

769. Hence it will be safe to add 28.14 per cent. in the ab-

sence of any other standard, to all returns of insanity, to arrive at anything like a correct number.

770. If to the number of insane reported in the last census returns, we add the 28.14 per cent. for omissions, it will give as the number of insane persons in the United States, 47,965, or very near an average of one for 806 of the population.

771. It is still more difficult to arrive at the number of insane persons, made so by alcohol, than at the aggregate number of the insane; for there is the same unwillingness of friends to reveal the cause of the insanity, even where they really know that it is intemperance.

772. Hence the insanity caused by alcoholic drinks can only be approximated by the reports of asylums, and the testimony of physicians.

773. About the year 1830, before the temperance question had claimed much consideration, insanity had increased two-thirds in twenty years in England, when there was one insane person in every 1,000 of the population; in Wales one in 800; in Scotland, one in 574. This may be justly ascribed to the general use of ardent spirits.

774. From the reports of the superintendents of the Pennsylvania Hospital for the Insane, the Massachusetts State Hospital at Worcester, and the Bloomingdale Asylum, New York, the nine principle causes of insanity are as follows:

Causes of Insanity.	No. of cases in Pennsyl. Hospital for Insane.	No. of cases in Mass. State Hospital.	No. of cases in Bloomingdale Asylum.	Total of cases in the three Institutions.	Per cent.
Ill-health,	601	695	237	1,533	32
Intemperance,	243	194	117	554	11
Grief at loss of friends,	193	72	43	308	6
Puerperal state,	152	141	99	392	8
Loss of property,	140	140	133	413	8
Religious excitement,	137	296	93	526	11
Domestic troubles,	87	413	65	565	11
Disappointed affection,	57	116	38	211	4½
Masturbation,	50	270	37	357	7½
Totals,	1,660	2,337	862	4,859	

775. By the above table it is seen that more than 11 per cent. of all the cases of insanity in those three institutions is directly caused by intemperance. To merely take into consideration the cases given in the reports as being thus caused, we shall not arrive at anything like an approximate estimate of the number; for the friends will in most cases strive to keep out of sight, if possi-

ble, the drinking habits of the subjects of insanity. Then again, the habits of an individual may not be what is generally called intemperate, yet he may be so continually under the influence of alcoholic drinks that the nervous and vital forces are so depressed and injured that some very slight circumstance, embraced under some one of the other causes of insanity, may produce *mental alienation*, and the causes may be given as being "ill-health," "Loss of property," &c., &c., while in reality it was alcohol.

776. The loss of property, and other reverses of fortune, are often the result of intemperance. Hence the difficulty amounting almost to impossibility, of arriving at the real cause of insanity.

777. Taking into consideration all the surrounding circumstances attending the use of intoxicating drinks, and the essential nature of alcohol, it will be safe to say that one-half of the cases ascribed to ill-health, or 16 per cent. and one-half of the cases of domestic trouble, or five per cent., are directly or indirectly chargeable to alcoholic drinks; then, the cases of insanity due directly or indirectly to intoxicating liquors, will be 9 per cent. directly from intemperance; 16 per cent. from ill-health; and domestic trouble, 5 per cent. or a total of not less than 30 per cent. or from 11,229 to 14,389 insane persons in the United States, whose afflictions are directly or indirectly due to the use of alcohol.

778. This is evidently no exaggeration, for it is much below the general average in other countries, under similar circumstances of race, habits, &c.

779. The following is an analysis of the causes of the mental affections of 83 out of 95 patients admitted into Liverpool Asylum in 14 months:

Drinking	50	Fit	2
Accident	1	Paralytic	4
Asthma	1	Pride	10
Consumption	1	Hereditary	12
Losses	2	Unknown	12*

780. From this report we find that more than one-half are directly from drinking, and it will be safe to say that at least 7 out of the 12 hereditary cases were due to the same cause; or 57 cases as the effects of alcohol, leaving but 26 cases for all the other known causes combined. Of these 26 cases, some of them, there can be no doubt, are secondary causes, connected directly or indirectly with alcoholics.

781. "Fits," it is well known, are entailed upon the children of drunkards. The daughters of drunkards are often *nervous*

---

* Parliamentary Report on Drunkenness, page 369.

and *hysterical;* and paralysis, we have already seen, is caused by the free and excessive use of drink; and it is therefore very probable that one case of the 'fits' and two cases of 'paralysis' were remotely due to alcohol.

782. There is another fact that should be well remembered: that the insane and idiots of a country are generally in proportion to the drunkenness of the people. For instance, Scotland is said to be a more drunken country than England, and we find a greater proportion of insanity. From the returns of the Scottish clergy, some few years ago, it was ascertained that the average number of insane persons, in every thousand of the population, was two and a half, or one in 400.

783. In Ireland, until Father Matthew awakened the people to the effects of alcoholic liquors, it was about 1 in 5000; in Scotland from returns of the clergy there were 2½ to 1,000 persons;* while in England and Wales it was about 1 in 496. By Dr. Crawford, in Richmond Lunatic Asylum, Dublin, in 1829, of 286 patients there were no less than 115 whose insanity was caused by drinking whiskey; of whom 58 were males, and 57 females; and he further says, one out of two of the patients of the asylum have become insane in consequence of ardent spirits.

784. It must be clear to every one, that the thirty per cent. allowed for *insanity* produced by alcoholic drinks, in the United States, must be below the real average. But even to estimate the production of insanity by alcohol at this evidently low rate, the 14,387, or even 11,229 cases of insanity produced by it, calls, in its national bearing alone, for the grave consideration of both legislators and people. It must therefore be apparent to every one that no question, political or financial, is so important, or so much affects the welfare and prosperity of our people, as that of the effects of alcoholic drinks upon their mental and social condition, and the future of our country and race.

DIPSOMANIA.

785. The various forms of insanity may be caused by habits of intemperance, without any previous existing predisposition to nervous disease.

786. Each special type of insanity depends mainly on individual peculiarity.

787. While dipsomania, though apparently due to vice only, is rarely unassociated with inherited neurosis.

---

* See "Bacchus," by Dr. Grindrod, p. 528, American edition. 1848.

788. DIPSOMANIA is a term employed to signify an insatiable desire for intoxicating drinks; which assumes three forms, viz., the Acute, Periodic, and Continuous.

789. In the *acute* form the person formerly temperate and sober, suddenly commences to drink to excess, and soon becomes careless and indifferent to all claims of business or family, and seems as if determined to drink himself to death as soon as possible.

790. The *periodic* form is mostly connected with some hereditary taint of insanity, intemperance, or injury of the head. The victim is abstemious and correct in his habits, and often after weeks or months of abstinence from alcoholic stimulants, becomes by degrees restless and uneasy, and begins to drink until he is intoxicated. He awakes from an uneasy and restless sleep, and returns to the intoxicating cup; and continues this course for weeks. Then a stage of depression comes on, and an utter loathing for the drink, and of himself for yielding to his appetite; but after a few months the paroxysms return: the same scenes are enacted, and the wretched experience is only too certain to be repeated. From these alternate periods of sobriety and drunkenness, unless they are checked, he falls a victim to the physical effects of intemperance, becomes a maniac, or an imbecile, or may run into the next form of the disease.

791. The *continuous* dipsomania, is the most common, the intemperance being associated with other vices, and always with the active form of moral insanity. It is distinguished by an amount of acute cunning, hypocrisy, and fearless lying. Indeed the victim will disregard every impediment, sacrifice comfort and reputation, withstand all the claims of affection, consign his family to disgrace and misery, and in fact deny himself all the common necessaries, in order to gratify the insane desire for drink. Without the drink, he is morose, fretful, disgusted with himself, and dissatisfied with everything. He is weak, tremulous, and incapable of exerting either his mind or body. His first feeling is a desire for the drink, with a dose of which he recovers a certain degree of strength, and feels comparatively comfortable.

792. Few hours of the day pass without the cravings for alcoholics, so that he drinks until he is intoxicated. Thus will continue the morning misery, and night's intoxication, until death or imbecility overtakes him.

The only chance for cure for this disease, says Dr. Carpenter, is attention to health, and abstinence from intoxicating drinks.

INTEMPERANCE A DISEASE.

793. By considering the morbid effects produced by alcoholic liquors upon the stomach, the blood, brain and tissues, it can readily be inferred that intemperance may become a disease in every sense of the term.

794. When the pathology of the alcoholic disease is clearly understood, when the drunkards, and others who have an intense craving for intoxicating drinks, are recognized as victims of disease, as they really are, we may expect to see more interest manifested, more efforts made to prevent and cure drunkards; not only by the temperance reformers, and by the medical profession, but by the law-makers, and by the masses. Now every one can understand that when a man has *delirium tremens*, he is in a diseased condition; but it seems to require more medical experience to discover that the intemperate use of strong drinks is a disease, and one that can only be cured by entire abstinence from the alcoholics that produced it.

795. When the use of alcohol has caused other derangements of the system besides that of intemperance, the aid of a physician is sought; but the fact not being generally known that the use of liquor is the effect as well as the cause of the disease,* the medical treatment of the habit is almost entirely overlooked. The fact that intemperance is one of the evil consequences of the consumption of alcoholic liquors, is known to every one, and also that the absolute specific for this disease is abstinence now, at once and forever, from the drink; is understood and advocated by temperance reformers.

796. This simple remedy has proved effectual in tens and hundreds of thousands of cases, many of which were apparently hopeless. Yet there are many persons, who from hereditary predisposition, derived from drinking parents or ancestors: or from the derangement of their system, by the use of liquor, are so infirm of purpose, or so much diseased, that they have not strength of will sufficient to enable them to abstain from drink, if by any means it can be obtained.

797. Now we are convinced that intemperance is as much a disease, as a sin; which in many cases, and indeed in all cases is induced by imbibing, at first, a very moderate quantity of alcoholic liquors, and very often in the form of beer or light wine, and even by home-made wine, pressed to the lips of a beloved child, by a fond mother; for the effects will be the same, however ignorant she *may* be of the evil she is inflicting upon her darling.

---

* The disease being established by the use of alcoholics, the victim is impelled to drink to allay the intense cravings; hence the use of liquor is the effect, as well as the cause of the disease.

The habit once established in the constitution, like any other disease, works independent of the *will* of the victim; and though he may, for a time, refuse to gratify his appetite, he cannot control the cravings that give rise to it.

798. There are in the medical profession, those who ignore the idea that it is a disease; for if they did not, they would often pause before prescribing such a dangerous remedy as alcohol.

799. We cannot be surprised that alcohol should produce so much mischief, when we consider, that the blood thus poisoned, the brain must cease to receive a proper supply of healthy nutrition, and thus becomes incapable of the proper performance of its functions.

800. The evil effects produced on the brain in this way, are intensified by the direct action of alcohol upon that organ; which is none the less injurious because of the special affinity of alcohol for the brain tissue, leading it to accumulate there. Hence it is impossible, if not absurd, to suppose that the mind can be preserved in a healthy state, so long as the brain is under the pernicious influence of alcohol; for the mind can only perform its healthy normal function, while the brain is in a healthy and normal state. But it may be said that the mischief referred to is the result of abuse; that small doses do not produce it, and that we must not simply avoid a remedy, because some do not exercise proper self-control in its use. To which we say, that the essential tendency of alcohol, even when given in small doses, is to produce all the results referred to; and we know, as a matter of experience, as well as of observation, that on account of some constitutional idiosyncracies, even very small doses are quite sufficient to produce in certain individuals the very worst effects named.

801. The experience of almost every physician must have furnished him with many instances of the recommendation of a *simple glass of beer*, perhaps at dinner, to "*strengthen and tone up*," the patient, ending in the production, or the reviving of physical craving for drink that has led to the physical as well as mental wreck of the unhappy persons. There are not many physicians, at the present day, who believe in the strengthening and tonic power of alcohol, who cannot furnish some such cases in their practice. It is in vain to ask a man to exercise self-control, and at the same time administer to him an agent whose nature, and physical properties, as well as psychological effects on his system deprive him of the power to exercise that virtue. These reflections should silence forever any arguments that the moderate or (so-called) judicious use of alcohol is harmless; which are arguments presented without thought on the part of the

person offering them, and are as injurious as they are false to science, reason, and experience.

802. Little do persons know of the danger connected with the daily or occasional use of those beverages that poison the brain, and subvert the intellectual powers. How often do men think themselves strong; that they are able to govern themselves, and can distinguish between the use and abuse, when they know not the power of drink, nor their own weakness.

803. By the annual report of the Board of Commissioners of Charities and Correction, for 1870, of New York, there were admitted during the year, into the Inebriate Asylum, 1,641 patients. The time since the opening of the institution has been too short to fully determine the value of the treatment as a cure for inebriates. The Report says:

804. "That it may be instrumental in the reformation of those who are earnestly desirous to reform, the experience of the past year has demonstrated; but it will probably be found that the sanguine expectations of the more ardent advocates of inebriate asylums, will hardly be justified by the results. Habitual drunkenness is a moral disease (also physical,) for which, as in other forms of licentiousness, there is no specific, except the resolute determination of the patient.

805. "So far as freedom from temptation is secured, the asylum may be regarded as a means of cure; but the mere isolation, or the temporary and compulsive abstinence from spirituous liquors, rarely provokes the desire of amendment. And even in some cases where reformation of the patients has seemed to be complete, they have, on their return to their former associations, lapsed into intemperate practices. Those addicted to drunkenness are in general too infirm in purpose to persist in their resolution of amendment, and this infirmity of purpose is one of the sad consequences of this vice. They are impatient for the term of their detention to expire, that they may again indulge their appetite. For the small number who desire to abstain from inebriety but cannot, and for such, as by their excesses disgrace their families and friends, the asylums are fitting retreats. But for the lasting cure of confirmed inebriates, it is apprehended they will be found of little practical value."

806. R. B. Grindrod, M. D., L. L. B., author of "Bacchus," a prize essay published in 1838, said: "I am more than ever convinced, that the view so long ago enunciated in "Bacchus," is correct; that drunkenness is a disease, physical as well as moral, and consequently requires physical as well as moral remedies. Until this view has been thoroughly ventilated and established, I am afraid that our efforts, in particular among the members of our Christian churches, will be comparatively fruitless."

PART IX.

ALCOHOL—ITS EFFECTS ON PROGENY.

807. Though we may be able to estimate approximately the influences of drinking habits as the causes of vice, pauperism, crime, insanity, etc., yet after all, we can only reach an imperfect calculation of the waste of human energy and material; but it is utterly impossible to approximately estimate the moral as well as the physical evils produced by them.

808. The part most overlooked, because least obvious, is the amount of the disease, weakness and imbecility that is transmitted from parents to their offspring, by the use of alcoholics. Children frequently inherit the diseases of their parents, and where the inheritance does not take the form of absolute disease, it often appears in defective mental or physical organizations, or in feeble development; and such feebleness and defect predispose to intemperance as well as to disease.

809. Aside from the expense resulting from the use of intoxicating drinks, it is a crime of the deepest dye to authorize by law a traffic in an article that destroys the minds of men and women, converting them into maniacs, and sinking them beneath the level of brutes. Society sows the seed and must reap a harvest, not only of insanity, but of idiocy, one of the sins that is visited upon the children of the intemperate to the third and fourth generation; for alcohol not only changes men and women of mind to demented beings; but contracts the vital nerve powers of the infant before it sees the light of day or breathes the life-giving oxygen. These unfortunate ante-natal victims of alcohol, live but to embitter the lives of their parents, a plague, and a mock to civilization, and an impediment in the world's progress to a higher, nobler state of society and human advancement.

810. The doctrine that drunkenness is transmitted to offspring is as old at least as Aristotle, for he said, that a "drunken woman brings forth children like unto herself;" and Plutarch affirms that "one drunkard begets another."

811. Dr. Caldwell says: "By habits of intemperance parents not only degrade and ruin themselves, but transmit the elements

of like degradation and ruin to their posterity." The constitutions of the children of intemperate parents are often physically and mentally weak and lax; they are predisposed to crave stimulants, often become drunkards, and transmit to their offspring, should they have any, still weaker mental organizations and more lax constitutions, and entail upon them liability to mental and physical diseases and a predisposition to their own vices.

812. The free use of intoxicating drinks, even if it does not produce drunkenness, is often sufficient to produce a predisposition in children to intemperance and various diseases of body and mind; and a continuance of the cause will transmit from generation to generation, feebleness, or imbecility of purpose, dullness of intellect, vicious habits, and deterioration of the race.

813. This can be seen in every race, in every country. No large city but presents numerous illustrations and evidences of this truth. The criminal and dangerous classes of every society are of this class, for the vast majority of them are but feebly organized, mentally or physically.

HEREDITARY EFFECTS OF INTOXICATING DRINKS.

814. M. Morel, a distinguished French writer, gives the history of four generations of a family. *First Generation.*—The father was an habitual drunkard, and was killed in a public-house brawl. *Second Generation.*—The son inherited his father's habits, which gave rise to attacks of mania, terminating in paralysis and death. *Third Generation.*—The grandson was strictly sober, but was full of hypochondriacal and imaginary fear of persecutions, etc., and had homicidal tendencies. *Fourth Generation.*—The fourth in descent had very limited intelligence, and had an attack of madness when sixteen years old, terminating in stupidity, nearly amounting to idiocy. Here we perceive the persistence of the taint, in the fact, that not even a generation of absolute sobriety will avert the fatal issue.

815. Dr. Yellowlees says:* "I believe the mere habit of intemperance in the individual rarely produces this condition (*dipsomania,*) but that it is usually a result and development of the baneful heritage entailed on their descendants by intemperate progenitors; the vice of one generation becoming the weakness of the next, liable to be invoked at any time by the present vice and then bring a double curse.

816. "The inherited tendency to intemperance may itself

---

* "Insanity and Intemperance," by D. Yellowlees, M. D., British Medical Journal, Oct. 4, 1873.

prompt to the habits which develop the disease; or these habits may be easily acquired in social life, the patient thoughtlessly tempting his fate, or, again, the inherited weakness may be evoked by brain disturbance from quite other causes, such as injury, sun-stroke, or moral shock.

817. "A host of facts might be brought forward to prove that drunkenness in parents, especially that form of drunkenness known as *dipsomania*, which breaks out from time to time in uncontrollable paroxysms, is a cause of idiocy, suicide or insanity in their offspring. It would seem to be truly a nervous disease, a kind of insanity. In its outbreaks it displays the periodicity which is a common character of nervous diseases, and exhibits its kinship to insanity, not only by the fact when occurring in one generation, it may become the occasion of mental derangement, or suicide in the next generation, but conversely by the fact that *insanity* in the parent may occasion *dipsomania* in the offspring."*

818. Dr. Elam says:† "All the passions appear to be distinctly hereditary: anger, fear, jealousy, libertinage, gluttony, drunkenness—all are liable to be transmitted to the offspring, especially if both parents are alike affected; and this, as has often been proved, not by force of example or education merely, but by direct constitutional inheritance.

819. "One of the most important of these, and the most easily illustrated, is that of the heritage of drunkenness. *Ebrii gignunt ebrios*, says PLUTARCH. Gall relates that of a Russian family, where father and grandfather had both died prematurely from the effects of intoxication, and the grandson manifested, from the age of five years, the most decided taste for strong liquors. M. Giron related an instance where the tendency was transmitted through the mother." A recent writer in the Psychological Journal, says:

820. "The most startling problem connected with intemperance is that not only does it affect the health, morals, and intelligence, of its votaries, but they also inherit the fatal tendency, and feel a craving for the very beverages which have acted as poisons on their systems from the commencement of their being."

821. M. Morel says, "I have never seen the patient cured of his propensity, whose tendencies to drink were derived from the hereditary predisposition given to him by his parents."

822. Before the parliamentary commission of Great Britain, in 1872, Mr. William Collins stated as a well-established physiolo-

---

* "Responsibility in Mental Diseases," page 43. Maudsley.
† On "Natural Heritage."

gical fact, that the drunkard's appetite, when once formed, never becomes completely extinct, but adheres to him through life. Dr. Hutchinson said: "I have seen only one case of (chronic alcoholism) completely cured, and that after a seclusion of two years' duration. In general it is not cured, and no sooner is the patient liberated than he manifests all the symptoms of the disease. Paradoxical as it may appear to be, such individuals are sane only when confined in an asylum."

823. A clergyman said, in his testimony to the Committee of the Lower House of the Convocation of Canterbury, "I have been directing my attention for some years to the more permanent effects of drinking habits, as tending to produce a depraved or debilitated offspring, not only making the parent '*nequiores*' but '*max daluros progeniem vitiosiorem.*' I have collected some very curious facts on this point, tending to prove that not only lunacy, but also other obscure diseases of the brain, may be traced to intemperance of parents." Another clergyman says, "My parish exhibits a high rate of mortality, chiefly among children, who are very often born in an imperfectly organized condition, and badly nourished afterwards, in consequence of the intemperance of the parents. I am continually called upon to sign papers for lunatics through drink." To the Committee, a superintendant of a Lunatic Asylum said: "the proportion of cases traceable to intemperance, cannot, I think, be much under 50 per cent. To these must be added an unascertainable number of idiots, imbeciles, &c., the offspring of intemperate parents, in whom the sins of the fathers are visited on the children." Dr. A. Mitchell[*] said, "I think it quite certain that the children of habitual drunkards, are in larger proportion idiotic than other children, and a larger proportion themselves habitual drunkards; they are also in larger proportion liable to the ordinary forms of acquired insanity, which comes on later in life."

824. Dr. Howe reported to the Massachusetts Legislature, "That the habits of the parents of 300 idiots had been learned, and that 145 of them were known to be habitual drunkards." He estimates that three-fourths of the idiots born are the offspring of intemperate parents.

825. M. Lunier estimated, that in great cities, at least, the parents of 50 per cent. of the idiots and imbeciles were notoriously drunkards. He also considers that the majority of the "children born of parents when drunk, or who are constitutionally drunkards, are weak in some way or other."

826. Dr. J. Ray says:[†] "Another potent agency in vitiating the quality of the brain is habitual intemperance, and the effect

---

[*] See Report of Committee on Habitual Drunkards, (House of Commons,) 1872.
[†] "Mental Hygiene," page 44.

is far oftener witnessed in the offspring than in the drunkard himself. His habits may induce an attack of insanity, where the predisposition exists; but he generally escapes with nothing worse than the loss of some of his natural vigour and hardihood of mind. In the offspring, however, on whom the consequences of the parental vice may be visited, to the third, if not the fourth generation, the cerebral disorder may take the form of intemperance, or idiocy, or insanity, or vicious habits, or impulses to crime, or some minor mental obliquities. The frequency with which intemperance is witnessed, both in parent and child, has come to be regarded not as accident merely, but as the result of hereditary cerebral defect. There have been cases enough, the circumstances of which excluded the influence of vicious example and training, and rendered no explanation possible but this. * * * As a cause of idiocy in the next succeeding generation, the potency of gross intemperance has been placed beyond a doubt. * ** The transmitted effect of intemperance may also appear in the form of a propensity to vicious courses, or a dullness of moral perception, or irresistible impulses to crime. One child may exhibit one or more of these traits, and another may be insane or idiotic, the former no less than the latter manifesting the legitimate effects of the parent's vice. The inmate of the penitentiaries, whose history is thoroughly known, present many examples of the operation of this pathological law."

827. E. Esquirol* gives the case of one Brikton. She was the offspring of a healthy mother, and a father who was habitually intoxicated. Her two brothers were never capable of learning to read. She came into the world in a pitiful condition, and it was only after two years nursing that she learned how to find the breast of her mother. In Combe's "Constitution of Man," there is a most striking case of an idiot who at the time was six years old. The only sign he gave of his wants was a wild shriek. Both the parents of the child were healthy and intelligent; one at least was habitually sober, but both were drunk at the time of inception and the result was this idiot offspring. In the town of Suffolk, England, two cousins married and lived on a small property. Their usual occupation was muddling themselves with alcoholics, not often, perhaps, actually drunk, but always more or less under their influence. In this state they usually went to bed. They had *five children*, and all were idiots of the *worst class*. That is, not only defective in intellectual capacity, but inherited from their senseless parents an excess of the animal propensities.†

828. The wife of the amiable clergyman of S——, in Staffordshire, Eng., was so addicted to drunkenness, that she had frequently to be carried to bed. Every effort of her distressed hus-

---

* "Mental Maladies," p. 489. 1845.
† See Levison's "Hereditary Tendency of Drunkenness," page 33.

band failed to reclaim her; till at last premature death cut short her career. She was the mother of *three idiotic children.*

829. Wm. Smith,* Governor of Ripon Prison, said: "Drunkards have generally come of parents who have led bad lives. In fact I have one case in particular, of a woman who has been in different jails 33 times, and she is now serving penal servitude for seven years. She had a drunken father and mother, was a drunkard herself, and had been drinking when she committed the felony." Dr. F. Winslow, said: "I was looking at some statistics the other day in a list of criminals; there was a father a drunkard, a grandfather a drunkard, a grandmother an idiot, and in the whole line there were in that family, drunkards, criminals, and idiots; all the forms of vice were hereditarily transmitted."

830. Dr. Macgill, Surgeon of Glasgow Police Station, says: "During sixteen years, had 600 cases of insanity from intemperate habits, or 30 or 40 cases annually, out of 12,000 intemperate persons brought before him."

831. Dr. F. E. Anstie, in his evidence before the Committee on Habitual Drunkards, said: "Of the kind of drinking which is entirely paroxysmal, it is a disease." That is not a fancied distinction. I know of several such cases. These persons are children of families where invariably, or almost invariably, insanity is hereditary; very often drinking has been hereditary in a marked degree. "The tendency to drink is a disease of the brain, which is inherited. Where drinking has been strong in both parents I think that it is a physical certainty that it will be traced in the children." "I have no doubt that many parents who were never drunk, in the old port-wine drinking period, have transmitted very unstable nervous systems to their children."

832. Dr. Richardson says:†—"The solemnest fact of all bearing upon the physical deterioration and upon the mental aberration produced by alcohol, is, that the mischiefs inflicted by it on man through his own act and deed cannot fail to be transmitted to those who descend from him, who are thus irresponsibly afflicted. Amongst the many inscrutable designs of nature, none is more manifested than this, that physical vice, like physical feature, and physical virtue, descends in line. But not one of the transmitted wrongs, physical or mental, is more certainly passed on to those yet unborn, than the wrongs which are inflicted by alcohol. Many specific diseases engendered by it in the parent are too often stamped in the child; while the propensity to its use descends also, making the evil interest compound in its terrible totality."

---

* Evidence before Select Committee of British Parliament, on "Habitual Drunkards," June, 1872.

† "Diseases of Modern Life," page 272.

PHYSICAL DEGENERACY IN CHILDREN BY INTEMPERANCE OF PARENTS.

833. The Lancet says: "A novel point in the consideration of this subject was brought under the notice of the PATHOLOGICAL SOCIETY by Dr. Langden Downe. This gentleman exhibited a case of arrest of development and growth in a child of five years of age, who had only the intellectual condition of one of nine months. She weighed 22 lbs., and measured 2 feet 3 inches. There was no deformity, but the child preserved its infantile character. Dr. Downe called attention to this case as a typical one of a species of degeneracy of which he had seen several examples. They all possessed the same physical and mental peculiarities; they formed, in fact, a natural family. He had known them to live twenty-two years, still remaining permanent infants, symmetrical in form, just able to stand by the side of a chair, to utter a few monosyllabic sounds, and to be amused with childish toys. Dr. Downe (who naturally, from large and rare experience, gained at Earlswood, speaks with peculiar authority on such a matter) has found so close a resemblance between the instances, even to the extent of facial expression and contour, that he had been led to regard this variety of degeneracy to have unity of cause. In several cases he has had strong grounds for holding the opinion that these children were procreated during the alcoholic intoxication of one or both progenitors. In the case presented to the society there were no antecedent hereditary causes of degeneracy to be discovered. The first child was healthy; then the husband became an habitual drunkard, and there is reason to believe that the second and third children were begotten during intoxication; and they were both cases of this peculiar arrest of growth and development. The husband then entered on an industrious and sober career, and the fourth child, now fifteen months old, is bright and normal in every respect.

834. Dr. Downe pointed out that these cases were an entirely different class from those which arise from being the offspring of parents who had become degenerate from chronic alcoholism. The question here broached is a very important one for the physician and the philanthropist.

835. Dr. F. R. Lees, speaking of the effects of alcohol on the *liver*, said, "And recollect whatever injury you inflict upon this organ, in your posterity the curse descends; and as is the father, so are the children. I know the delusion in reference to this matter, and I wish we could get rid of it."

836. "It is not long ago, that a tall stout man, now happily a reclaimed drunkard, invited me to his house. He had had

thirteen children, and only one was living. 'Doctor,' said he, 'how is it all my children have died of decline when young? None of them reached more than twenty. My wife wasn't an unhealthy woman, and see how stout I am.' I asked him a question, and saw at once. He had been for many years an excessive drinker. He had a giant's constitution, which apparently prevented him from being destroyed, but drinking had destroyed the beginnings of life, so that he transmitted a corrupted type to his children. *He* was saved, for a while, by reason of strength, while his children perished.

837. "Doctors themselves are blind on this point. I recollect lecturing some years ago in St. Ives, and taking supper afterwards with some of the chief persons in the town, three or four doctors and two lawyers. A doctor said he thought I exaggerated the matter. I said, 'Why do you think so, sir?' 'Oh,' says he, 'we have such cases of free drinkers, who nevertheless, are in good health.' I said, 'Have you any particular person in view?' 'I have Mr. W., a friend of mine. Only the other day he told me he had drank at least a bottle of wine a day for the last fifty years.' 'Well, of course it is good wine he gets, because he is wealthy?' 'Yes, none of your adulterated stuff.' 'Well, is he a fine-looking man?' 'Oh, very! We have not a finer in the town.' 'What is your argument?' 'That wine cannot be so bad a thing as you represent, when a man is so hale at eighty, after taking so much drink.' And the rest of the doctors looked hard at me, 'Now for your opinion,' said the lawyer. 'Well,' I said, 'I cannot give you an opinion without knowing the *facts*. This gentleman lives in a good situation?' 'The best in town; the only eminence in the district.' 'He lives well, and not extravagantly?' 'Just so.' 'And what sort of a lady is his wife?' 'Oh, she is a very moderate woman.' 'Pretty healthy?' 'Yes.' 'Well, I should think, then you have not much to do in this family?' 'O yes,' said the doctor, 'but I have.' Proceeding on this hint, I asked, 'What family have they?' 'Oh, they have had eleven.' 'Indeed! how many have they now?' 'Six.' 'That is very singular,' said I, 'for I suppose you believe in the law that like produces like? Is there any more certain principle in physiology than that good food makes good blood, good blood, good structures, and good structure transmits good structure? When the parents are healthy the children must be healthy. 'I cannot deny that,' said he. 'Now,' I replied, 'there is something to be accounted for; six children are living, five are dead. But what is the constitution of the six?' 'Oh,' said he, 'for that matter, they are hipped, *nervous*.' 'Oh,' says a lady over the table, 'you know Miss —— was touched in the head.' 'And Mr. George,' says another, 'was in the Asylum.' 'And Mr. William you know is certainly queer,' says a third. 'Gentlemen,' I said, 'without going further; nothing is more certain than that *some great* and *serious*

law of *life must have been violated;* and upon the face of it, the one bottle of wine a day for fifty years may have been the agent. *That is my case.*' A silence followed. The sequel of this story I did not learn until many years after. One of the sons died in a low despairing state of lunacy. A granddaughter subsequently consulted me as to her health, which was bad, when I learned that her grandfather died of apoplexy at eighty-three! And fifteen years later, being in the house where this conversation occurred, I was told that the last grandson had spent all his money, but a small pittance, on which he had retired to the country town."

838. "When chronic diseases," says Darwin, "arise from the use of ardent spirits, they are liable to become hereditary, even to the third generation: and if the cause is continued, to increase till the family becomes extinct."

839. Intemperance is increasing especially among females. It is stated by medical gentlemen and others, that even among the upper and wealthy classes of England, female intemperance has greatly increased within the last ten or fifteen years. From the evidence presented, this increase is due to the increased facilities of obtaining wine and other intoxicating drinks, by granting licenses for their sale by grocers, confectioners, &c. Within the last twenty-five years, there has been an increase of drinking by females, and consequent intemperance in the United States and in Great Britain. As a result of this, there will certainly be still greater liability to intemperance in the next and even succeeding generations, unless some great change is made in our land relative to the traffic in alcoholic liquors.

840. "It is very clear," says Dr. Chambers, "that alcohol, taken in the dram-drinker's fashion, in small divided doses, by no means increases metamorphosis. It rather tends to diminish it, and this diminution is not sudden or immediate, but is more and more, for a certain period, till the retention reaches a point at which a critical discharge takes place in healthy persons."

841. Again he says, "I have never yet met a forenoon tippler, even though he never got drunk in his life, without a condition of stomach which most infallibly shortened his days." Though the effects of moderate tippling may not be so apparent as downright intemperance on the individual, yet "his sin will find him out."

842. The effects of injury upon the mind and body may not always show themselves on the drinker, yet we very much doubt if ever the progeny entirely escapes the effects in one form or other. They may be manifested in insanity, intemperance, or with a tendency to take the form of some disease of the stomach, liver, bowels, lungs, or other organs and tissues; for it is thus

imposssible that an agent so foreign to the animal economy can be habitually used without inflicting injury on its delicate tissues.

843. H. P. Ayres, M. D., of Fort Wayne, Indiana, in relation to the cause of imbecile and idiotic children, says;* " Of three hundred and fifty-nine idiots, the condition of whose progenitors was ascertained, ninety-nine were the children of drunkards. But this does not tell the whole story, by any means. By drunkard is meant a person who is a notorious and habitual sot. Many persons who are habitually intemperate, do not get this name even now, much less would they have done so twenty-five or thirty years ago. A quarter of a century ago, a man might go to his bed every night muddled and sleepy with the effects of alcohol, and still not be called an intemperate man. The men who in that day, abstained from alcoholic drinks, were remarkable exceptions to the general rule. They would be known. We shall come nearer to a true estimate, therefore, by ascertaining how many such there were. By pretty careful inquiry, with an especial view of ascertaining the number of idiots of the lowest class whose parents were known to be intemperate persons, it is found that not one-quarter can be so considered." The effect of habitual use of alcohol, even in moderate quantities, seems to be to lymphatize the whole bodily organization; that is, to diminish the proportion of the fibrous part of the body—that which gives enduring strength—and to make the lymphatic or the watery particles to abound in all tissues. The children of persons so lymphatized, are apt to be of the scrofulous character above described; and their children again are apt to be feeble in body and weak in mind. Idiots, and simpletons, are common among the progeny of such persons, either in the first or second generation. Thus directly and indirectly, alcohol is productive of a great proportion of the idiocy which now burdens the commonwealth. If, moreover, one considers how many children of intemperate parents there are, who, without being idiots, are deficient in bodily and mental energy, and predisposed by their very organization to have cravings for alcoholic stimulants, it will be seen what an immense burden the drinker of one generation throws upon the succeeding one. Many a parent, by habitual stimulus applied to his own nervous system, forms and fashions his child in such wise, that he is more liable, much more, to be made a drunkard, by the ordinary temptations of life, than the child of a temperate man would be, even if living from his youth upward within the extraordinary temptation of a bar-room.

844. Viewing the effects of Alcohol on Progeny, it becomes a three-fold question of vital importance which forces itself alike on

---

* "Report on the Education of Imbecile and Idiotic Children," by H. P. Ayres, M. D. Transactions of the American Association, page 628.

ALCOHOL—ITS EFFECTS ON PROGENY.

the attention of the Political Economist, the Social Reformer, and the Medical Professor.

845. The main facts in relation to the effects of intoxicating drinks on progeny lie too deep in the secret recesses of domestic life to enable us to catch but a mere glimpe of their terrible results. And though, occasionally, we may be enabled to trace the effects of the downright intemperance of the parent to the *dipsomania*, insane and idiotic inheritance of the children, yet we are unable at all times to trace the disorganizing and degenerating effects of the (so-called) moderate use of alcoholics, upon the children to the third and fourth generation.

846. For be it remembered, that its hereditary physical effects may neither show themselves nor end with the second generation, but may be exhibited in the third or fourth most unmistakably. Hence, whatever may be the effect traceable to the use of alcohol, the great bulk of the evil results will remain unknown, though not unfelt.

PART X.

IS ALCOHOL A MEDICINE?

847. WE believe that it has been clearly shown that *Alcohol is not a food*, in any sense. We now come to that other important question: *Is it a medicine?* With our present views, if we were to answer by a simple negative or affirmative, we should most emphatically answer, No! For we are very much inclined to say, with that brave, noble, and conscientious gentleman, Dr. John Higginsbottom, of Nottingham, Eng., "It is neither *food* nor *physic*."

848. In the opinion of many practitioners, the use of Alcohol as a medicine, is an open question: while many have the notion that it is indispensable as a medical agent. Yet, it is gratifying to know that the most learned of the profession, in all countries, are beginning to look upon its use as a medicine with distrust; while many discard it altogether, even as a remedial agent. The signs are hopeful when doctors begin to doubt, and pause to investigate the nature and the real action of a remedy on the human body.

849. Not having space or time to discuss the nature and pathology of disease, we shall take it for granted, that when a man is sick, that *something is wrong*, and *needs to be made right*.

850. A sick man generally calls in the aid of a doctor, whom he supposes to be well versed in the Medical Science. Science knows nothing of authorities, and as the Medical Science, it is said, takes nothing for granted that cannot be demonstrated; we will present a few facts, and the testimonies of physicians of learning and great experience.

MEDICAL SCIENCE—WHAT IS IT?

851. SCIENCE, from the Latin *Scientia*, from *Scio*, to know, means literally *a Systematic species of Knowledge*. MEDICAL means *to heal, to cure*. Then by the term *Medical Science*, we understand to mean literally (to know-how-to-cure-disease:) the knowledge of healing.

852. First, then, the nature and philosophy of the medical science demands that the doctor should discover in what the disease or wrong state consists; and secondly, What cause gave

rise to it. These discoveries made, it naturally follows that the physician should pursue one or all of the courses open to him, viz.—the *curative, preventive*, and *palliative*. It is the physician's duty to cure, by any and all the means in his power, and as soon as possible. But how is this to be done? Some one has said: that the whole secret of medicine was to know what to use, how to use it, and when.

853. In answer, we would say: First, by removing the cause, that being found.

854. Second, by the use of and the application of such remedies as will cure the wrong state of the system. Third, by avoiding what originally produced the wrong condition. The first may be done by strengthening the vital forces, by supplying the natural elements of the body, associated with the conditions necessary for the proper assimilation of those elements, and to excite normal action by administering substances having specific power to suppress injurious, or promote remedial processes. Will, or can, alcohol fulfil any of these conditions of supplying the natural elements, aid in their assimilation, suppress injurious, or promote remedial processes?

855. If it can do any of these, we may admit that it may be a medicine, though a very dangerous and an unsafe one; which can easily be dispensed with.

856. Dr. Anstie says:—"On the part of the medical profession, I think I may say that we have long since begun to believe that those medicines which really do benefit our patients, act in one way or another as food," etc.

857. Though we may agree with the above doctrine in the main, yet we are not ready on that account to admit that alcohol is a food, or acts like a food; or that it is a medicine to be used with less caution than we use any other potent poison. Now if the medicines that really benefit our patients can act in one way or another as food, can alcohol, in any of its forms, as alcohol, act in any way as a food?

858. The French experimenters—M. M. Lallamand, Perrin, and Duroy, concluded from their experiments, that 1st. "Alcohol is not a food." 2nd. "Alcohol is a special modifier of the nervous system. It acts in a feeble dose as an excitant; in a larger as a stupefiant." 3rd. "Alcohol is never transformed, never destroyed in the organism." 4th. "Alcohol accumulates by a sort of elective affinity, in the brain and in the liver." 5th. "Alcohol is eliminated from the organism in totality, and unchanged in its nature. The channels of eliminations are: the lungs, the skin, and especially the kidneys." 6th. "Alcohol has a pathogenetic influence, material and direct, upon the develop-

ment of many functional disturbances and organic alterations of the brain, liver, and kidneys." 7th. "Spirituous drinks owe to the alcohol they contain their common properties, and the specialty of their effects. The use of fermented and distilled liquors is often noxious: it should be always very restrained: it should never be tolerated save in exceptional circumstances."*

859. It must be borne in mind that these are not the conclusions of ultra-teetotalers, nor teetotalers at all, but the conclusions of the advocates of light wines, etc., in moderation, of course. It is pitiful that practice and knowledge should so differ, or that the practices of these experimenters should lag so far behind their science.

860. Common sense would pause and ask: "What is the use, either in health or disease, of taking something into the body that will not stay there long enough to do any good; and more especially if, during the period it remains in the body, it irritates and injures all the organs, tissues, and fluids of the body, and particularly the stomach, liver, kidneys, and brain? The late English *Medical Declaration*, signed by Drs. Burrows, Busk, Paget, Watson, etc., etc., says: "No *medical practitioner* should prescribe it without a sense of grave responsibility," and "it should be prescribed with as much care as any powerful drug," etc.

861. This is a step in the right direction, an advanced movement toward a rational and common-sense view of the use of alcohol as a medicine; for the nearer we can approach to the point of entirely dispensing with the use of alcohol in our medical practice, the better it will be for our patients. In the first years of our practice of medicine, when the patient or friends—as is too often the case even now,—thought something was needed to strengthen, we allowed some alcoholic liquor to be given, but ever failed to perceive any good result from it. Never having any faith in it, we do not remember voluntarily to have prescribed it, but for the last eight or ten years, since leaving the army at the close of the war, we have entirely forbidden its use in every case, and have seen no reason for regret. Once and only once, in all this time, have we been tempted to use alcoholic beverage, when suddenly called upon: but even in this case, we got along without it; and feel satisfied that the patient recovered much better than she would have done, had we given her brandy.

862. From our experience, if as a rule, all alcoholics were banished from the sick-room, the bills of mortality would be very much lessened; and we are also sure that the sooner alcoholic tinctures, etc., are substituted by non-alcoholic preparations, the

---

* Dr. F. R. Lees, in "Meliora," April, 1862.

better will it be for our patients, the welfare of our race, the honour of the medical profession, and the progress of *true medical science*.

863. We know that the opinions of the vast majority in the medical profession are against us in this; and most unfortunately they are not only in favour of the use of alcohol as a medicine, but also as a beverage. The history of medicine is a history of the change of the theory and of practice, and each change has been met by the profession with furious denouncement. To-day we have no settled scientific treatment of disease.

864. "We see now," says Dr. Trall, "where the error is with learned men. They have mistaken *vital resistance* for a physiological process; they have mistaken *morbid action* for *normal function;* they have mistaken inflammation for nutrition; they have mistaken fever for food; they have mistaken waste and expenditure for accumulation and supply; in short they have mistaken disease for health. * * * It is an error which utterly confounds all distinction between foods, poisons, and medicines. In fact it makes a rational distinction impossible. Must I tell you that medical authors do not give us any definition of the word food."

865. Sir Henry Holland, in his medical notes, speaking of wine, said, "We have not less assurance that it is in numerous other cases habitually injurious in relation both to the digestive organs and to the functions of the brain. * * * Modern custom has abridged the excess, but much remains to be done before the habit is brought down to a salutary level: and medical practice is greatly too indulgent on this point, to the weakness of those with whom it deals. It is the part of every wise man, once at least, in life, to make trial of the effect of leaving off wine altogether; and this even without the suggestion of actual malady. To obtain them (the results) fairly, the abandonment must be complete for a time, a measure of no risk even where the change is greatest."

866. It is a fact well known, that the medical practice is greatly too indulgent, and men in all countries and of every class, testify to the evil wrought by the medical prescription of alcoholics; and that it is antagonistic to the temperance reformation.

867. That the medical faculty has, doubtless, with the very best of motives, lent itself unconsciously to the fostering of the drinking habits of the people of this country, cannot successfully be denied.

868. There is no profession that deserves more honour and receives less than the medical, yet the truth must be told. The

medical practice has its fashions, as the milliner, the tailor, and dressmaker have their fashions. As the fashions for dresses change, so do the fashions in medicines change; nor are diseases without their fashions. At one time everything with some doctors is *neuralgia*, at another, *liver complaint*, and a third, dyspepsia; and with this class of doctors, alcohol in some of its forms is generally a panacea. If the minister whose nervous system is deranged by too much work applies to them, he is ordered *pure Bourbon* whiskey. The merchants and lawyers also, are ordered *Bourbon*, and everybody who does not feel well, drinks whiskey: and all shield themselves behind, the "doctor ordered it."

869. But the drink, ignorance, and superstition must not all be ascribed to the profession. The public must take some share of the blame. Dr. Edmunds said in his lecture in New York: "Now when some of you go to your doctor, you say, 'What do you think, doctor? Had I better take a little spirits?' The doctor has a wife and family at home; he is not always a man well up in real estate in the city of New York, and he has worked twenty years. You may pay your accounts regularly and your fees are very adequate. He looks at you, and says, 'Yes, you need a little brandy,' just as the wife who says, 'Doctor, do you think that going to Saratoga would do me any good?' 'Yes,' he replies, 'I think it is the best thing you could do.' The wife replies, 'Then I wish you would write husband a note, and say I must go.' But you must not go to the doctor in that way. You must recollect that he has to look after his wife and family, and he may think he will lose his reputation if he tells you you must not drink. Some medical men would say, 'So and so is a well-meaning man, but he is a little cracked. Yours is a constitution that would run down rapidly if it had not a little wine. You came to me in time to save you.' You did not die but got well in spite of the wine, and you would have got well much better if you had not taken wine. As things now stand, the doctor is put in an extremely uncomfortable position. But I tell you if you go to your doctor and say to him: 'These alcoholic beverages do a great deal of harm; do you think I need them?' Nineteen times out of twenty the doctor would say, 'No, I think you would be better without them.' There are some who would not say so, but who are they. Some of them are men who tell you that which they have been told before.

870. "It is quite natural that the young ones should be influenced by the weight of opinion of their elders. Many medical men really have no well defined belief, but they have seen the old gentleman from whom they learned their profession do things in a certain way, and they remember what has been taught them at the hospital, and they continue to do the same way without thinking of the matter.

871. "You will do them a great deal of good if you follow them up and question them. Ask them why they order you spirits? What it is to do? What doses you are to take? And how long you are to take them? It is so strange, that if we go to a physician, and get an ordinary prescription, if we take it for two or three weeks, we think we have done very well: but if he orders us a glass of wine, we take it all our lives *as a medicine*, not only with commendable punctuality, but increase the dose! If you ask your doctor questions, you very often do him service; you call his attention to this matter. My attention was called by a rough-handed teetotal abstainer. I ordered him stout. I said, 'You must take a little beer.' He sat down in my dining-room and said, 'Doctor, I am sure you have a reason for everything; if you can show me it is good for me, I will take it. I have taken nothing for a dozen years, and I am a great deal better without. What do you think it will do for me?' I had never been cornered in my life in that way. I really found I had no answer: and so you will find that your doctor will have no answer for such questions. When they appeal to experience, resting upon dogma, recollect the facts with regard to it? Medical dogma, as such, has never been anything but a delusion and a snare."

872. To the truthfulness of these statements, every physician can testify, who has had the manliness and courage to speak out against medical drinking, or has dared to refuse to recommend alcoholic beverages in his practice.

873. We have never yet met with an advocate of alcoholic medication that could give us a satisfactory reason for its use; or could point us to a single case, that he could positively say was cured by alcoholic drinks. This is a part of our experience, and will, we believe, be the experience of every one who will discard medical dogma and seriously investigate the subject.

874. Dr. Higginbottom, F. R. S., of Nottingham, Eng., says, "If a medical man has practised his profession for some years, and becomes a teetotaler, he soon suffers persecution and loses his reputation; his friends and his practice leave him; in short, he receives the common wages of a reformer; he is under the necessity of recanting to gain his former status or quit his profession and seek some other employment for a living! Some of my medical brethren, several of eminence, have acted with more policy, thereby preserving their reputation and practice. They have not been ultra-teetotalers; they have allowed or prescribed a little drop of alcohol, prescribed it in fever, or in extreme cases; they have publicly acknowledged they were not teetotalers. That is enough; they have escaped scatheless."* "In some

---

* "Alcohol, Medical Men." &c. By John Higginbottom, Hon. F. R. S., F. R. C. S.

countries," says the doctor, when the patient has been suffering from disease of the heart, and other cases, in which stimulants were totally inadmissible, I have waited to hear the physician's directions, which have seldom been completed until permission was gained for the patient to take a little wine or brandy, evidently as a *placebo* (I will please.) A daughter has asked in a beseeching manner, 'Shall my mother take a little brandy?' The answer has been, 'Just a drop, to flavour the gruel.' The drop is often somewhat between a drop and a tablespoonful or more. I once remonstrated with a physician, who answered, 'Let them take what they like.' One celebrated physician told me that he never prescribed to a patient more than two or three teaspoonsful of brandy, and only that quantity, in one or two particular cases. Such admissions are sufficient; the doctor is a fine clever fellow, and not a scrub of a teetotaler. Some of my friends, in order to save me from persecution and pecuniary loss, wished me to admit that I might prescribe a little alcohol, just a little, sometimes; but not having 'expediency' in my temperance vocabulary, they importuned me in vain." Dr. Higginbottom abandoned the prescription of alcohol as early as 1832.*

875. Dr. Henry Mudge, M. R. C. S., says: "The causes which retard the adhesion of members of the medical profession to the temperance movement may be considered to be both *proper* and *common;* as ignorance, fashion, gain and professional status."

876. Henry Barker, M. D., says: "The honest medical practitioner, whose convictions may lead him to follow the non-alcoholic treatment of disease, has to bear with the results of years of ignorance and prejudice, and he will be fortunate if he escapes a large amount of spiteful misrepresentation on the part of contemporaries and the drink-loving public. Such pleasant observations as the following are sure to be made and circulated freely in his neighbourhood. He is said to 'let down his patients for the want of proper nourishment,' to keep them 'too low,' or if they die, which occasionally happens, he has 'allowed them to slip through his fingers.' Persons are advised not to consult him, as 'he will be sure to stop their beer,' or else, 'drench them' with 'cold water;' and, if not required professionally he is not invited to many social gatherings, for fear he should inflict upon them a teetotal lecture."

877. A correspondent of the "Medical Press and Circular," April 5, 1871, said: * * "Admitting that the administration of alcohol has been carried to a faulty and injurious extent, on whom shall we lay the blame? Partly, certainly, on the doctors,

---

* "International Temp. and Prohibition Convention Report," Manchester, England, 1862.

whose error is of a twofold kind. They may, in blind deference to authority, or on mistaken views of the action and power of alcohol, have given it too freely, or on the other hand, it may be given in too great compliance with the popular prejudice of the day. One thing is certain, that the public likes a doctor who 'does something.' If years ago the doctor bled, purged, and sweated a patient well before he died, every one was satisfied, and the physician extolled for his energy and assiduity, without which none can say what might not have happened to the patient.

878. "Now people's views, so far as methods are concerned, are changed, and they look with a great deal of distrust on a physician who talks of bleeding and water gruel diet; but the man who, at a glance, says at once: 'You must take a bottle of champagne with your dinner, and a half-dozen glasses of port afterward,' is the man for the public purse. 'Never mind,' says the doctor, 'if wine makes your head ache; it is because you don't take enough of it.' The cautious, pains-taking man, who has been gradually but slowly getting his patient out of some exhausting nervous malady by two or three glasses of Manganilla Sherry at dinner-time, soon is bowled out by such a go-a-head brother as the one just described; and for a time, the patient perhaps goes ahead also, the difficulty being to keep his tongue quiet on the virtues of the alcoholic method. At last, however, down he comes, all at once in a fit, and a long convalescence and terribly shattered nerves are the best results then to be looked for. * * * But the object of this letter is to hint at the way in which respectable drunkards and drunkenness are sometimes made; and to entreat medical practitioners to follow the teachings of experience and of physiology as much as possible in their practice, rather than to make fashion and popular prejudice in any way a rule of action."

THE USE OF ALCOHOL AS A REMEDY FOR DEBILITY.

879. *The use of Alcohol as a remedy in Debility* is not at all rare. The belief in its stimulating and tonic virtues is not alone confined to the general public, for we find many in the medical profession, who seem to labour under the idea that alcoholics are useful, if not absolutely necessary in cases of *weakness* or *debility*. This, we regret to say, is a far too common delusion, and tends to produce much mischief.

880. Dr. Samuel Wilks, in a clinical lecture in Guy's Hospital, said: "Endeavour, if you can, to erase from your minds, that it is a proven fact, that alcohol is a tonic or a necessary part of every one's beverage. This is assumed by a large mass of people, and the meaning of the question which your patient puts

to you when he says, 'What shall I drink?' is not, 'Shall I take a stimulant or leave it alone?' but 'Shall I take wine, or beer, or spirits?' He often confesses that he is in a great difficulty; he finds none of them agree with him: but that he must take 'something' appears as necessary as eating his daily food; the questionability of the alternative never having formed a part of his calculation. I say it is assumed that a 'strength-giving property' lies in these drinks, that just in proportion to a man's feeling of weakness, so will he require one of them. In ordinary health he may only want his beer; but ill, his wine; and if very ill, his spirits.

881. "This popular error is shared, I am free to say, by many in the profession. If the patient is weak, he wants support—this term carrying too frequently with it the necessary idea of wine or spirits. I should be sorry to say that the doctor panders to the public taste, since he too often accords with it; but the consequence of such agreement between the patient and the medical man resolves itself into this,—that an extra stimulant is prescribed. You may ask to what complaints do I refer, when I speak of this too common advice; I need only repeat the word, 'patient' for it matters little what is the nature of the disease, since the reasons for treatment are applicable to all complaints, and are founded on this simple proposition. All persons who are ill, are weak; they have lost strength; they require it to be restored; alcohol is a supporter and a tonic, therefore alcohol is a remedy for all diseases!

882. "This is no parody, for I have heard this argument set forth in so many words; and practically, it is adopted by many, for I constantly hear medical men say they give brandy to their patients, for they always find them low! Brandy, indeed, with some becomes as much a universal remedy as 'Revalena chlorodyne,' 'Morrison's pills,' or any other quack medicine.

883. "Moreover, it is a medicine of which patients approve, assuming, as they do, its supporting and strength-giving powers. You therefore cannot do better, if you fear no compunctions in converting your profession into a mere trade, than to say to all your patients, after feeling their pulse, that they are very low—that you are sure they do not take enough; and order them several glasses of wine daily. Should they be exceedingly ill with some desperate organic complaint, then you must turn your remarks to the friends, and speak of the necessity of supporting the patient by giving him as much brandy as can be poured down his throat. By this method you are sure to give satisfaction; for should the patient die without such treatment, you may have the credit of 'letting the patient slip through your fingers;' while, if he die with it, you have done your best. If you kill a dozen patients with brandy, you need have no fear; you have done your

best. This I say would be a very comfortable and lucrative mode of practice."

884. In relation to the debility of patients in many diseases, it is true of only a certain class of continued fevers, in which there is generally found a peculiar depression of nervous and muscular power, accompanied often with a degeneration of muscular tissue, as well as disease, attended by an increase of temperature. All practitioners are now agreed that the powers of the patient should be sustained. What the physician has to do is to find out the cause of the weakness, and whatever will remove the weakness, whether food or medicine, is a tonic.

885. But it does seem to be a strange infatuation, that of all the many poisons in the materia medica, that alcohol should be the only one, within the profession and out of it, that is esteemed a sustainer of vitality; a tonic, a stimulant, and possesses many other virtues and curative properties too numerous for one little head to contain.

886. Though it may be very absurd for either doctors or patients to conceive that because a drug may be good in disease, it must be relatively good in health; yet it is nevertheless a fact, that the medical profession, and the people, carry into every day's practice this absurd assumption.

887. And why not? If alcohol can give strength, it is right that it should be used. The doctor says it will make weak persons strong; and the doctor is very good authority in the eyes of the people. Yet we have seen that it is not food, and cannot, in the remotest degree, aid the assimilation of food. Call it what you please, narcotic, stimulant, tonic or what else; unless it can be assimilated by the blood, the natural source of power in the system; it is an imposture, a mocker.

ALCOHOL IMPAIRS THE VITALITY OF BLOOD DISCS.

888. Numerous experiments have been made, clearly proving, that when alcohol is absorbed into the blood and it becomes surcharged with it, that not only the blood corpuscles are affected, but that the liquor sanguinis itself, suffers deterioration; that alcohol produces in the blood discs an increased and unnatural contraction, which hurries their development, inducing their premature decay and death; and as a consequence the colouring matter disappears, and they lose their vitality; less oxygen is absorbed, and less carbon carried out of the system; thus the devitalization of the tissues takes place.

889. It is clearly an unsafe and too powerful a chemical agent to be used in order to make up for the fatigue occurring in the every-day wear and tear of ordinary life. The cases for which alcohol is generally prescribed in some of its forms, are those in which weakness or debility is a prominent feature. This weakness is never a disease in itself, but is invariably the result or the symptom either of some constitutional or local, abnormal or morbid action, which it may be safely said can never be cured, but may be injured, and very frequently is by the use of alcohol. The trouble is increased, for the only scientific and proper treatment is to remove the cause.

890. True, the use of alcoholics often imparts a feeling of support and comfort to persons who are suffering from weakness or fatigue, but this relief is many times dearly bought, for the original cause *often* remains, and is perhaps aggravated by the alcohol. We have no faith in the supporting or sustaining power of alcohol on the diseased system. When we reflect that it causes deterioration of the blood, brain and tissues, it does really seem impossible that it can in any way nourish or act as food.

891. From the fact that alcohol can be found unchanged in the brain and other tissues of the body, for some time after it is ingested; and that its derivatives have never been discovered, it is improbable that it can benefit the body; the only rational and natural inference is, that the system endeavours to get rid of it as quickly as it can, as it does to eliminate every other poison: and the organism, in the words of Sam. Weller says: "Out with it, as the father said to the child, when he swallowed a farden;" and it is very doubtful if the "farden" would do as much harm to that child as alcohol will to a weakened and debilitated system; and I feel certain that the said "farden" would be just as nourishing as the alcohol. For Dr. T. K. Chambers said in his 'Clinical Lectures on the Renewal of Life:' "It is clear that we must cease to regard alcohol as in any wise aliment, inasmuch as it goes out as it went in, and does not, so far as we know, leave any of its substance behind." Aside from alcohol, no one ever thinks of supporting vitality and of receiving strength and vigour of body, except from fresh air, water, food and refreshing sleep.

IS ALCOHOL A STIMULANT OR A NARCOTIC?

892. Among the many reasons alleged for using alcohol both as a beverage and as a medicine, is, that it is a stimulant. When a clergyman or merchant is overworked by the high-pressure system of the times, it is said a little stimulant is needed to help them to get up steam for their work.

IS ALCOHOL A MEDICINE?

893. What is a stimulant? Dr. T. K. Chambers, says: "It is usually held to be something which spurs on an animal operated upon to more vigorous performance of its duties." According to this definition, it is something that takes out of the animal what is in it. Or it acts on the principle of applying a whip or spur to the jaded nag, instead of giving the animal rest, and a supply of oats, hay, and water. Then we come to this fact, that food is what gives strength, while stimulants take it out; and that when we use stimulants they extract the remaining portions of strength from the system, that otherwise would not have been parted with.

894. Dr. Brinton says: "Even a moderate dose of beer or wine diminishes the maximum weight which a person can lift, to something below his teetotal standard. In like manner, it is not too much to say that mental acuteness, accuracy of perception and delicacy of the senses, are all so far opposed by alcohol, as that the maximum efforts of each are incompatible with the ingestion of any moderate quantity of fermented liquors."

895. It is therefore clear that if we attempt to work on alcoholics we shall wear ourselves out in a few years, and ultimately be a loser by the speculation.

896. A *true* stimulant may be said to be an agent which, while it acts in harmony with the powers of the organism to resist the action of external force, will also increase the activity of the functions, and the development, and aid in the proper distribution of the vital forces. The best of all stimulants, is easy digestible and nutritious food. If we live abnormally and violate hygienic laws, and must have others, nature has furnished us with medical stimulants, as cayenne pepper, and numerous acro-aromatics.

897. But nature never intended us to live on stimulants; for the same law governs them all, and they must be reserved for a time of actual need, and not used at all times; for the too frequent use of any stimulant will impair the sensibility and finally produce debility.

898. Hence, Sir Benj. Brodie, says: "Alcohol removes the uneasy feeling and inability of exertion which want of sleep occasions. But the relief is only temporary. Stimulants do not create nervous power, they merely enable you, as it were, to *use up* that which is left, and then they leave you more in need of rest than before."

899. Dr. Archibald Billing, M. A.,* says: "Tonics give

---

* "Principles of Medicine," (4th edition, 1841.)

strength, *stimulants call it forth*. Stimulants excite action, but action is not strength." From these distinctions of stimulation and strength, it does seem evident that alcohol cannot strengthen the system.

900. But in the light of science, is alcohol a true stimulant? If it is, it must increase the activity of the functions. Does it do this? It is certainly, in large doses, a narcotic, a paralyzer. Hence, we must decrease the dose in order to change the effects.

901. Dr. Chambers says: "It seems doubtful if on the healthy nervous system, this (to spur on the animal to a more vigorous performance of its duties) is ever the effect of alcohol, even in the most moderate dose, and for the shortest period of time. A diminution of force is quite consistent with augmented quickness of motion; or, may it not be said that in involuntary muscles, it implies it. The action of chloroform is to quicken the pulse, yet, the observations of Dr. Bedford Brown on the circulation in the human cerebrum during anæsthesia, clearly show that the propelling power of the heart is diminished during that state." (See "Experiments of Drs. Parkes, Count Wollowicz, Richardson," &c., 136 to 162).

902. We have no evidence to prove that alcohol is any more a stimulant than that opium, chloroform, and ether are stimulants.

903. Alcohol we believe to be an *anæsthetic* and narcotic, and not a stimulant; and if it has any medical virtues, it owes them to the fact of its being a narcotic, and not as a stimulant. You ask, what is a narcotic? It is a substance which, when taken into the animal organism, possesses the properties of stupefying, or of partially or entirely paralyzing the nerve forces; or we may say that it will partially or entirely destroy life.

904. We have shown that alcohol is an acrid-narcotic poison; that Dr. Percy destroyed dogs almost instantly by giving them two ounces of alcohol; that men have dropped dead after taking a quantity of ardent spirits. Let a man drink a pint of whiskey, and he will lie on his back, in a helpless, senseless state. What shall we call his condition? He is not stimulated. His powers are certainly not spurred on to a 'more vigorous performance of their duties." He is paralyzed, body and mind. His muscles and nerves are paralyzed through and through. He is narcotized, and not stimulated; hence, we certainly conclude that the agent that produced these results, is a paralyzer, a narcotic, and not a stimulant

905. Alcohol is therefore an agent which in large doses paralyzes, stupefies and narcotizes the mind; and if life is not entirely destroyed, the whole system will suffer from its effects for days, perhaps weeks, even when no more of the narcotic is taken. Hence, alcohol is nothing more or less than a narcotic, equal with opium, chloroform and ether. We may be reminded that the late Dr. Anstie classed alcohol as a stimulant in small doses and a narcotic in large ones.

906. Now the fact is simply this. If a pint of brandy or whiskey will kill a man by entirely paralyzing the system, a half-pint will half paralyze him. And as we reduce the dose the effects are proportionately diminished. And whether we take a pint or a teaspoonful, the effects are those of a narcotic and not of a stimulant.

907. Another evidence is that alcohol, like other narcotics, demands an increase of the dose to produce the effects, after being used for some time; which arises, we conceive, from the nervous sensibilities being blunted and narcotized by the paralyzing poison, whether opium, alcohol, or chloroform.

908. This fact is too well known to dwell on. We are not able to distinguish any of the effects of alcohol from those of other narcotics; all, like alcohol, have their peculiar characteristics and modes of action, which do not make them any the less narcotics or the more stimulants.

909. But even admitting it to be a stimulant, we cannot really expect any good results from the use of alcohol, for Prof. Muller says, in his Physiology: "A stimulant, too often repeated, deadens the excitability of the organs and renders them insensible to the same stimulus for a long time. Hence may be explained a part of the phenomena observed in the effects of habit; although many things, to whose action, after long repetition, we become insensible, produce at first, not merely the phenomena of excitement, *but afterwards a durable structural change*, to which alone their subsequent inefficiency can be explained.

910. "*A great error has been committed in classifying the vivifying stimuli, with other stimuli which do not really contribute to the composition of organic bodies, and do not renovate their power.* A mechanical stimulus which modifies the condition of a membrane endowed with sensiblity (for example pressure) *excites*, it is true, a vital phenomena—sensation—but does not *vivify*, does not invigorate the organic force; while on the contrary the essential vital stimuli, viz., nutriment, water, etc., contribute to the formation of organic matter."

911. Dr. Edmunds said :*—" Alcohol in the blood diminishes the osmosis or permeation of its fluids through the membranous tissues of the body, and thus the extra-vascular circulation or soakage of the fluid parts of the blood is interfered with. The alcohol blunts the chemical affinities, by virtue of which tissues of the body, and the fluids of the blood, react upon each other. These two effects obstruct the onward passage of the blood through its capillaries, and the blood accumulating behind distends the arteries and stirs up the heart to force on the current. Thus we get what is called the stimulating action of alcohol;— *i. e.* a fuller pulse and a more laborious action of the heart—the real fact being that more heart labour is required to keep the circulation going, just as when respiration is interfered with, the breathing becomes more laborious.

912. "I can see nothing in the action of alcohol in the human body, in any case, or at any time, but that of a paralyzer; and I see in that view the key by which we can explain all the contradictory benefits which have been ascribed to the influence of alcohol.

913. "By giving alcohol as a stimulant in exhausting diseases, I believe we always do, as we should, in giving a dose of opium and brandy and water to comfort a half suffocated patient; *i. e.* increase his danger. If that be so, we reduce alcohol not only from the position of food medicine, but we reduce it from the position of a goad; and we say that the suppositious stimulating or goading influence of alcohol is a mere delusion; that in fact alcohol always lessens the power of the patients and always damages their chance of recovery, when it is a question of their getting through exhausting diseases.

914. "There are some cases in which alcohol is invaluable in staving off certain kinds of convulsions, or in lessening the sensibility of the body under a painful operation. But these are cases which happen but rarely, and which do not come within the scope of that class of ailments for which we now see brandy and wine indiscriminately prescribed and relied upon. * * * But I think alcohol should be restricted to such cases as are usually treated by opium or chloroform. * * *

915. "We conclude by simply affirming these propositions:— That alcohol never sustains the forces of the body as food-medicine; that alcohol never acts as a goad to the body; that it has no stimulating properties whatever, in the sense of increased action either in rate or quantity; that alcohol always acts as a narcotic, and is always a paralyzer of sensation and a lessener of action."

---

* In a Lecture in Manchester, Eng.

916. These views of Dr. Edmunds are much more reasonable than the theories of Dr. Anstie, and others already presented.* "On a certain occasion, a gentleman, was talking about his horse. He said he could not get it into a right state at all.' He had tried all kinds of specifics, condition powders, and all the rest of them in vain, and the bystanders were wondering what he could do next, when a little stable boy asked : ' Sir, did yez ever try corn ?' If people would just really try food,—such food, using the word in a large sense, as is adapted to their condition, not drugs or drink, but food for increasing their strength or maintaining and recovering it; if in battling with disease, they would try the natural means that God has connected with bodily health, they would find that method wonderfully successful."

EXPERIMENTS ON THE USE OF WINE.

917. The researches of Dr. Parkes and Dr. C. Wollowicz, show that alcohol and brandy are neither necessary nor useful, but that they derange the action of the heart. As those experiments were confined to pure alcohol and brandy, a doubt was expressed, whether the alcohol in wine would act in the same way. To satisfy this doubt, they made a series of careful experiments with wine. These experiments were continued for thirty days. The first ten days, the subject was confined to water at dinner; during the next ten days, red Bordeaux wine was taken instead of water, a half-pint of wine being given for the first five days, and a pint on the last five days. The wine was taken only at dinner, at a quarter past 1 o'clock. During the last ten days, only water was again given. The wine was analyzed, and was declared to be claret, the quantity used being what is considered moderate.

918. The experimenters say:—"The result of all the observations was, that in the water period of ten days, the mean temperature was $97°.726$, and the wine period, was $97°.56$, or $0°.166$ less, a difference so slight as probably to fall within the limits of unavoidable error."

919. It will be seen that the results on the temperature, do not agree with the results of Professor Binz and other experimenters: neither do they support the warming power of alcohol, though it is still used by persons as a heat-giver. They also say : "We conclude that in health, the apparent heat after wine must be owing, as in the case of alcohol and brandy, rather to subjective feeling connected with the quickened circulation, (?) than with an actual rise of temperature ; but that on the other hand, wine in

---

* "Stimulants and Strength," page 12. A Lecture by Rev. Hugh Sinclair Patterson, M. D., London.

the above quantities causes no appreciable lowering of temperature."

920. Though the change of temperature was so little, yet there was the most marked effect upon the pulse by wine. For we find that during the water period :—" The daily mean of the pulse was uniform, the mean of the ten days being 76.3 beats per minute; the extreme daily variation was from 74.2 to 77.87." The heart did its work properly without alcohol, but an irritating action was soon shown when wine was taken, for the experimenters say :—" The wine increased the frequency of the heart's action by 4¼ beats every minute during fourteen hours in the day, and doubtless also in the remaining ten, for the pulse at 8 A. M. was still too frequent during the wine period. In the twenty-four hours there was an excess in the heart's action of 6.120 beats, or nearly 6 per cent. As the amount of alcohol was 1.1 ounces, in the first five days, and 2.2 ounces in the other five days, the increase in the number of the heart's beats was slightly more than in the days when an equal quantity of pure alcohol was taken."

921. The wine was taken shortly after one o'clock each day. The effect of which will be seen by examining the following extract from the tables :

	Water period.	Wine period.
Mean number of pulse at 10 A. M., after breakfast	78.4	79.1
Mean at 2 P. M. after dinner	83.7	86.8
,, ,, 4 ,, ,, ,, ,,	75.8	87.6
,, ,, 6 ,, ,, after tea	78.8	88.1
,, ,, 8 ,, ,, ,, ,,	76.5	82.1
,, ,, 10 ,, ,, ,, ,,	71.3	74.9

From the above table it is very clear, that whatever else alcohol may be able to do, it certainly deranges the action of the heart, and causes a waste or expenditure of force.

922. These experiments also show that alcohol is eliminated by the breath, the perspiration, and the urine.

923. Drs. Parkes and Wollowicz said :—" The general results of these experiments are in all respects identical with the experiments on alcohol and brandy; that is to say, that there was a marked effect on the heart, coinciding tolerably well in amount with the effect produced by pure alcohol in the former experiments."

924. In other words, the claret wine in the above quantities, cannot so far be distinguished in its effects from pure alcohol.

Its most marked effect, the increase of the heart's action, must be ascribed to the alcohol, in great measure, though the ethers may play some slight part.

925. These researches of Drs. Parkes and Wollowicz, clearly prove that alcohol is not a necessity of life, but may do a great amount of mischief. These facts, which scientific men have ascertained now by improved means of investigation, aided by scientific apparatus, were arrived at long ago, by total abstainers, by studying, and trying both the use and non-use of alcoholics, upon themselves. We have now the declarations of both science and experience, that alcoholic beverages are unnecessary and injurious.

926. None of the scientific experimenters have yet been able to give a logical reason for the use of alcoholic beverages in health, nor to show that total abstinence ever produced disease or injured the health; but there is ample reason for believing that alcohol is injurious in sickness and in health.

RECOVERY RETARDED BY THE USE OF WINE.

927. Dr. Charles Maclean, writing to the editor of the British Medical Journal, said:—"I was much struck, last spring, with the effect of wine on myself as a patient. I had emerged from enteric fever, and, there being all the indications for its use, I was ordered and took wine. Now instead of benefitting me, it seemed to do just the reverse. I took two glasses during the twenty-four hours.

928. "It stimulated the heart's action, in a remarkable manner, and always produced, more or less, a feeling of cold, which latter effect is interesting, as showing that wine influences the contractility of the minute as well as of the large vessels, although probably it is indirectly through the nervous system. But that such stimulation was unnecessary, and indeed injurious, appeared from the fact that, when I was out and walked a few miles, after taking a glass of wine, a cold perspiration would break out generally, and a feeling of exhaustion come on, compelling me often to sit down at the roadside during my walk; whereas, going to see the same patient another day, before taking the stimulant, I felt quite another being. All the time that I was taking wine, for two months after I got out of bed, my pulse could not be coaxed below 120; but, at the end of this period, I stopped the wine; and from that time I date my satisfactory convalescence. I soon noticed a lowering of the pulse, and certainly, before a fortnight passed, it was down to seventy-two, and faintness and other disagreeable symptoms belonged to

the past. My pulse soon came down to sixty, which is my normal number. Now I cannot but think that the wine materially retarded my recovery." "To escape the evils arising from the use of alcohol," says Dr. B. W. Richardson, F. R. S., "there is only one perfect course, namely, to abstain from alcohol altogether. No fear need be entertained of any physical or mental harm from such abstinence. Every good may be expected from it. A man or woman who abstains is healthy and safe; a man or woman who indulges at all is unsafe; a man or a woman who relies on alcohol is lost."

VIOLENT INFLAMMATION EXCITED BY ALCOHOL.

929. Dr. Martin, after giving the history of the case, says: "This case shows:—1st. That alcohol has a tendency to excite inflammatory action. We have seen this proved crucially. The inflammation was increased while wine, etc., was being given; it declined rapidly, when alcohol was withdrawn; it recurred when the use of wine was resumed; it again declined when wine was prohibited. 2nd. The administration of wine aided in keeping up the disease, not only by poisoning and deteriorating the blood, but by destroying the desire for food. The patient had been urged to take beef-tea, etc., before I was called in, but she manifested an utter aversion to food of any kind. Soon after the stoppage of the wine, however, she not only began to take a fair supply of milk, beef-tea, etc., but to relish it. When the wine was resumed, her appetite gradually declined, and disgust for food returned; when it was once more banished, she once more was induced to take food, and soon began to crave it. 3rd. I would remark on the extraordinary extent to which the minds of all concerned were dominated by the belief in the invigorating properties of brandy and port-wine.

930. "Although they saw that the poor girl was snatched from the grave when the wine was given up, their old faith was not shaken; although the disease returned '*pari passu*,' with the return to the use of wine, there was no disposition manifested to leave it off, until I insisted on it when again called to see the case.

931. "Lastly, there is every reason to believe that if the administration of alcohol had been persisted in, the patient must have continued to endure agonizing pain until she had lost her leg by amputation or succumbed to the exhausting effects of the disease."

932. "If you value your happiness," says Dr. Callenette, "if you value your lives—banish from your houses, from your tables,

from your sick-rooms, every drop of intoxicating drinks; for be assured they produce weakness—not strength; sickness—not health; death—not life."

INFLUENCE OF ALCOHOLISM ON TRAUMATIC LESIONS.

933. In a recent discussion on the influence of alcoholism on this subject at the Academie de Médecin,* M. Béhier stated, that in his opinion this influence was disastrous, and he added that the same observation was applicable in the case of internal maladies. That this influence was not to be regarded as an instance of poisoning; and independently of the acute symptoms of alcoholism, the different morbid results observed in persons addicted to drink are to be referred to the changes produced by alcohol in the different organs of the body.

934. These changes are of different kinds, according to the period of the disease; and in order to estimate the influence exercised by alcoholism on diseases and wounds, the different phases of alcoholism must be distinguished.

935. At first, alcohol produces transient congestion; at more advanced stages induces sclerosis (hardening of the cellular tissue) of certain organs, symptoms varying according as attacked; as in the liver signs of obstruction of *vena portæ;* in the nervous centres, trembling, dulness of the senses, loss of memory, local paralysis; and at a still more advanced state it induces fatty alteration of the tissues, and steatosis of different organs. *Sclerosis* and *steatosis* represent, according to M. Béhier, the important terms of the ifluence of alcoholism, and these *lesions* (injuries) constitute in the economy a condition of degradation which sensibly lessons the force of resistance to depression produced either by disease or injuries.

936. The alterations caused by prolonged alcoholism are very extensive, *steatosis* having been demonstrated in the glands of the stomach, in the liver, in the kidneys, in the heart, and other muscles, and even in the blood. The question may be asked, how can it be ascertained that the economy has arrived, under the influence of alcohol, in excess at the period of organic *alteration* just mentioned?

937. M. Béhier, considers the answer a difficult one, but he points to a coincidence which deserves notice, viz., an excess of fat in the areolar tissue, and he adduces two facts which seem to

---

* Archives Generales de Medicin, January, February, and March. And in the British and Foreign Medico-Chir. Review, October, 1871.

be established. 1st. An excess of fat in the heart, the mesentery, and some other regions, in persons addicted to alcohol; and 2nd, the marked *embonpoint* of subjects in whom the serious symptoms in question are manifested when they suffer from disease or injury. *Delirium tremens*, he considers, belongs to a different, and less advanced stage of alcoholism.

938. As alcohol vitiates the blood, wastes the nervous energy, and disturbs the natural functions, it cannot reasonably be expected to heal wounds or repair lesions of any kind; for as Dr. Trotter said:—"Intoxicating liquors, in all their forms, and however disguised, are the most productive cause of disease with which I am acquainted."

STIMULANTS DURING HEMORRHAGE.

939. Dr. Cooper Foster says:*—"Cases of hemorrhage require very careful management with regard to stimulants. On the one hand you have to guard against any excess of circulatory activity when reaction is established. I was not sure in the case where brandy might not possibly increase the hemorrhage, and therefore I did not continue it.

940. "Be careful in these cases. In all abdominal injuries with rupture, however slight, of any viscera, there is always collapse. The public are very fond of pouring in the alcohol, and it certainly rallies the patient; but with the reaction comes also a quickened and excited blood current, forcing the clot, which may have become lodged during the time of feeble or nearly stagnant flow, and insuring a fatal termination; whereas, perhaps if the case had been left quietly alone, the rent might have become consolidated, and valuable life saved."

941. Dr. Richardson said in the Lancet:† "There is another class of cases of hemorrhagic kind in which the administration of alcohol is, according to my experience, indifferent practice. I refer to the cases of * * recurrent hemorrhage in women. * * The patient, under these circumstances, greatly reduced in power, is easily misled by her own sensations to think well of alcohol. She is mentally and physically feeble. She takes, in periods of lowness, a glass or two of *wine*, or a large draught of *stout*, and for a time she feels so much relieved by the assumed remedy, that she returns to it again and again. * * The results of this treatment are at the best dangerous; at the worst, disastrous. There is engendered a dislike for natural good food, a depraved appetite, and a persistent dyspepsia. * * The action of the heart is feeble and irritable.

---

* In a Clinical Lecture, Guy's Hospital. In the Lancet, June 29, 1872.
† "Notes on the Administration of Alcohol in the Treatment of Disease." January, 1876.

942. "The mind is depressed, and the emotions are either excited into hysterical elations or lowered into despondency. With these symptoms there is the continuance of the hemorrhage, for a time passively, at periods actively and copious. * * * My experience of this class of cases now is that the first point of practice in their treatment consists in withdrawing the alcohol. As soon as the unrest which alcohol induces is set up, the vascular depression at one moment, the quick excitement at another, is allayed, and the cure commences. Peace is secured. The current of the blood flows on in a steady stream; the blood regains its plasticity; the weakened vessels have rest; the nutritive changes are more naturally carried out; the nervous system is toned to even tension and the signs of amendment begin to appear. * * *

943. "Patients suffering from chronic loss of blood, and who are in the habit of taking alcohol to meet the sensation of exhaustion * * are often difficult of treatment. They hold by the assumed remedy, hard and fast, so that it is necessary to be most firm in relieving them from its bad influences. As a general fact, I find that no half measures are of avail. If one glass of wine be permitted occasionally, two will be taken, and that means a continuance of the vicious system.

944. "The argument used by the patient against the withdrawal * * * is that some kind of undefined, but terrible danger must or will occur if all the alcoholic support is withdrawn. The only danger I know of, and that is real, is to the practitioner, who runs the risk of losing the confidence of his patient, if he too determinedly maintain his position. * * But so far I have not yet the slightest evidence before me of any harm whatever accruing from the entire and sudden withdrawal of alcohol in the class of cases under consideration.

945. "On the contrary, when the appetite for stimulant is appeased, and the mental worry and fear which attend the withdrawal are calmed, I have never seen anything but good as the result of the practice. My experience further is that the lower a patient feels, the greater is the reason, as a general rule, for the enforcing total abstinence. The chances are large that the lowness which alcohol relieves will be intensified when the effect of the brief stimulation it has produced has passed off. * * I include, however, under the same class of diseases, others where blood is recurrently lost. Cases of loss of blood from piles are treated with much greater success, and with much more certainty of cure, when total abstinence from all alcoholic drinks is enforced."

946. The doctor having detailed several cases of severe hemorrhage being successfully treated without alcohol, said: "From

this time forward, I have substituted *warm milk* for *alcohol* in every *case* of *hemorrhage* I have been called to treat, and I am satisfied that the new treatment is the safest and soundest." Thus we find, that even in cases of loss of blood, in which alcohol was thought to be of the utmost importance and service, warm milk can now be substituted with advantage to the patient, and to the satisfaction of the physician.

ALCOHOLIC STIMULANTS IN TYPHUS FEVER.

947. Dr. W. T. Gairdner,* (physician to the Royal Infirmary, and Professor of the Practice of Physic in the University of Glasgow), shows that the mortality from typhus fever might be greatly reduced, by reducing the quantity of alcoholic liquors usually given; that this reduction in mortality may take place at all ages, but in a marked degree among the young; that young and temperate persons may be advantageously treated, with a diminished mortality, *without one drop of wine or spirits being given, from the beginning to the end of the fever, except in the rarest casualties.*

948. The reduced mortality under Dr. Gairdner's mode of treatment, is highly encouraging. It appears, that in 595 cases of all ages treated by him, the mortality was only 11.9 per cent., whilst under the liberal use of stimulants, the mortality of all ages was $17\frac{1}{2}$ per cent. These results are extraordinary, as the average mortality in the hospitals of England is little less than 18 per cent. It is well known that typhus fever is not so fatal to the young as adults, and we see that in 189 unselected cases among the young, treated by Dr. Gairdner without stimulants, the mortality was less than one per cent. He says:

949. "I confess I am strongly persuaded that, to the young, in typhus, and very probably in most other fevers, stimulants are not less than actively poisonous, and destructive, unless administered with the most extreme caution, and in the most special and critical circumstances."

950. He further shows that, had the 189 young persons formerly mentioned, been in the hands of the late Dr. Todd, under a routine of such extreme stimulation as is indicated in Dr. Todd's book on Acute Diseases, it seems probable that instead of one death in 189 cases, there must have been no fewer than thirty or thirty-five." It appears very reasonable that if alcoholics can be so advantageously dispensed with in typhus fever, they can be equally so in every other disease. We find by these statistics of Dr. Gairdner, that when the wine was reduced from

---

* Lancet of March 12, 1864.

an average of 34 ounces to 2¼ ounces per patient, and spirits from an average of 6 ounces to 2½ ounces, it was followed by a reduction of the death-rate from 17 per cent., to 10.

951. In 210 cases of children under the age of fifteen, treated without alcoholics, all *except one recovered*, which one had no medicine given, being 'moribund' when brought into the hospital. These conclusions do not rest alone on statistics, but on observations combined, for Dr. Gairdner in a series of lectures published in the Lancet, January, 1865, says: "The habitual exhibition of drugs and stimulants has a great tendency to *mask* the disease, to disturb or retard the crisis, and to increase the mortality.

952. "This is an opinion formed after most careful *observations of particular cases in detail, over many years*. I venture to put forward AS A LAW, that in a large proportion of cases, typhus fever, left to its natural course, and treated with abundant milk diet, and without drugs or stimulants, will have its natural crisis before the twelfth day. *Milk or buttermilk* is with me the staple food in typhus.

953. "I know no other food that can be depended on. To give wine, whiskey, and beef-tea, withholding milk, is simply, in my opinion, to destroy your patient; and the more wine or whiskey you give, while withholding milk, the more *sure* you will be to destroy your patients, because you are thereby superceding the natural appetite (or what remains of it) for a nourishing and wholesome diet—if that can be so called,—which poisons the blood and checks the secretions, and alter for the worse the whole tone of the nervous system, and of the digestion and assimilations."

954. Dr. Cotting, in a paper read before the Massachusetts Medical Society, says: "In the epidemics of 1847-8, we took care of 307 cases of typhus fever without administering drugs. The cases were taken indiscriminately, including those in a dying state when first seen. The result was 31 deaths (10 per cent.)."— *Boston Medical Journal*, Sept. 1865.

955. Dr. John Jeffrey of Axton, Eng., on the use of stimulants in typhoid fever, said, "That fevers were better treated without stimulants. He had just had a fair trial of it on a girl of six years who had typhoid fever. An aunt, with whom the girl lived, was a most intelligent woman, and he thought he would try to give the girl nothing but milk and nutritious diet. The aunt agreed to do so; and the case went on well, although it was a severe attack of fever. The little girl was recovering favourably, when one day he found to his amazement, a great increase of fever. He questioned the aunt, as to what was the cause of it; when she burst into tears, and replied, that she had been foolishly

prevailed upon by a neighbour to give her a glass of wine. This neighbour had said to her, "Oh, never mind the doctor; he's a teetotaler." But when she saw the child was worse, she traced the effect to the proper cause, the use of alcohol. However, he was happy to say the fever passed off in a few days and the girl made a complete recovery.

956. Dr. Erasmus Wilson* said, "I must not be supposed to undervalue light, air, cleanliness, and exercise, the kindred of food; but if it were my commission to improve the human race, to produce finer, stronger, and better men; to *extinguish* disease, I should begin with food; and if it were my duty to lay down rules for the *prevention* of disease, I should first endeavour to secure the co-operation of man's first and best friend—his stomach."

ALCOHOL AS A CURE FOR DYSPEPSIA.

957. We know of no disease in curing which alcoholics gain more credit, or are a greater delusion, than in that of dyspepsia. We have already seen that alcohol is the direct cause of some of the worst forms of the diseases of the stomach, so that it cannot be really needful to say much about the irrational practice of attempting to cure dyspepsia by alcohols. But as lager beer, ale, porter, and whiskey have received credit for their wonderful medical powers in curing this disease, we will give them a passing notice.

958. Dr. Watson says: "Again you will be continually asked whether you would recommend malt liquors or wine, wine or brandy and water; white wine or port, sherry or Madeira. It would be very easy to propound some general rules, but it would not be so very easy to vindicate them. * * *

959. "I believe, however, most dyspeptic persons would be better without any of these drinks, and even when a favourable effect, for the time, seems to be produced, there is always a risk of ultimate detriment to the powers of the stomach from its habitual excitement."

960. Dr. Budd, F. R. S., says, concerning Gastric Irritation: "The most effectual remedies are (1) Sedatives, and other means which lessen the irritation from which *gastric* disorders spring. (2) Alkalies and astringents. The diet should consist chiefly of milk and farinaceous food, and little should be eaten at a time.† Alcoholic drinks, and all stimulating articles seldom fail to aggravate the disorder, and should be strictly forbidden."

---

* " Medical Times," January 7, 1865.
† Medical Times, June 14, 1854.

ALCOHOL IN CONSUMPTION.

961. Dr. F. R. Lees* says: "That the use of alcohol should either prevent or help to cure consumption, is a wild and ignorant notion. Tubercle is an inflammatory condition, originating in perverted cell action. * * The young cells begin by granulating; an arrest of their growth has happened, and they are dwarfed and shrivelled, and sink into 'fatty degeneration' at the central and oldest parts, *furthest removed* from the springs of nutrition.

962. We see this in the meninges and bones. Now alcohol produces precisely analogous effects, and must therefore aggravate the general diathesis of weakness and perversion so favourable to the production and development of phthisis."

963. The researches of Virchow, Niemeyer, Burdon, Sanderson, Andrew, and Clark, have shown that there are different kinds of phthisis, and that the pathological changes that occur in the lungs are of more than one kind. We have not space to examine particularly the effects of alcohol upon the lungs, but may here remark, that it is absorbed by the veins of the stomach and carried to the liver, from thence to the heart, lungs, brain, and kidneys.

964. The chief exciting causes of consumption are malnutrition and inflammation. By the statistics of 1000 cases of consumption given by Dr. C. J. B. Williams, we find that nearly one-third had their beginning in pleuro-pneumonia or bronchitis.

965. If to these be added the number arisen from congestions, from colds and other irritating causes, which might with very little care, be avoided, the majority of those who annually die of consumption, are free from hereditary taint.

966. The full force of alcohol is expended first on the stomach and liver, then on the lungs and circulatory system. The lungs are subjected to a double source of irritation; for besides the alcohol contained in the blood vessels, a large quantity is exhaled in the breath, presenting another source of irritation, which being kept up for any length of time, must damage the tender structure of the lungs. Then again the alcohol interfering with the nutrition of the lungs, renders them more susceptible to cold and other irritants. Cases to illustrate these facts may be presented by any physician of ordinary observation.

967. Now alcohol used in these cases, must certainly aid in

---

* See "An Inquiry into the Reasons and Results of the Prescription of Intoxicating Drinks," &c., &c., page 115.

hurrying the disease to its final termination ; for we need not say the spirits will interfere with the processes of the nutrition of the system, beside increasing the irritation of the tissues.

THE INFLUENCE OF ALCOHOLIC DRINKS ON THE DEVELOPMENT AND PROGRESS OF PULMONARY TUBERCULOSIS.

968. Dr. N. S. Davis, of Chicago, in a very valuable paper, read before the American Medical Association, said: "To show the results in reference to this point, I have been obliged to divide the whole number of patients into three classes. The first class embraces such as had used some form of alcoholic beverages almost daily, from one to twelve years previous to the active signs of tuberculosis. The second, such as had used these drinks occasionally. And the third, such as had wholly abstained from their use. Of the 210 cases, 68 belonged to the first class ; 91 to the second, and 51 to the third. Although so large a proportion as 68 out of 210 cases were habitual drinkers of alcoholic liquors, only 15 of the number were such as are usually called drunkards. Five of these were admitted into the hospital while affected with delirium tremens, and also in the advanced stage of phthisis. Among the 53 cases occurring in those habitually using alcoholic drinks, yet not to the state of producing drunkenness, there were many presenting circumstances as favourable for determining the question, whether these drinks are capable of preventing pulmonary tuberculosis, as though they had been selected purposely for an experiment to last through a series of years. * * * The ten already given from the first division, include some in which the drink used was beer or fermented liquors; some chiefly distilled spirits in moderate quantities, but being long continued; and others in which all kinds of liquors were used not only for a long time, but in large quantities.

969. * * * "In the first class, numbering 68 cases, the disease uniformly commenced, and regularly progressed through its first and second stages, while the subjects of it were, at the time, and had been for from one to twelve years previously, regularly and habitually using alcoholic drinks, either fermented or distilled. In 33 of these cases, the disease was developed between the ages of 16 and 30 years; in 18, between 30 and 40 years; in 7, between 40 and 50 years; and in 10, between 50 and 60 years. The average duration of the disease in those who remained under observation until a fatal result was reached, was 19 months, dating from the time when the patient began to be troubled with cough.

970. "In the second class, numbering 91 cases, were included many who had long used alcoholic drinks, and sometimes in excess, but not as a daily habit; while others in this group, drank but very sparingly, and only on some social occasion.

971. "In 50 of these, the disease was developed between the ages of 16 and 30 years; 28 between the ages of 30 and 40 years; 6 between 40 and 50 years; and 7 between 50 and 60 years. The average duration of the disease, in those who remained under observation until the fatal result was reached, was 23 months.

972. "The third class, numbering 51, includes a larger relative proportion of females than either of the other classes. In 21, the disease commenced between the ages of 16 and 30 years; in 17, between 30 and 40 years; in 9, between 40 and 50 years; in 4, between 50 and 60 years. The average duration of the disease in those who had died, is 25 months.

973. "From the foregoing collection of facts, it will be observed, that in one-third of the whole number of cases, the tubercular disease commenced and progressed through all its stages, while the subjects of it were, at the time, and had been from one to twelve years previously, habitually using either fermented or distilled spirits. In but little less than one half of the whole number, the disease was developed while the subjects of it were only occasionally using these drinks. While, in less than one-quarter of the whole number, the disease was developed in subjects who had for years totally abstained from all such drinks. It is thus clearly demonstrated that the use of alcoholic beverages, however uniform in their administration, and however long continued, neither prevents the development of tubercular phthisis, nor retards the rapidity of its progress.

974. * * * "By a series of experiments commenced in 1849, and continued at intervals, until the present time, I have fully satisfied myself, that the presence of alcohol in the human system positively diminishes the great functions of respiration, capillary circulation, calorification, and metamorphosis of tissue; and, as a necessary consequence, leads to diminished excretion, and to the accumulation of effete matter, both in the blood and in the tissues. This is corroborated by the experiments of Dr. Boker, showing that the presence of alcohol in the system, diminishes the sum total of all the excretions and eliminations; and by the almost uniform tendency to fatty degeneration in the muscles, the liver, the kidneys, etc., in those who have been long accustomed to use alcoholic liquors. If the presence of alcohol thus diminishes the exchange of oxygen and carbonic acid in the lungs, diminishes the sum total of all the excretions, and retards both capillary circulation and calorification, it is easy to see how

its habitual use would lead to deficient oxydation and metamorphosis of tissues, and consequently, to accumulation of adipose matter, fatty degenerations, and morbid deposits, but extremely difficult to conceive how it should act as a tonic or invigorating agent. * * * From all the facts, experiments, and clinical observations that have come under my notice, I am led to the following conclusions, and to them I invite the critical attention of the section on Practical Medicine.

975. "1st. That the development of tubercular diseases is facilitated by all those agents and influences, whether climatic or hygienic, which directly or indirectly impair or retard the metamorphosis of the organized structures, and the efficiency of the excretory functions.

976. "2nd. That observations and carefully devised experiments, both show that the presence of alcohol in the human system, notwithstanding its temporary exhilaration of the cerebral functions, positively retards both metamorphosis and elimination.

977. "3rd. That neither the action of alcoholic stimulants on the functions of the human body, nor the actual results of experience, furnish any evidence that these stimulants are capable of either preventing or retarding the development of tubercular phthisis."

978. Dr. John Bell, of New York, in his admirable Essay* on Alcoholic Liquors in Tuberculous Diseases, or on constitutions predisposed to such diseases; after presenting a vast amount of statistics on various points connected with the use of alcoholics in these cases, said:

979. "I am well aware, that the statistics presented in this essay, are by no means sufficiently extensive to set the question at rest. But after a careful consideration of the facts presented by others, and also from the results of the observations here presented, I think the following general conclusions may be regarded as probably true:

980. 1st. "The opinion so largely prevailing as to the effects of the use of alcoholic liquors, viz., that they have a marked influence in preventing the deposition of tubercle, is destitute of any solid foundation.

981. 2nd. "On the contrary their use appears rather to predispose to tubercular deposition.

---

* For which the Fiske Fund Prize was awarded, June 1, 1859.

982. 3rd. "Where tubercle already exists, alcohol has no obvious effect in modifying the usual course run by that substance."

983. 4th. "Neither does it mitigate in any considerable degree, the morbid effect of tubercle upon the system, in any stage of the disease."

ALCOHOL IN BRONCHITIS AND HEART DISEASE.

984. Dr. Charles Elam,* says: "I have reserved for this late consideration one monstrous and gigantic source of evil, a compound of theory and resultant practice, which I believe to be the cause of more avoidable deaths than all the other errors combined.

985. "The Theory is, that all diseases tend to death, and therefore the powers of life must be supported.

986. "The Practice is, the great prevalence of feeding, and excessive stimulants. Space does not allow me to enter upon any scientific investigation. I must content myself with giving the result of long and careful thought, with ample test and experiment in hospital practice.

987. "The result is that nothing can be more erroneous than the theory, nothing more fruitful or productive of evil than the practice.

988. "I have stated in a previous paper that the deaths from bronchitis have increased from 2067 in 1838, to 41,000 in 1866; and that those from heart disease, have increased during the same time from 3,319 to 21,197.

989. "Now bronchitis is not, or rather ought not to be an essentially fatal disease, in the sense that cancer, pyæmia, or phthisis may be considered; such disease of the heart is likely, in some degree, to shorten life; but it is by no means essentially and speedily fatal, as is often supposed. It is almost always by the production of secondary and congestive affections, that disease of the heart proves fatal, and if these can be warded off, life may be prolonged indefinitely. I have known many patients with valvular obstructions live a long term of years, and at the end be hurried off by indiscreet zeal in treatment.

---

* Article, " Medicine, Disease and Death." Lancet, June 12, 1869.

990. "With regard to these two diseases, bronchitis and heart disease, the increased mortality in which is so enormous as to account for the whole average increase in deaths, I have not the slightest hesitation in attributing the fatal result, in a vast proportion of the cases, to the vicious system of treatment that has become more and more prevalent for many years, and especially to that most pernicious habit of fashion, of giving stimulants largely and indiscriminately. Alcohol is poison in bronchitis, speaking generally: and in affections of the heart there is nothing that so much favours the development of local congestion as these stimulants.

991. "Another serious evil connected with this practice is its ultimate results on individuals and families, apart from the disease. By the loose method in many of our own profession to order wine or brandy, for even slight neuralgic affections, a taste for drinking is established, the consequences of which are often not easily to be calculated.

992. "Most assuredly I have seen large families swept off entire, all by affections connected with alcoholism, the original use of the stimulant having been by 'medical order.'"

ALCOHOLIC STIMULANTS IN CHILD-BIRTH.

993. The following table shows the rate of mortality for the five years ending Feb. 28, 1868, when a large quantity of liquors were used:

BRITISH LYING-IN HOSPITAL IN-DOOR PATIENTS.

Date.	Total deliveries.	Maternal deaths.	Children's Deaths.		
			Totals.	Born dead.	Born alive.
1863. March to December 31	120	1	7	3	4
1864. January to December 31	200	0	15	10	5
1865. January to December 31	232	5	21	10	11
1866. January to December 31	192	4	29	8	21
1867. January to December 31	290	7	24	13	11
1868. January to February 28	12	1	2	2	0
Ratios		1 in 58	1 in 10⅔	1 in 23	1 in 20

994. During the next year, March 1, 1868, to February 28, 1869, inclusive, the hospital was under the sole charge of Dr. Edmunds, and only a few shillings were spent for liquors. The results were as follows:

| | | | Children's Deaths. ||
| | | | Born dead. | Born alive. |
Total deliveries.	Maternal deaths.	Totals.	Born dead.	Born alive.
167	1	8	6	2

995. The maternal death was a poor woman who entered the hospital in an advanced stage of consumption, who having passed safely through the delivery, died on the eleventh day afterwards.

996. Of the two deaths among the living born children, one was due to congenital abscess of the brain, dying the third day. Yet counting these deaths, the mortality for the preceding five years had been three times as great among the mothers, and four times among the children live born. While during the twelve months immediately preceding, there had been 259 deliveries, with eight deaths among the mothers, and ten deaths among living born children—a disproportion much more startling. These figures were investigated very carefully, in consequence of the various reports that were circulated that Dr. Edmunds had injured the patients by depriving them of stimulants; and afterwards, to account for small mortality, that the patients had been sent out earlier, so as to lessen the risk. The matter was investigated, when the results were:—The 167 patients were in the hospital, 2,974 days, or an average term of 18 days each under Dr. Edmunds; while the 259 patients the previous year were in the hospital a total of 4,147 days, or an average term of 16 days for each. The Council of the British Medical Temperance Association report as follows for the 9 months ending March 31, 1877:

RETURN I.—DATA OF OBSTETRIC PRACTICE.

		Ab-stainers.	Non-ab-stainers.	Total.
1.	Total number of labours	91	284	375
2.	No. of cases of post-partum hemorrhage	2	13	15
3.	" " Powerless labour	1	30	31
4.	" " Rupture of uterus			
5.	" " Febrile attacks within four weeks after birth	0	19	19
6.	" " Maternal deaths	0	1	1
7.	" " Deaths of live born children, within four weeks after birth	0	7	7

The above figures clearly show the advantages that are derived from total abstinence from alcohol by females; and as clearly indicates the non-alcoholic treatment in all cases of parturition.

THE USE OF ALCOHOL BY NURSING MOTHERS,

997. Is perhaps as grave and fatal an error, as any we have yet mentioned. The infant, for its nourishment and growth, must be provided with the same food elements as the adult, which must be adapted to less perfect masticatory and digestive apparatus. The solution and primary assimilation of the infant's food is prepared by the organs of the mother; hence she requires a greater supply of food elements when nursing, than at other times, to nourish her and the child. The secretion of the mammary glands, or *milk*, is the natural food of an infant.

998. This secretion is essentially the same in all animals. The milk, as it is discharged from the gland, is a white opaque fluid, with slightly alkaline reaction. The proximate chemical constitution of milk is as follows:

COMPOSITION OF COW'S MILK.

Water	870.2
Casein	44.8
Butter	31.3
Sugar	47.7
Soda	
Chlorides of sodium and potassium	
Phosphates of soda and potassa	
" " Lime	6.0
" " Magnesia	
" " Iron	
Alkaline carbonates	
	1,000.0

999. Human milk is distinguished from the above by containing less casein, and a larger proportion of oily and saccharine ingredients. The entire amount of solid ingredients is also somewhat less than in cow's milk. The casein is one of the most important ingredients of the milk, and is an extremely nutritious organic substance.

1000. If, as is very frequently the case, the mother's masticatory and digestive apparatus are imperfect, or the processes of assimilation are so imperfectly performed, that sufficient nourishment cannot be supplied for herself and infant; the question then arises, what shall be done to make up the deficiency?

1001. She very naturally, in the emergency, applies to her physican, who perhaps may order her some ale, beer, stout, or some other alcoholic beverage. After taking it, she has an abundant flow of a secretion she calls milk.

1002. It is very true that alcohol, and especially malt liquors, are powerful exciters of the secretion of the mammary gland, followed by a corresponding reaction. But this increase in the secretion, is only the watery portion, for alcoholic liquors do not contain any of the constituent elements of milk, as seen by the following analysis of wine, beer, ale, and porter.

1003.

Name.	Wine.	Beer.	Ale.	Porter.	Number of ounces in a pint of beer.
Alcohol	14 to 23	4.00	5.85	3.00	1. 9-25 ounces.
Extract	....	5.66	5.00	6.09	1.16-25 ounces.
Acetic acid	....	.17	.15	.21	
Water	86 to 76	90.17	89.00	90.70	13. ounces.
Total.	....	......	100.00	100.00	16. ounces.

1004. By comparing the analysis of the milk with any of the liquors named, it will be seen they contain nothing in common, except the water—none of the elements of the milk. There is no casein to make muscle, no butter, oily matter, no sugar, none of phosphates to form bone, iron for the blood, soda or potassium, or other salts of the blood and secretions. The liquors are minus every element necessary to build up the tissues of the growing infant.

1005. In the milk of a healthy woman, the water ranges from 879 to 905, the solid matter from 94 to 120, The butter, oily substance, ranges from 25 to 42; casein, from 15 to 39. Sugar of milk, from 31 to 45, and the salts from one to 4 parts in 1000.

1006. "Alcoholic drinks materially alter these proportions, for on the analysis of the milk of the same woman,* a few hours before and after the use of a pint of beer, it was found that the alcohol increases the proportion of the water and diminishes that of casein; and that alcohol is very perceptible in it.

1007. "The only rational mode to be adopted by mothers, to increase the supply of nutrition for their infants, is to secure plenty of suitable nutritious food, prepared in the way that it will be most easily digested, while they at the same time avoid as far as possible all fatigue, and mental excitement. It is impossible that alcoholic beverages can add anything to the nutrition of either the infant or mother."

---

* Dr. Bessey, "On the Use of Stimulants by Nursing Mothers."

1008. Dr. James Edmunds* says: "The supply of milk may be increased in the following ways:—First, by the transformation in the mother's system of some substance into milk, which requires no digestion; for instance, if by any magic, water, which will soak through the stomach as it will soak through a sponge, without tax on the masticating, digesting or assimilating organs, could be transformed into blood, or milk; it is clear that any quantity of milk could be supplied by the mother in whose system such transformation took place. But that would virtually be equivalent to water being poured into a tube at one end, and coming out as blood or milk at the other—a feat which, as far as I know, medical men have hitherto discovered no means of accomplishing.

1009. "Second, by such use of any stimulant to the mother's digestive organs as would temporarily cause them to digest a larger quantity of food than they would naturally do. If in this way a large quantity of food be forced into the mother's system, a larger supply of milk would be produced for the infant; and in that case the only drawback is that the mother's digestive apparatus would be strained and injured in order to produce this result. Such injury might not be felt at the time, but it certainly would be incurred, and it would manifest itself in the long run, whether or not it were ever credited to the real cause, *i. e.* the use of alcoholic beverages as an unnatural goad to the digestive organs.

1010. "Thirdly, a greater supply of milk might be produced at the expense of the mother's blood and constitution, although without involving either of the two foregoing suppositions.

1011. "Just as a horse in good condition may be worked down by an amount of labour, more than equivalent to the food it can digest, or—if the mount of food be stinted—more than equivalent to the force yielded by the food which it consumes. In short, the results would be precisely equivalent to those which are exemplified every day in London cow-houses, where, by stimulating but comparatively innutritious foods, such as the refuse of breweries and distilleries, healthy cows are made for a few months to produce an inordinate quantity of milk. The cows gradually waste away, lose their health, and are only saved from dying of consumption by the knife of the butcher, after a brief reversal of the treatment.

1012. "Fourthly, the quantity of milk may be increased at the expense of its quality, by mere dilution, and this will readily take place, if the mother be induced to drink an inordinate quantity of watery fluid. In this way the London cows are made to produce ready-made milk and water, which needs no further dilution.

---

* "Alcoholic Drinks an article of Diet to Nursing Mothers."

1013. Fifthly, there are many substances which, when taken into the human system, are treated by the system as foreign and poisonous agents, and are immediately eliminated by the excreting organs. * * * Many medicines which ordinarily act as purgatives will, when taken by a nursing mother, act as lactagogues (milk drivers); *i. e.*, they will be eliminated by the breasts instead of by the intestines of the mother; and the child,—its system being a much more sensitive index than that of the mother—will often suffer greatly from crude and improper food, although the more callous system of the mother may not have shown that any impropriety of diet had been committed.

1014. Alcohol, the essential principle of all intoxicating liquors, will, under different circumstances, act either as a purgative or as a diuretic, as well as act as a lactagogue, according to the circumstances and conditions of the alcoholized subject. It is a matter of common observation that a glass of spirits taken at bed-time by a nursing mother, not merely increases the flow of milk during the night, but causes the child to sleep heavily. The spirits, under these circumstances, act as a lactagogue, because the breasts are then in a state of great activity, and form the readiest channel through which the mother's system can eliminate the alcohol, and for that elimination the breasts have to discharge a profuser quantity of milk; but the increased quantity of milk is produced by a mere addition of alcohol and water, or it is produced by impoverishing and straining the system of the mother. In either case the poisonous influence of alcohol is manifested in narcotizing the child, and it cannot need much reflection to show that children ought not to have alcohol filtered into them as receptacles, which the mother's system finds it necessary to eliminate, and that probably nothing could be worse than to have the very fabric of the child's tissues laid down from alcoholized blood."

1015. These views of Dr. Edmunds should commend themselves to the serious consideration of every mother; and whatever may be the circumstance under which she labours for the lack of milk for her child, she may rest assured that alcoholic drinks can in no way benefit herself and the child, or make up the deficiency.

1016. Dr. E. Smith says: "Alcoholics are largely used by many persons in the belief that they support the system and maintain the supply of milk for the infant; but this is a serious error, and not unfrequently causes fits and emaciation in the child."

1017. We have seen that alcohol is not food, and never yields up force in the body; is not even a stimulant, but a narcotic, a paralyzer. If ever it does yield up some of its force by undergoing oxydation, we have seen it is a very poor food as well as a very dangerous one. This much is very certain, that whether it is food or not, every time it is taken it enters the circulation, and causes the degeneration of the blood and tissues, and constitutes one of the main sources of all diseases at the present day.

1018. There can be no doubt in the mind of every intelligent physician, but that the food value of alcohol at the best is far outweighed by the physical and mental injury inflicted by it. Hence it is a very unsafe food for men, women, or children. That which would not be able to nourish a hard-working man, would clearly be useless to a nursing mother.

1019. But alcohol is not only useless but injurious; for children whose mothers try to keep themselves upon beer, &c., very frequently suffer from vomiting and diarrhea, and often from convulsions. Sometimes a single glass of whiskey taken by the mother will produce sickness and indigestion in the child for twenty-four hours after.

1020. Dr. Lees, F. S. A., says: "It is the real cause of so many ill-balanced minds neither insane nor sensible; and in its higher use, it is the teeming fount of the sad idiocy which depresses and disgraces our boasted civilization."

1021. Dr. Condi says: "The only drink of the nurse should be water or milk. All fermented and distilled liquors, as well as strong tea and coffee, she should strictly abstain from. Never was there a more absurd or pernicious notion than that wine, ale, or porter, is necessary to a female while giving suck, in order to keep up her strength or to increase the quantity and improve the nutritious properties of her milk. So far from producing these effects, such drinks, when taken in any quantity, invariably disturb more or less the health of the stomach, and tend to impair the quality and diminish the quantity of nourishment furnished by her to the infant."

1022. The above instruction is the rational and natural guide for a nursing mother. We have only to follow nature, which is the true axiom, and rational medicine. Look at the lower animals; the cow and other mammalia require no stimulating drinks.

1023. Every farmer knows that all a healthy cow requires to give good milk and butter, is, give her good feed and pure water to drink; and he also knows that the way to make a cow give poor watery milk, which they might churn until doomsday without obtaining butter, is to feed her on distillery slops or grains from the brewery. It is also well known that cheese cannot be made from such milk, it being deficient in curd or casein.

1024. A writer in the Pall Mall Gazette, signing herself "a Mother," says: "I visit a young nursing mother, who tells me she is obliged to take, for the sake of the baby, a half pint of stout three times a day. To her second, eighteen months old, she is admininistering half a teaspoonful of brandy in his food. 'Oh, he takes it regularly by the doctor's order.' Her oldest, a girl of five, quaffs at dinner the daily half glass of port-wine with considerable relish. 'My children require it,' sighs the mother, "they are so delicate.' No wonder.

1025. "To preach usefully one must practice. Nor is it so very difficult. There is more strength even for poor tired women —and we often are very tired, we mothers of families,—more real strength in a bit of brown bread and a cup of milk, or even a glass of water, than in a half pint of sherry; and oh, if every young mother did not believe, in spite of doctors and nurses, that stimulants are necessary to herself or her babe, what a difference it would make in the health of the next generation, and how it might nullify a frightful fact which everybody knows and nobody speaks of, that among the middle and upper classes, there are many confirmed drunkards, who become such simply because as mothers of large families, they got into the habit of comforting themselves in their physical weakness and mental cares by taking 'just a little more than was good for them.' For the children dosed with wine and brandy from babyhood, by the doctor's orders—God help them—their parents might as well have fed them upon poison. * * *

1026. "When I look at my own bright, healthy, merry child, who knows not the taste of either wine or physic, I long to say to every mother: 'Defy doctors, old women, and all the world. Bring up your children Nazarites, till they are old enough to refuse the evil and choose the good. Any one who has ever known the wholesome cheerfulness and healthy strength of mind and body produced by a constitution which has always been kept pure from alcohol, and which, even if delicate, is sound, and owes nothing to the fictitious stimulant of any spirituous liquors—any one, I say, who from youth upwards has known the blessing of a life like this, will never be in doubt which to choose. Pardon this letter, sir. I give you my name, but to the public it matters not. I am neither a man nor a philosopher, but

ONLY A MOTHER."

STIMULANTS AND DEATH RATE.

1027. At a meeting of the West Derby Board of Guardians, held June 22, 1873, Mr. Sickle brought before the board the following returns, showing the consumption of stimulants at Walton, and Mill Road Workhouses, during the years 1871-1872, with the weekly average number of inmates, cases of infectious diseases, and the proportion of deaths to the population per week.

1028.   WALTON.

	Average weekly inmates.	Cost of stimulants per quarter.	Average cases of infection	Proportion of deaths to population, weekly.
1871.		£. s. d.		
Quarter ending March,	1178	495 4 10	....	1 in 147*
Quarter ending June,	1051	313 5 0	....	1 in 191*
Quarter ending Sept.	935	191 10 2	....	1 in 297
Quarter ending Dec.	943	62 6 2	....	1 in 377
1872.				
Quarter ending March,	943	35 13 5	....	1 in 343
Quarter ending June,	878	37 13 9	....	1 in 351
Quarter ending Sept.	839	34 17 0	....	1 in 280
Quarter ending Dec.	895	38 1 9	....	1 in 447

1029.   MILL ROAD (HOSPITAL).

	Average weekly inmates.	Cost of stimulants per quarter.	Average cases of infection	Proportion of deaths to population, weekly.
1871.		£. s. d.		
Quarter ending March,	231	240 13 9	200	1 in 19
Quarter ending June,	200	305 19 8	162	1 in 22
Quarter ending Sept.	161	255 0 8	76	1 in 36
Quarter ending Dec.	297	177 5 6	108	1 in 42
1872.				
Quarter ending March,	354	145 8 2	87	1 in 67
Quarter ending June,	298	82 6 4	34	1 in 66
Quarter ending Sept.	267	90 4 10	19	1 in 59
Quarter ending Dec.	314	132 5 8	36	1 in 51

1030. Mr. Sickle remarked that the medical men had reduced the consumption of stimulants both at Walton and Mill-Road, since the report of the committee on the use of stimulants had been presented. He had prepared the figures because he thought it was important that the public should known the whole facts of the case, and also that the guardians might have the information for their guidance. He was gratified with the result not only of

---

* Small pox cases in house included in these returns.

the reduction in the use of stimulants at the Walton work-house, but also the reduction in the death-rate.

1031. The bill for liquors to supply the Guernsey Hospital for one year was $1,790. A new doctor was elected, and not a drop of strong drink was administered to the patients during the whole year, thus saving $1,790. At the close of his term the health of the patients was so much improved that the authorities testified their gratitude by electing him for a period of five years.

THE USE OF ALCOHOLIC LIQUORS IN WORK-HOUSES.—*England.*

1032. A committee of the West Derby Guardians of the Poor, in a Report censuring the use of stimulants in the work-house of the Union, embody a return from twenty-two Unions and parishes, of the consumption of stimulants in their respective work-houses showing the total population, the yearly cost of stimulants per head, and the death rate on an average of two years, which will be seen in the following table:

1033.

Parishes and Unions.	Total Population.	Total Deaths.	Cost of Stimulants. £ s. d.	Cost per head. £ s. d.	Deaths one in
West Derby............	4,588	400	1257 6 0	0 5 6	11
Liverpool..............	22,780	1,952	1590 17 11	0 1 5	12
Lambeth...............	5,950	850	1690 5 11	0 5 9	17
Islington..............	2,948	225	816 12 11	0 5 6	13
St. Pancras...........	6,557	491	2103 4 2	0 6 5	13½
Marylebone...........	5,266	501	2050 10 0	0 7 9	10
Halifax................	....	131	249 1 11	0 2 11	13
Sheffield..............	2,493	251	378 15 0	0 3 0	10
Charlton..............	5,748	424	500 3 9	0 1 8	14
Leeds..................	4,219	224	202 7 4	0 0 11½	18
Manchester Hospital...	8,194	750	485 0 0	0 1 2	11
" Crumpsall	6,033	160	273 0 0	0 0 11	38
" Workhouse	....	......	....	0 6 10	
Birmingham..........	8,912	446	373 5 0	0 0 10	20
Aston.................	....	60	102 1 2	0 0 9	27
Preston	3,858	153	116 3 7	0 0 8	21½
Edinburgh............	4,448	151	104 8 7	0 0 5	30
Dublin	6,526	488	751 8 9	0 2 5	13
Cork..................	....	......	594 9 11	0 1 4	
Newry.................	....	102	Nil	Nil	30
Armagh...............	2,012	98	Nil	Nil	20½
Lurgan (1871).........	2,868	111	Nil	Nil	26
Glasgow (Govan)	1,955	180	75 9 7	0 0 9	11
West Derby (1871)....	6,531	693	2388 4 0	0 7 3	9

1034. By examining the above figures it will be seen that the death-rate is in proportion almost to the cost of the liquors per head, clearly showing that the more liquor used as a medicine, the greater is the number of deaths.

MEDICAL EXPERIENCE.

1035. Speaking of alcohol as a medicine, Dr. Higginbottom said: "Sir Astley Cooper himself declared his ignorance to a temperance physician whom I knew, by saying: 'We used to call brandy a tonic; we have all been deceived, it is only a stimulant.' During my long and extensive practice, I have not seen a single case of disease cured by alcohol. On the contrary it is the most fertile producer of diseases, and may be considered the bane of medicine and the seed of disease. It is entirely destitute of any medicinal principle implanted by the Creator, as in genuine medicine."

1036. Again he says: "The subject of alcohol as a medicine has occupied my attention ever since the year 1810. * * For twenty of the first years of my practice, I ignorantly gave alcohol in some diseases, as was customary with the profession, yet at so early a period as 1813, I discontinued it in typhus, typhoid, and other fevers, with the most marked and beneficial results; in 1818, in all cases of midwifery, and at a later period in delirium tremens, and in all other diseases, from full conviction of its injurious properties, so that I lost all faith in alcoholic stimulants, and discontinued their use several years before the formation of the Temperance Society.

1037. "For about thirty years, I have not prescribed alcohol as a medicine, so that I have fully tried both ways, with and without alcohol; and I perfectly agree with the Scotchman who said honesty was the best policy, for 'he had tried baith ways,' and he had really found out that honesty was the best policy. I only differed from the Scotchman in acting dishonestly with my patients from ignorance. I am now fully of opinion that a more dishonest or cruel act cannot be inflicted on a patient, than to prescribe or order alcohol as a medicine. Why is alcohol prescribed at all, when it is such a disease producer? * *

1038. "The answer will be what a medical man once said to me: 'I like it.' The general answer has been, when I have asked medical men, personally, why they ordered it as a medicine? 'We could do without it, but it is so convenient, always at hand, and the patients like it.'

1039. "My greatest trouble has been, for many years, in preventing patients from being destroyed by alcohol. I do not say the abuse, for I consider to use, is the abuse." Again he says: "I have discovered a great truth, and have made a great discovery—that alcohol in every form may be dispensed with in medical and surgical practice, and is not required in a single disorder or disease. What evidence can be clearer or more satisfactory? My practice has been open to hourly inspection and observation for thirty years, in the centre of a large populous town, surrounded by more than forty surgeons and physicians, most of them intelligent, discerning men. Surely some one of them would have informed me of my insufficiency or malpractice had I been in error; but I heard of no such remark from a single individual, although in daily communication with them."

1040. At a medical conference, held in London, May 25, 1869, the following experiences and testimonials were presented in letters, papers, etc.

1041. Dr. Munroe, of Hull, Eng., said: "It is now (1869) seven years since I have ordered any alcoholic drink either as a medicine or diet; and the success attendant upon its disuse, in cases where, in former years, I should have ordered it largely, and condemned myself if I had not done so, is so gratifying as to lead me to its entire abandonment in the treatment of disease. In typhoid fever, as well as in other cases of fever of the worst character; in cholera, and in sudden and violent hemorrhages, in delirium, in rheumatism, in gout, and in many other diseases, the success of this treatment, without the use of alcohol, has been most marked and satisfactory. Our profession is now beginning to doubt the vaunted efficacy of alcohol as a therapeutic agent. Its reputation for the cure of disease is becoming exceedingly problematical. I have no doubt, that, in a few years, alcohol will no longer be administered as an internal medicine, but will take its proper place as an external remedy!"

1042. R. L. Bayley, M. R. C. S.: "So far as my own testimony goes, and I may say it accords with others, I have treated successfully nearly every form of disease without alcohol, and with the best results for years. Time would fail here to enter into particulars; suffice it, that we should be content with a general result. So pleased am I with the success of the plan, that I should be sorry to go back to the use of alcohol."

1043. J. R. Scatliff, M. D., London, wrote:—"But in this paper, I am to give my own experience of the treatment of disease. Having been practically an abstainer nearly all my life, I had been led to give the habit of ordering alcoholic drinks for my patients more than ordinary attention, and from the experience of a large practice for twenty-five years, during nine of which I held public appointments, giving me vast opportunities of observing disease, I have gradually grown stronger and stronger, in my opinion as to the mischievous effects of alcoholic drinks taken in moderation by persons in a state of health, or disease. Did the time allow, I could enumerate a large number of cases of successful treatment of delirium tremens, fever, pneumonia, bronchitis, erysipelas, and almost every other disease, some of them of extreme gravity, where no stimulants were ordered."

1044. Dr. B. Collenette, L. R. C. P., Guernsey: "For the first four or five years of my professional life, I like others, followed the usual practice, and administered brandy, wine, and beer to my patients; but some twenty-nine years since, I became convinced that alcoholic drinks were both injurious as articles of diet and unnecessary as a medicine, and I have ever since been a personal abstainer, and have also banished them from my practice; and I have never had cause to regret having done so. Occasionally, indeed, I have had to yield to the wishes and opinions of some of my medical brethren, who in consultation have thought that the case we were treating would be benefitted by the administration of alcoholics, and in some half-dozen cases, when away from all other stimulants, I have been compelled to have recourse to them. But I cannot in truth say that I have derived such benefit from their use as would induce me to again administer them except under compulsion. It is my firm and deep conviction, that as a medicine, they are for the most part injurious, and almost if not altogether unnecessary; and this opinion I have formed after having attended and successfully brought through, without their use, cases of typhus fever, malignant scarlet, and other fevers, cholera, small-pox, delirium tremens, floodings, exhaustive and other diseases; and the only patient lost after operation was the only one not strictly treated on the non-alcoholic principles. I may be permitted to say that I have thus for the last twenty-nine year treated without alcoholics all cases of patients, the rich and the poor, sober and drunkards, the over-fed and the half-starved, the over-worked and the idler, the moral and the grossly immoral, the inhabitants of well-ventilated and well-drained dwellings, and those huddled together in miserable hovels without ventilation or drainage of any kind; the patients of an hospital for many years (fourteen) and the paupers of a populous parish for twenty-eight years. Under all these different circumstances, and in all these different cases, I have not found it necessary (except as previously stated) to administer alcoholic stimulants, and I am more than ever convinced that the practice is right, and more firmly resolved than ever to continue in the same course."

1045. L. M. Bennett, M. R. C. S., Winterton, said: "I am proud to be able to state that I can rank myself among the earliest of the medical men who upward of thirty years ago, advocated and practised total abstinence, and at the same time discarded alcohol as a medicine in the treatment of disease. * * I have myself for thirty-five years practised in the country with a large Poor Law Union appointment, and now have not the least hesitation in stating that I more than ever believe there is no curable disease that cannot be treated and cured without the use of alcohol; and I will go further and say I believe there are many diseases that cannot be cured without the disuse of it, even in moderate quantities, such as rheumatism, and even consumption; and I have found the greatest benefit result from their disuse. * * I have attended 3000 cases of child-birth, and have had many cases of severe flooding and exhaustion, still without the use of alcohol in the treatment. I feel proud to say I have never lost a single case from these causes. During the last two years, I have had under my care upwards of 400 cases of fever, typhoid in type, all treated without wine or brandy. The deaths from that cause were under five per cent.; and I believe the recoveries more rapid than those treated with stimulants."

1046. A. W. Wallace, M. D., Parsontown, writes that: "He has had a pretty full experience of alcoholic and non-alcoholic treatment in his own person. He has for some years been subject to attacks of dyspepsia, apparently dependent on want of due supply of nervous energy to the stomach. They come on from over-fatigue; begin with nausea, loss of appetite, pyrosis, and sometimes vomiting of undigested food. After a few days this goes off, abdominal pains come on, sometimes in the epigastrium, going through the back, sometimes lower down. The pain comes on about four hours after a meal. For some years brandy at dinner-time was taken, whenever the attack came on. The attacks used to last at least three months. For the last three years, whenever the attack came on, a milk diet was adopted, and the attack went off in ten days or a fortnight."

1047. Simon Nicholls, M. D., Longford, had been for twenty-eight years medical officer to the Longford Union Workhouse: "For the first seven or eight years," he says, "I used porter, wine, and spirits in the usual way, and with the usual results; a large mortality among the sick, and much confusion, irregularity and misconduct among the attendants. * * It is now more than twenty years since wine, spirits or porter were used in the hospitals under my care, and the result in every way has been satisfactory. Putting economy entirely out of view, in my opinion the disuse of alcoholic stimulants tends much to promote the health and morals, even in a workhouse hospital. I have for a length of time considered the use of alcoholic stimulants to be the fruitful source of murder, robbery, prostitution, poverty, destitution and disease."

1048. Caleb H. Yewen, M. D., London, says: "How is it, then, that in my obstetric practice, puerperal fever is unknown, hemorrhage readily controlled, and deaths from malignant and typhoid diseases, affections of the bronchia, delirium tremens, phthisis, &c., do not amount to two per cent.? The answer is contained in the fact, that during the past eleven years, I have not in a single instance prescribed alcohol, either in the form of brandy, wine or malt liquor. * * I will not intrude further upon the time of the CONFERENCE than to express my thorough convictions that the daily imbibation of alcoholic stimulants in any form is opposed to health and longevity, and their employment in disease (especially of the arterial system, and cerebral organs,) is bad practice, and generally attended with the most lamentable consequences."

1049. Benjamin Townson, M. R. C. S., Liverpool, said: "It is my most firm conviction from fair experience in a mixed practice, that life is safer, and health generally better, in the abstainer than in the moderate drinker. * * I know of no disease which in its treatment demands the use of alcoholic drinks, and which cannot be as successfully treated without them."

1050. Alfred Prideaux, M. R. C. S., Liskeard, said: "The evils that follow the indiscriminate use of alcohol in treating disease are worse than the malady it is intended to cure. Strong beef tea and other strengthening diet, ammonia, &c., can generally be substituted for brandy, or any other alcoholic drink."

1051. R. M. Forsyth, M. M., Templemore, said: "I have been an abstainer for several years, and am consequently convinced of the important benefits and results of withholding alcoholics as remedies in numerous diseases where generally indiscriminately administered; fevers, eruptive diseases, confinements, hemorrhage, gout," &c., &c.

1052. J. J. Ritchie, M. R. C. S., Leek, writes: * * * "Although I know beforehand that their united testimony must be in favour of the practice of total abstinence from all intoxicating drinks, being most conducive to health and longevity of their patients, but very inimical to the pocket interests of themselves, my own experience is, that my teetotal patients are seldom ill, and that they get well very soon again, if they are attacked by disease. A higher principle than that of gain must influence a medical man's mind, or he will never advocate the doctrine of total abstinence."

1053. COUNCIL OF THE BRITISH MEDICAL TEMPERANCE ASSOCIATION.*

An extract from the Report of the Council of the BRITISH MEDICAL TEMPERANCE ASSOCIATION, for the nine months ending March 31, 1877, which is made up from returns of physicians who are members:

"RETURN II.—DATA OF INFLUENCE OF ALCOHOL ON THE MORTALITY.

1. Total Number of deaths from all causes, certified by members and coroners.. 228
2. Number of deaths in which intemperance is assigned in the certificate as the primary cause of death 8
3. Number of deaths in which intemperance is assigned as a secondary cause of death 7
4. Number of deaths in which although intemperance is not mentioned in the certificate, the use of alcoholic beverages is believed to have contributed to the death 38

1054. "RETURN III.—CASES TREATED WITHOUT ALCOHOL.

	Cured.	Died.	Total.
No. of Cases of Post-mortem hemorrhage	15		15
„ Important Surgical operations†	21		21
„ Compound fractures	1	1	1
„ Smallpox	22	2	24
„ Measles	272	9	281
„ Scarlatina	145	4	149
„ Diptheria	52	5	57
„ Typhus fever...........................	12		12
„ Enteric	38	3	41
„ Erysipelas	46		46
„ Carbuncle	9		9
„ Rheumatic fever	75		75
„ Delirium tremens.......................	21	1	22
„ Acute pneumonia	51	2	53
„ Infantile bronchitis	265	11	276

1055. This Council, elected by the Association, met May 16, 1876, and resolved that an attempt should be made to discover the effect of the use of alcohol upon the process of *parturition*,

---

* Medical Temperance Journal, July, 1877, pages 226, 227.

† Cæsarian section, 1 case; ovariotomy, 1; amputation of hip-joint, 1; of thigh, 2; of hand, 1; ligature of right common carotid, 1; removal of mamma, 2; excision of tumours, 9.

and as a primary and secondary cause of death, and the treatment of well-defined diseases without alcohol.

1056. Before closing this part of our subject we will give a few extracts from the REPORTS OF THE LONDON TEMPERANCE HOSPITAL. The special purpose of this hospital is to treat the sick without alcoholic liquors; and the administration of alcohol even as a drug has been dispensed with during the year, by the medical officers, without incurring any risk or delay of recovery, but with decided advantage. The medical staff has ignored alcohol, even as a pharmaceutical solvent and vehicle. The in-patients numbered 129; and the out-patients treated were 1260; among which were some extreme cases, wherein the general practice considers large quantities of alcohol to be needed. The death-rate for the whole period of hospital work was only six per cent., which is far below the average in hospitals. Dr. Edmunds, who had under his charge 683 cases, says: "I have not in any case thought it necessary to prescribe the use of alcoholic beverages as medicine. * * The results of the non-alcoholic treatment, have been, in my judgment, entirely satisfactory, and the treatment has moreover done much good in directing attention to the errors in diet, work, regimen, &c., which were the real cause of the disease; and by dispelling mischievous illusions as to the supposed advantages of resorting to alcoholic beverages."

1057. Dr. S. W. Moore, who had charge of the surgical work during the year, had 306 patients under treatment. Thirty-four persons suffering from the severer maladies, were under his care as in-door patients, who in every case recovered. A number of important operations were performed, including one resection of the hip-joint, one resection of the elbow-joint, and one excision of the spine of the scapula. One patient suffering from disease of the bones of the foot, was attacked twice with erysipelas, the limb being left in such a condition that amputation at the hip-joint or at the thigh was contemplated; but the limb was eventually restored, and by means of Syme's operation of the ankle-joint a most perfect result was obtained. Several cases of chronic ulcers were successfully treated. In one case the patient had been suffering for five years, and had been treated in one of the largest hospitals for six months without the least benefit. She was cured in ten weeks.

1058. Dr. Moore, in his report, says:—"Amongst the 306 patients who have been under surgical treatment, it has not been deemed necessary in one instance to administer alcohol in any shape or form.

1059. "By the third report, for the year ending April 30, 1876, we learn, that during the seven months ending April 30, 1874, the in-patients were 73, and the out-patients 482. In the year ending April 30, 1875, the in-patients were 129, and out-patients 1,260. In the year ending April 30, 1876, in-patients, 123, and out-patients 1,164. Total since opening of the hospital, 325 in-patients, and 2,906 out-patients.

1060. "From April 30, 1875, to April 30, 1876, there were 123 in-patients—cured 55, relieved 46; died 6; remaining under treatment, 16. Males, 68; females, 55; under 15 years, 12; over 15, and under 45, 85; above 45, 25. Abstainers, 74 (7 all life,) non-abstainers, 49. The report says: 'The medical staff, who regard this question from a strictly professional point of view, have had no reason during the year to administer alcohol in any form or degree; and the rate of mortality continues so low, as further to confirm all other evidence of the wisdom of the non-alcoholic treatment adopted.

1061. "By the fourth annual report, the number of in-patients, 30, out-patients, 1,300. From the opening of the hospital, Oct. 3, 1873, to April 30, 1877, the in-patients have numbered 455, the out-patients, 4206; a total of 4,661.

1062. "The fifth annual report was made May 30, 1878, when the meeting was addressed by Cardinal Manning, Dr. James Edmunds, Dr. Norman Kerr, Dr. G. B. Longstaff, and others. The report read by Rev. Dawson Burns, says: 'The year's proceedings have in all respects been confirmatory of the conviction derived from previous experience that the non-alcoholic principle of treatment is as scientifically sound as it is morally safe.' The in-patients recovered, 130, making 585 since its opening, four and a half years ago; the out-door patients number 1,272, or a total of 5,478 in the same period. 'The medical and surgical cases of a severe type have been quite equal to the average proportion in other hospitals, and such as, according to traditional usage, would have been treated with a liberal supply of alcoholic liquors; but the absence of these has not been considered by the visiting physicians to have been attended with any disadvantage, but to have conduced to recovery, or to an abatement of disease.' The number of patients during the five years ending April 30, 1879, was 735, of which 355 were cured, and 253 relieved, with 35 deaths, or less than five per cent. of the whole; while the cases being fully up to the average in general hospitals, and many of them have been peculiarly severe. These cases, as already said, include surgical operations, one a *Cæsarian* operation, in which both mother and child were saved."

1063. The limit of this work will not allow us further space for this branch of the question. A mere glance has been taken, though volumes of facts and testimonies could be given, to show that disease is more easily cured without alcohol than with it.

1064. We trust that the facts presented, though few, may induce the *medical profession* to investigate more closely the use of *alcohol* as a *medicine*, that they may be better able to free mankind from the avoidable diseases and sufferings that now afflict it.

PART XI.

CONCLUDING REMARKS.

1065. MY task is done. To my medical brethren I will say, that the question of alcohol as a medicine is perhaps more important than any other before the *medical profession*. Upon its right solution, the present and future of our race greatly depends.

1066. There is no article in the Materia Medica, that produces such baneful effects, when outside its medical necessity; wherever the boundary line of its necessity may lie.

1067. It is a fact not to be ignored, that our profession is charged with aiding to keep up the delusion that alcoholics are not only necessary *as a medicine*, but *useful* as beverages and harmless as luxuries.

1068. This charge is not without some ground of truth; for the common people not having been generally aware that alcoholics used moderately are really injurious, are confirmed in their ignorance by the precept and example of their medical advisers.

1069. As the medical profession is the guardian of the public health, it must teach what will prevent disease as well as cure, if it would fulfil its whole duty; but having generally neglected to teach the masses the true nature and effects of alcohol, if it truly understood them, the medical profession is not wholly unblamable for much of the popular delusion regarding it.

1070. We cannot claim ours to be a god-like and philanthropic profession if it fail to use its great power and influence to

1071. It is only the medical profession that can free the world from the false ideas regarding alcohol.

1072. The warnings of Scripture, the teachings of nature, and lessons of experience alike proclaim the evils of alcoholics. Shall the medical profession, with its results of scientific research, and its vast experience, be silent, and behold the tears of the widow and orphans with chilling, heartless indifference? Or will they not teach the people the true nature and effects of these drinks? The medical profession possesses the knowledge the people lack, to free them from the dangers and influences of strong drinks.

1073. It may be said, that all the medical men do not agree as to the nature and value of alcohol. Let there be no doubt when it is administered as a medicine. Let no medical man be ignorant of the action of anything he may use, and far less of alcohol, whose nature and action has claimed the attention of the most careful investigators: who have proclaimed it to be a *poison* and a disorganizer of the blood and tissues.

1074. It must also be borne in mind, that the advocates of the use of alcohol as a medicine, cannot claim any special advantage, that cannot be claimed in a much higher degree for the non-alcoholic treatment by those who have stricken it from their list of curative agents. Then again alcohol has been known to retard recovery, and often prevent it entirely. While, on the other hand, it has yet to be shown that any evil whatever has resulted from its prohibition, either as a beverage, or as a medicine; but on the contrary the results have always been every way satisfactory.

1075. Now brethren, which treatment should commend itself to an educated, conscientious Christian physician?

1076. This question we leave with you, believing that you will appreciate the great responsibility resting upon you, not only as citizens, but as medical men, and that it will spur each and all to greater zeal and activity, in behalf of *true medical science*, and also in the promotion of the welfare of the human race.

1077. Then again, whilst we may have reasonable doubts on many subjects, it must be remembered, that *nutrition* is the only source of power, and that *no force can be derived from the animal organism*, but only from some substance that has been previously taken into the animal system *capable of giving up such force*.

1078. Alcohol, we have seen, cannot nourish, give strength, or impart force to the body; hence in periods of sickness and danger, when the powers are sinking, and we are on the brink of death, alcohol, which prematurely exhausts the forces of the body, must be a very unsafe agent to be used to sustain the animal system already sinking under exhausting disease.

1079. Having carefully considered the chemical nature of alcohol; its physiological action, its effects on the animal body in health, and disease, we can but conclude with Dr. John Higginbottom, F. R. S., that:

"ALCOHOL IS NEITHER FOOD NOR PHYSIC."

1080. As briefly as the importance of the subject would permit, we have traced the origin and nature of the alcohols, with some of their actions within the animal organism.

1081. We have seen that alcohol has its origin in the putrefaction of organic substances; and that in every sense of the term, *alcohol* is a *poison*, and not a *food* in any sense. For:

1082. INSTEAD OF NOURISHING, IT POISONS.

1083. INSTEAD OF STRENGTHENING IT WEAKENS.

1084. INSTEAD OF STIMULATING IT NARCOTISES AND PARALYSES.

1805. INSTEAD OF INCREASING THE VITAL FORCES, IT DIMINISHES FORCE; PRODUCES DISEASE; AND IS AN AGENT OF DEGENERATION AND DEATH.